NORTH OVE

D1554949

RY

North Over South

Northern Nationalism and American Identity in
the Antebellum Era

Susan-Mary Grant

University Press of Kansas

© 2000 by the University Press of Kansas
All rights reserved
Published by the University Press of Kansas (Lawrence,
Kansas 66049), which was organized by the Kansas Board of
Regents and is operated and funded by Emporia State
University, Fort Hays State University, Kansas State
University, Pittsburg State University, the University of
Kansas, and Wichita State University

Library of Congress Cataloging-in-Publication Data

Grant, Susan-Mary.
North over South : northern nationalism and American identity in the antebellum era /
Susan-Mary Grant.
p. cm.
Includes bibliographical references (p.) and index.
ISBN 0-7006-1025-1 (cloth : alk. paper)
1. United States—Politics and government—1849–1861. 2. Northeastern States—Politics
and government—19th century. 3. Nationalism—United States—History—19th century.
4. Sectionalism (United States)—History—19th century. 5. National characteristics,
American. 6. Political culture—Northeastern States—History—19th century. 7. Southern
States—Civilization—1775–1865—Public opinion. 8. Public opinion—Northeastern
States—History—19th century. 9. Southern States—Description and travel. 10. United
States—History—Civil War, 1861–1865—Causes. I. Title.

E415.7 .G73 2000
973.5—dc21
00-021245

British Library Cataloguing in Publication Data is available.

Printed in the United States of America

10   9   8   7   6   5   4   3   2   1

The paper used in this publication meets the minimum
requirements of the American National Standard for
Permanence of Paper for Printed Library Materials Z39.48-1984.

For my mother

MAGDA

and to the memory of my father

JAMES GRANT

(1913–1997)

We are so young a people that we feel the want of nationality, and delight in whatever asserts our national "American" existence. We have not, like England and France, centuries of achievement and calamities to look back on; we have no *record* of Americanism and we feel its want.
— George Templeton Strong, 8 November 1854

I fear Northerner and Southerner are aliens, not merely in social and political arrangements, but in mental and moral constitution. We differ like Celt and Anglo-Saxon.
— George Templeton Strong, 2 December 1860

Contents

Acknowledgments

This book has been many years in the making. It originated as a doctoral thesis that set out (somewhat ambitiously, with hindsight) to examine northern images of the slave South between 1820 and 1860. It ended up as a study of the development of a phenomenon that historians have paid little attention to: northern nationalism in the antebellum period. In the process of researching and writing over a long period, I have accumulated a number of debts, both academic and personal.

My thanks, above all, go to my Ph.D. supervisor Peter J. Parish, whose unfailing kindness and encouragement have made all the difference in the world to me. His own work on American nationalism and the American Civil War has been a continuing source of inspiration; in both intellectual and personal terms, he set a standard that I can only continue to aim for. His willingness to read and comment on this book in its final stages went above and beyond the call of duty.

I am also extremely grateful for the intellectual and financial support I received at the outset of my research from the Massachusetts Historical Society. Without the help and encouragement of the MHS staff, this book would have been much poorer and the process of research much less rewarding. I particularly wish to thank Conrad Wright, Peter Drummey, and Virginia Smith for their faith in a naïve graduate student, and special thanks to Virginia for checking my citations (any mistakes that remain, however, are my own).

My thanks, too, to the staff of the Library of Congress for their help during my visits to Washington. The librarians at the New Hampshire Historical Society, the Congregational Library in Boston, and Dartmouth College were, similarly, both encouraging and helpful to a junior researcher who turned up, unannounced, on their doorsteps on more than one occasion. As far as librarians go, however, top honors must go to Alison Cowden, formerly of the Institute of United States Studies in London (where all this began) and now at the University of London Library. Her range of knowledge, her attention to detail, and her continuing friendship never fail to amaze me, and I have been grateful for all three on more than one occasion.

I am grateful, too, for the efforts of my editor at the University Press of

Kansas, Nancy Scott Jackson, who showed remarkable patience. She has been encouraging and supportive of both me and my work.

The community of nineteenth-century American historians in Britain has been a great and continuing source of support in my research and in my academic life in general. Several of them were kind enough to read through parts of the manuscript. I would particularly like to thank Martin Crawford, Robert Cook, and Brian Holden Reid for their time and patience (and tact). I also wish to thank Iver Bernstein, who read the manuscript for the University Press of Kansas. His support for what was at the time a rather rough manuscript gave me a much-needed boost, and his thoughtful suggestions for future areas of research will keep me busy for years to come. My thanks, too, to Nina Silber, whose detailed reading of the manuscript in its later stages not only caught several errors but also encouraged me to rethink the organization of some material and expand on certain crucial issues.

Over the years, I have been fortunate to be able to present my research findings at various conferences in both the United States and England and would like to thank the many people who commented on my work on such occasions. Thanks are due, too, to the several anonymous readers who commented on parts of the book that first appeared as articles in *Nations and Nationalism* and the *Journal of American Studies*. The editors of these journals and Cambridge University Press kindly allowed me to reproduce some of that material here.

Two grants from the British Academy supported my doctoral research and funded a research trip to the United States in 1993. The American Embassy also showed great kindness and generosity by funding one of my research trips to America, as did the University of Newcastle-upon-Tyne. I am grateful for their support of my work.

Friends and family were a continuous and much-needed source of support (both emotional and financial). Elizabeth Clapp shared the problems of trying to function as a female historian in a world where the past sometimes seems too close for comfort. She manages to tolerate the quirks of the very masculine world of British academia with better grace than I do. Giles Alston, with whom I had the privilege of working at the University of Essex many years ago, has continued to support my work since he moved to the United States, and I greatly value the sharpness of his intellect as well as the warmth of his friendship. My former colleague at the University of Newcastle, Peter Wilson, was a source of intellectual stimulation and good humor, which I continue to miss. My mother, of course, has been my strongest inspiration over the years and has supported me in countless practical and emotional ways. I dedicate this book to her and to my father, who, sadly, saw neither it nor his grandson—both arrived too late, to my lasting regret. My husband Mike is famed for his patience, which has been sorely tried over the past few years. Undoubtedly he would have preferred that I write a decent science fiction novel, but he supported my work on this book nonetheless. I could not do what I do without his love and support. Last, but definitely not least, I want to thank my son, Joshua Tárlach Howard. Joshua is not only an absolute joy, but without him this book would never have been completed.

Introduction

> The significance of the section in American history is that it is the faint
> image of a European nation and that we need to reexamine our history in
> the light of this fact. Our politics and our society have been shaped by
> sectional complexity and interplay not unlike what goes on between
> European nations.
> — Frederick Jackson Turner, *The Significance of Sections in American History*

Northern nationalism is not a concept that historians of America are familiar
with. Southern nationalism is another matter entirely. Although its origins
and development remain a source of debate—southern nationalism is vari-
ously interpreted as both a cause and a consequence of the Civil War—most
historians, and even most scholars of nationalism, would concur with Hugh
Seton-Watson's assertion that at some point during the antebellum period,
"something [developed] which could seriously be called southern national
consciousness."[1] Indeed, in the absence of much interest in American nationalism, its southern variant is virtually all that scholars do recognize. Although
Hans Kohn perceived that "the chief movements endangering national unity
in the United States . . . sprang from the very two sections which had formed
the core of the nascent nation—New England and the South," he concluded
that, "except in the case of the South," the various sections never developed
a national consciousness.[2]

So if southern nationalism—however that is defined—existed, why not
northern nationalism? Indeed, if southern nationalism existed, how could a
parallel northern nationalism have failed to exist? If a sufficiently large or
influential group of southerners felt so out of touch with the American nation
in the antebellum period that an attempt to secede from the Union was made,
on what grounds did the North maintain support for the Union in the same
period? In short, how national was American nationalism in the pre–Civil
War years? The search for an answer to this question was not the original
motivation for the present study. In examining northern reactions to and images of the South in the antebellum period, I aimed to fill an acknowledged
gap in the historiography and explain what appeared to be a contradiction in

our understanding of how northerners viewed the South in mid-nineteenth-century America.

In an article that first appeared in 1977, Patrick Gerster and Nicholas Cords observed that the subject of the northern origins of the southern myth "has seldom been given more than passing attention. . . . Though widely noted, it has never been given the focused study it deserves."[3] They acknowledged that they were not the first to recognize this lack. Gunnar Myrdal, in his seminal study *An American Dilemma,* suggested that scholars might wish "to investigate in further detail the role of . . . [the Yankee] in the original creation and the tenacious upholding of the myth of the 'Old South.'"[4] C. Vann Woodward likewise suggested that there was "a need for a history of North-South images and stereotypes, of when and how and why they were developed, the shape they took, the uses that have been made of them and how they have been employed from time to time in regional defense, self-flattery, and polemics."[5] Little has been done since then to fill this historiographical gap. Not only does our understanding of northern reactions to the antebellum South remain incomplete, but to date, it has been hampered by an unresolved contradiction.

Gerster and Cords argued that in the antebellum period, many "northerners began to cast their eyes southward because it appeared that an Old World aristocracy there had somehow discovered a way of assuring stability and cultivating a sense of gentility and decorum while maintaining a commitment to the public good under a republican government." This was also the essence of William R. Taylor's argument in *Cavalier and Yankee.* In his study of "the Old South and American national character," Taylor identified a "hankering after aristocracy in the North which took the form of eulogizing the social system of the South."[6] Admiration, however, was hardly the extent of the northern response to the South. The alternative response has been presented most comprehensively by Eric Foner in his analysis of Republican ideology before the Civil War. According to Foner, antebellum "northerners came to view slavery as the antithesis of the good society, as well as a threat and an affront to their own fundamental values and interests."[7] In addition, Foner uncovered evidence that supported his contention that northerners—particularly Republicans—were overtly hostile toward the South. It would seem, then, that antebellum northerners were at best confused in their reactions to the South: on the one hand, they admired it and saw in southern society a stability and conservatism missing in the North; on the other hand, they criticized it, seeing it as a threat to both their way of life and northern values.

This apparent contradiction rests, in part, on which group of northerners and which period are under discussion. The work of Taylor and Foner—in terms of the evidence they used, the arguments they employed, and the conclusions they reached—represents two extremes. In *Free Soil, Free Labor, Free Men*, his study of the "Republican critique of the South," Foner relied mainly, but not exclusively, on political evidence garnered from the 1850s.[8] Although he argued that this critique had developed over a twenty-year span, the impression one gets on closer inspection is that the Republican outlook did not come to fruition until the mid to late 1850s, along with the party itself. Foner concluded that, for northerners, the "whole mentality and flavor of southern life . . . seemed antithetical to the North. Instead of progress, the South represented decadence, instead of enterprise, laziness. . . . To those with visions of a steadily growing nation, slavery was an intolerable hindrance to national achievement." In *Cavalier and Yankee*, Taylor used mainly, but not exclusively, literary evidence and arrived at the conclusion that northerners, faced with a choice "between the predatory Yankee and the genteel Southern slaveholder . . . were quick to indicate their preference for the latter."[9]

In another study, *The South in Northern Eyes*, Howard Floan utilized mainly literary evidence to arrive at a conclusion that fell somewhere between the extreme positions of Taylor and Foner. Most antebellum northerners, Floan argued, knew little about the South and cared less. The only subject that interested them was slavery. "Having no conception of the fullness and variety of Southern culture," Floan averred, northern "attitudes toward the South were in reality attitudes toward slavery. Their emotional and imaginative attitudes arose from the awesome gap between their ideas of what life ought to be and their view of life in the South as colored by abolitionism." New Englanders in particular projected an image of the South that was "vivid, less complex, and therefore more acceptable to the popular mind" and succeeded in convincing many antebellum northerners of the backwardness of life in the South; that image has had a pernicious influence ever since.[10]

Yet there is more to these seemingly contradictory responses than is suggested by the evidence cited by these historians. Although common sense suggests that neither extreme view is entirely accurate and that it is more likely that the majority of northerners felt a certain ambivalence toward the South, one has to pull these conflicting images together to understand how northerners viewed the South in the antebellum years and, more importantly, why they saw it that way. Both images of the South—the positive and the negative—existed in the antebellum northern mind. The question one must address is why, and to an extent how, did the negative come to dominate? Clearly not every northerner concurred with the "Republican critique of the

South." Democrats, for example, did not, and according to Taylor's evidence, neither did many other northerners. It is undeniable, however, that such a critique existed. In order to understand how this critique came to have the impact it did, I set out to examine the negative and positive views of the South to see how, and at what points, the latter interacted with and was eventually overtaken by the former. In the process, it became obvious that northerners were increasingly using the South to define, first, a northern identity and, second, an American identity. From northern responses to the South in the antebellum era it is evident that northerners, no less than southerners, were engaged in a quest for self-definition that ultimately led to the development of an ideology predicated not on the American nation but on a northern one.

Historians have been aware of the existence of a northern ideology in the antebellum period but have failed to examine it closely. Foner set the terms for a potential debate on the subject, but that debate never materialized. In the two decades prior to the Civil War, he argued, conflicting sectional ideologies emerged, "each viewing its own society as fundamentally well-ordered, and the other as both a negation of its most cherished values and a threat to its existence. The development of the two ideologies," he suggested, "was in many ways interrelated; each grew in part as a response to the growth of the other."[11] Historians of America and scholars of nationalism have resolutely focused on the development of southern ideology and ignored the northern variant, with two important exceptions. In 1969 Larry Gara argued that "a self-conscious North" emerged after the 1848 election, but no study since then has either taken up or developed Gara's analysis of this phenomenon. Similarly, Reinhold Niebuhr and Alan Heimert suggested in 1963 that in the 1850s the "Northeast and Northwest moved toward a sense of common identity distinguishable from the character of that section which seemed, at the time, conspicuous in light of its 'peculiar institution,'" but the idea was not pursued further.[12]

One of the clues to this lacuna lies in the fact that our understanding of northern reactions to the antebellum South is derived from studies of the politics of the era. Although the work of Foner, Michael Holt, William Gienapp, and others acknowledges the existence and the destructive impact of the "northern critique of the South," their analyses are confined mainly to the political sphere. There is no real attempt, except in Gienapp's work, to trace the development of northerners' belief that southern society was "both different from and inferior to their own" and, more importantly, to show how a concentrated form of that belief became the core of Republican ideology.[13] In addition, as Bruce Collins has argued, Republican ideology, as Foner defined it, was remarkably optimistic in its view of northern society and "represented the self-satisfied affirmation that the proper maintenance of existing Protestant and entrepreneurial values in the socially harmonious North was essential to America's future growth."[14] Although Foner recognized that northerners considered the South to be a threat, his study downplayed the impact that this "alien and threatening" society might have had on the North. Foner's Republicans, it seems, did not take the threat very seriously, being convinced that the slavery-induced ignorance, decadence, backwardness, and laziness of the South could never pose a real threat to the "economic development, social mobility, and political democracy" of northern society.[15]

Paradoxically, many northerners, particularly many Whig-Republicans, managed to combine an overweening optimism regarding the bright future of northern society with an apparently deep-rooted pessimism regarding the dangers of what they identified as "the slave power conspiracy," the attempt by the South to dominate the federal government. Yet for many northerners, the idea of such a conspiracy seemed less a threat than a convenient rallying cry against all the nation's ills.[16] Specifically, it provided a means by which many of the contradictions inherent in nineteenth-century American society could, theoretically, be resolved. The notion of the slave power conspiracy enabled northerners to bridge the gap between the ideals expressed in the Declaration of Independence and the reality of slavery in the nation by sectionalizing the dominant moral dilemma of the age. In sum, the image of the southern slave power conspiracy provided Whig-Republicans with a powerful and persuasive symbol of aristocratic tyranny against which to define their own political and social vision.[17] So, far from undermining the Whig-Republicans' faith in the merits of northern society, the notion of the slave power only strengthened their arguments in favor of northern superiority and ultimately reinforced their belief that northern ideals should, and in time would, become national ones.

On the whole, historians have seen this Republican optimism as justified. As a result, they have accepted as valid, and therefore failed to examine, the pro-Union rhetoric espoused by the Republicans. Although the Republican Party advertised itself as the party of the Union and of republican government and claimed to stand for true American nationalist principles, it was, as David Potter reminded us, "totally sectional in its constituency, with no pretence to bisectionalism."[18] Rather than promulgating a truly national ideology, the Republicans revealed themselves to be conditional nationalists; in other words, "they were committed to the Union on northern terms" alone.[19] This idea is not entirely new. David Brion Davis concluded in 1984 that "Republican leaders agreed that the South must ultimately be 'Northernized,'" but historians have neither picked up on this theme nor examined the process whereby Republican leaders arrived at this decision.[20] By the 1850s, the common ground on which North and South could meet was diminishing fast. Therefore, the construction of American nationalist ideology in the mid-nineteenth century was not a process undertaken jointly by both sections, as had been the case during the revolutionary era and following the War of 1812. Instead, as Foner noted, two alternative ideologies emerged, each reliant on the other for definition.

It was not the case, however, that the northern ideology of the antebellum period was American, truly national, and supportive of the Union and the southern ideology was wholly sectional and destructive of the Union. As Potter indicated, to portray the North as national and the South as sectional "has the effect of prejudging the question which is purportedly under examination, settling by ascription a point which ought to be settled by the evaluation of evidence." Potter's focus was, of course, on the South. Nevertheless, as he argued, "the equation of Northernism with nationalism and Southernism with sectionalism not only denies by prejudgment, and without actual analysis of group feelings, that the Southern movement could have been national: it also leads to an easy assumption that all Northern support for federal authority must have been nationalistic rather than sectional."[21]

Our recognition of the development of a specifically northern ideology in the antebellum period has been further hampered by the lack of attention devoted to the United States by scholars of nationalism. In light of the fact that several of the most prolific writers on the subject of nationalism—including Walker Connor and Benedict Anderson—work in the United States, it is difficult to understand why the process of national construction in America remains relatively neglected. Part of the problem is that the subject of American nationalism attracts the attention of two very different groups of scholars: those whose primary interest is the study of nationalism, and those who are, first and foremost, historians of America. The opportunity for a fruitful exchange of ideas between them exists, but to date, nationalism scholars and American historians have for the most part talked past rather than to each other. Consequently, studies of nationalism have failed to build on the work of those such as Paul Nagel, Fred Somkin, Rush Welter, and Major Wilson, who in the 1960s and 1970s produced broad-ranging studies of the development and nature of American nationalism.[22] One explanation for the general unwillingness of nationalism scholars to engage with the American case has been proposed by Peter Parish, who sees it as a result of the combined forces of academic specialization, ideological inclination, and Eurocentrism. As he points out, it is nationalism scholars' loss, because America offers the prime example of the voluntaristic nation, as defined by Ernst Gellner, and "was well ahead of the field in meeting many of the conditions—political democracy, education, mobility, and so on—for the creation of the kind of 'imagined community' which Anderson describes."[23] Whatever the reason, the American example is conspicuous by its absence from most of the early studies of nations and nationalism, and recent works on the subject have not been more forthcoming.[24]

If American nationalism is discussed at all, it tends to be in one of two ways. Scholars of nationalism who do address the American version tend to emphasize the colonial and revolutionary periods and concentrate on the process whereby the thirteen colonies broke away from Britain. This is the case in the work of Hans Kohn, Liah Greenfeld, and Anthony Smith, the only three nationalism scholars who pursue the American example at any length.[25] Alternatively, America is mentioned only in passing, either to dismiss American nationalism altogether or to suggest that it is in America as well as in Europe that the "roots of modern nationalism are to be found."[26] Among historians, the scholarly approach to the subject of American nationalism remains diverse. Initially, the colonial and revolutionary periods were seen as crucial in the development of a distinctive American nationalism. The act of revolution against Great Britain was regarded as both the outward expression of and the catalyst for a fledgling but fast-growing sense of national identity.[27] More recent studies, although they take the Revolution as their starting point, examine the early Republic, or what used to be called the early national period. They emphasize the role played by festivals and celebrations, such as Fourth of July festivities, in national construction in the years before the Missouri Compromise.

The focus of the most recent studies on the development of American nationalism is the emergence of the American political system. The growth of American nationalism is examined in the context of the development of party politics and the creation of a "national popular political culture."[28] Such studies reveal that it was conflict rather than consensus that encouraged the growth of national sentiment, "as contestants tried to claim true American nationality and the legacy of the Revolution." The danger is that, from this perspective, American nationalism can be interpreted as little more than "a political strategy, developed at different times by specific groups" within American society.[29] There is no doubt that the different parties frequently sought to make political capital out of national images and ideology. It would be wrong, however, to conclude that the ideology itself was either produced by or contained within the parameters of partisan debate. From the outset, the process of American national development was entangled with wider sectional impulses that drew on, but at the same time undermined, an overarching national ideology.

By far the largest problem faced by anyone seeking to understand the clash of northern and southern ideologies in mid-nineteenth-century America lies in the central event of that century—the American Civil War and specifically its outcome. Regarded as, in Abraham Lincoln's words, a "fiery trial," the Civil War is perceived to be the event that formed the American nation, that finally united, once and for all, the states of the Union, abolished the institution of slavery, and set America on the path to modernity. However, the fact that the "right" side—in the moral sense—triumphed prevents an accurate assessment of the ideological and political processes of the antebellum period. This problem is most acute when it comes to our understanding of American nationalism, in particular the emergence of the Republican Party and the use it made of the national "idea." In order to understand the process of nation building that was undertaken by the Republican Party in the antebellum and Civil War years, American historians and scholars of nationalism need to look beyond Republican rhetoric and beyond the outcome of the Civil War. Only then can one isolate and identify more accurately the means by which the American nation was re-created.

Certainly scholars have recognized that the Civil War was an important part of the process whereby Americans sought to define their national ideals, but the background to this conflict and the role nationalism played in it have not been fully examined. Kohn's analysis, which concentrated for the most part on the earlier period, led him to conclude that the Civil War "can well be understood as a war for national independence with nationalism as its chief issue," but unfortunately, this was not a point he pursued.[30] Greenfeld's study also identified the Civil War as a crucial factor in the nationalizing process. American nationalism, she argued, "was idealistic nationalism," and it was the Civil War that "marked the line between the dream of nationality and its realization."[31] Even Greenfeld, however, did not examine the background to this conflict and, as a result, failed to identify which group promulgated these idealistic national sentiments. American historians, in a similar vein, tend to ignore the role that northern ideology played in the Civil War and therefore fail to perceive that the antebellum years saw the development of an extremely aggressive nationalist ideology that offered no role for the South, an ideology that may accurately be termed northern nationalism.

Northern nationalist ideology was predicated on the northern image of the South in the antebellum period. This image was never consistently negative, although the use to which it was ultimately put was destructive. At its core was the belief that the South was a world apart from the North, and that the differences between them did not derive from slavery alone. Although northern, like southern, nationalism rested on opposition to the other section, in both its ambitions and its concerns, northern ideology went beyond what might be understood as sectionalism. The Republican Party in the 1850s was engaged in, and was partly the result of, a process of national construction by which the American national idea became associated with the North in general and the Republican Party in particular. It is instructive to note, in this context, that some scholars have detected a substantive shift in the concept of European nationality in the nineteenth and early twentieth centuries, from a Romantic-Liberal to an Imperialist-Darwinian nationalism. Wolfgang Mommsen, for example, argued that between 1870 and 1914, it "appeared to be no longer possible to allow national or other minority groups any substantial degree of autonomy with the nation state."[32] It is clear from the development of a northern ideology rooted in opposition to the South that a similar process was under way much earlier in the United States. This process eventually found political expression in the Republican Party in the 1850s and a conclusion of sorts in the Civil War. Convinced that their democracy was, in Abraham Lincoln's words, "the last, best hope of earth," northerners could no more allow the secession of the southern states in 1861 than they could permit the South to remain in the Union unchanged. In its attempts to reshape the American nation in a northern mold, the North created this paradox for itself, and it was one that even the Civil War proved unable to resolve.

In order to trace the development of this essentially antisouthern ideology, this study examines northern attitudes toward the southern states throughout the antebellum period and concludes with a brief examination of the impact of the Civil War on northern nationalism. The approach to such a large subject had to be selective. This work concentrates on the northeastern part of the United States, specifically Massachusetts and New York, although it also examines Pennsylvania. Boston, New York, and Philadelphia were all major publishing centers in the mid-nineteenth century and were selected for specific attention in part because newspapers, journals, and periodicals were crucial to this study. The simultaneous growth of the publishing business and the rise of popular literacy in nineteenth-century America offer historians unparalleled opportunities to trace the development of the national idea. As Somkin pointed out, in the years prior to the Civil War, there was an identifiable "unity of public utterance." Political speeches, religious sermons, and public orations were not only listened to by mass audiences but also widely reprinted in newspapers and periodicals, as well as appearing individually as pamphlets and collectively in anthologies and edited volumes. Indeed, as far as American national identity is concerned, there was a great deal of truth in, and more than one way of interpreting, Carl Bode's pithy description of the antebellum period as one in which the "people and the printed word came together."[33]

As historians have long recognized, much of this literary output, although disseminated throughout the North, originated in the New England states. Certainly New England can be viewed as a region that embodied many of the attributes that came to be considered peculiarly northern during the antebellum era, since it "best reflected" the social and economic trends that separated North and South in the years before the Civil War.[34] Although the present study acknowledges New England's impact on northern views of the South, the images and opinions that were instrumental in the construction of a northern nationalism can be identified in New York and, to some extent, in Pennsylvania as well.

This is not to suggest that sources from other areas of the United States might not shed light on northern reactions to the South. However, other regions—notably the Midwest—were frequently battlegrounds between the Northeast and the South (at first ideologically, and later literally) over the future direction of the nation. The increasingly negative image of the South provided a valuable weapon in the Northeast's battle with the South for influence in the West, but this, together with the more positive image of the slaveholding states that Taylor identified, was developed not in the West but in the Northeast. The decision was therefore made to concentrate on that part of the North in which the critique of the South was first constructed and later most fully and articulately developed. In addition, because this study is concerned with the background of what became the "Republican critique of the South," the focus is on the Whig-Republican viewpoint and does not, except for comparative purposes, examine Democratic ideology.

It should be emphasized that this work is not concerned with the reality of the antebellum South. It focuses on what some northerners believed the South to be and on how this belief—often the product of ignorance about the complexity of southern life—was instrumental in the creation of a distinctly northern sectional outlook. It is important to stress, too, that this study is not concerned with the abolitionist critique of the South. Since a significant amount of work has already been done on the abolitionist movement, it was deliberately avoided here, except insofar as aspects of the abolitionist critique found their way into Whig-Republican rhetoric after 1830. In short, "political abolitionism" is examined, but not abolitionism as a movement. Nor is this work primarily concerned with the politics of the antebellum period, on which a great deal has been written. Rather, it is an examination of a particular viewpoint that one party—the Republican Party—developed and refined as part of its political creed in the 1850s. In an attempt to trace the evolution of northern attitudes toward the South, I used a wide range of material, only a fraction of which relates to the political sphere. It is, of course, no easy matter to trace the development of something as essentially abstract as attitudes, or to link these to any particular ideology. However, it should be made clear that the term "the North" is used in the sense in which it was understood by those who employed it at the time—to refer to a particular sectional awareness defined and sustained by its opposition to "the South." Studies that attempt to trace changing opinions are always open to criticism on the grounds that generalizations are at best unwise and at worst wholly indefensible. I proceeded with that potential flaw firmly in mind, and although phrases such as "the North" and "northern" or statements about northern attitudes are not always qualified by the reminder that they refer to a particular, and often fluctuating, section of the North, that is what is meant.

In attempting to isolate and understand "the thought of an era," Phillip Paludan suggested that a concentration on the various written documents alone was insufficient. The material selected by such an approach, he argued, "offers too many opportunities for culling from a body of thought only those comments that conform to the historian's generalizations." Instead, he recommended the selection of "representative thinkers of the era," an approach that both "respects the reality of an enormously complex past" and "recognizes that the thought of an age is a composite, not a homogenization, of the thoughts of individuals."[35] In an attempt to cover as many bases as possible, I sought to combine a variety of source materials with a selection of nineteenth-century thinkers. The book therefore comprises chapters that examine literary, political, and media evidence, as well as chapters that focus on representative thinkers of the day.

However, in searching out the phenomenon of northern nationalism, it was important to identify and examine source material that either had not been used before (no simple matter when it comes to nineteenth-century America) or had been used in a different way. Seeking to identify the middle ground between the extreme northern positions identified by Taylor and Foner, the present study does not reexamine ground covered in their landmark studies, except in a very general sense. I deliberately sought material that provides an alternative perspective on North-South interaction in the antebellum period. Specifically, the book concentrates on essentially conservative views and on conservative publications, such as the *North American*

Review. I also used material, most notably *Hunt's Merchants Magazine* and the papers of various northern businessmen, that clearly had no particular political ax to grind in an attempt to identify the "typical" view of the South that predominated in the pre–Civil War North. Since the subject has already been covered in depth by Taylor, the nineteenth-century literary representation of the South is not examined here. Instead, a number of manuscript, newspaper, periodical, and political sources were combined with travel writings on the South by, among others, William Cullen Bryant, the Democratic-Republican editor of the *New York Evening Post*, and Frederick Law Olmsted, the South's most famous antebellum visitor, to uncover the prevalent image of that region.

Historians have been reluctant to utilize the full range of travel accounts written in the antebellum period partly because such accounts—with the exception of Olmsted's—are regarded as limited in both outlook and argument. Further, their influence over northern opinion of the South, it has been argued, was slight at best.[36] But to dismiss them on such grounds is to miss the point. Rather than influencing northern opinion, the wealth of travel accounts of the South *reflected* northern opinion. If travelers to the South "took their preconceptions with them," then their reports must be adjudged especially informative as far as the northern view of the South is concerned.[37] In the 1830s, 1840s, and 1850s, northerners traveled south for a wide variety of reasons. Some went south for business, some to visit friends, some for health reasons, some simply for pleasure, and some, of course, with the specific intention of condemning the region in print and thereby profiting from it at the same time. Some reports, too, were written to counter the negative image of the United States that appeared in some foreign travelers' accounts. Consequently, travelers' reports provide an extremely varied and more revealing appraisal of the antebellum South than many other sources.

Olmsted's original series of dispatches for the *New York (Daily) Times* and the *New York Tribune* formed the basis of his three later volumes on the South: *A Journey in the Seaboard Slave States* (1856), *A Journey through Texas* (1857), and *A Journey in the Back Country* (1860).[38] The image of the South that emerges from Olmsted's work is, in general, a negative one. His views varied, however, between the original letters and the subsequent volumes based on them—a fact that Olmsted scholars are aware of, but historians too often ignore.[39] In common with the response of many other northern visitors to the South, Olmsted's was firmly rooted in a concern for the American republican experiment. His ultimate conclusion—that the South posed a threat to the nation—was no more than a confirmation of concerns that had been expressed by many visitors to the region between 1830 and 1860.

Indeed, as far as the northern critique of the South was concerned, William Cullen Bryant was probably more influential in its development. Bryant had visited the South some ten years before Olmsted, and their criticisms of the region were closely parallel. This is unsurprising. Bryant and Olmsted, although not normally associated with each other, actually had much in common. Bryant was an editor as well as a poet; Olmsted was an editor, a writer, and a landscape architect.[40] Both published their impressions of the South, first in newspapers and later as books. Both were descended from Puritan New England stock, and both operated within New York's social and literary circles. They had in common friends, Free-Soil sentiments, and moderate antislavery views, but more importantly, they shared an increasingly hostile view of the South. Both were, consequently, active in the construction of a distinct northern nationalism during the 1840s and 1850s, a nationalism that was predicated on the belief that the South represented a threat to the nation's future. Olmsted's most recent biographer touches on this point when he argues that in their search for an identity, Olmsted and his peers struggled to "define not only their own identity but also a national identity."[41] In the South, both Olmsted and Bryant perceived a clear threat to American republican ideals and to the nation's fledgling identity.

Olmsted and Bryant were not, of course, the only northerners to visit the South, nor were they the only ones to publish their impressions. Between 1830 and 1850, travelers' reports on the South appeared sporadically. Usually they took the form of an article in a newspaper or periodical, sometimes stretching as far as a short series. Only occasionally did a full-length work appear. As sectional tension increased after 1850, so too did northern interest in the South. More northern travel accounts were published in the 1850s than in the previous two decades. Several of them were not travel accounts at all, although they were presented as such. They were actually composite volumes of writings taken—usually without acknowledgment—from a variety of sources, including genuine travel reports, Republican propagandist pamphlets, political speeches, and, in some cases, southern publications. Olmsted's letters to the *New York Times* were a favorite source of firsthand material prior to 1856, although his *Journey in the Seaboard Slave States* was less popular among antebellum plagiarists. Instead, most of them turned to Hinton Rowan Helper's *The Impending Crisis of the South* (1857), with additional material drawn from other Republican propagandist works such as George Melville Weston's pamphlets on the South and published congressional speeches. Almost all relied heavily on the census of 1850 for statistical evidence of southern backwardness.

The amount of borrowing that went on between the various negative accounts of the South reveals that, at least in part, the northern critique of the South was a contrived effort. Such works sought to show the South in the worst possible light and frequently did so. The contrived nature of such accounts does not make them worthless, however. What is often overlooked is that a great many northern travel accounts found significantly more to praise than to criticize in the South. Historians have largely ignored the positive images to focus instead on the negative view advanced by Olmsted and others. Without taking the positive views of the South into account, however, the development of the northern critique of the South can be only partially understood. By comparing Olmsted with both Bryant and other travel writers from the 1830s onward, one can better appreciate how the northern critique of the South developed and, more importantly, why it had the impact it did.

When it came to a "representative man" who might best express the northern viewpoint, the most obvious figure was Horace Mann, for various reasons. Mann is best known as the architect and founder of American public education. Consequently, historians have left Mann to the social scientists, who have written several volumes on his educational thinking and on his contribution to the development of the public school system in the United States.[42] Although it has been acknowledged that Mann's impact on the nineteenth century was rooted in a reform outlook that he shared with many Whigs of his generation, as well as some Democrats, historians have not thought to link this aspect of Mann's career with his stand against the "slave power" between 1848 and 1852.[43] Historians have therefore missed an opportunity to examine in detail the opinions of a man who functioned at the heart of nineteenth-century northern society. Mann represented that society in a very broad sense—its outlook, its concerns, its ambitions, and its fears—and as an educator he enjoyed a position of considerable influence. More significantly, given that he was not a professional politician and therefore had no political ax to grind, his views reveal a great deal about the issues and concerns behind what eventually became the "Republican critique."[44] Mann was a reformer who had developed a clear idea of America's mission in the world and how, through education, that mission might be realized. In common with other reform-minded northerners, Mann believed in "the American dream of unlimited material progress for the society at large, of upward mobility for all its people."[45] And like many others, he saw in the South a real and tangible threat to that dream. Between 1848, when he was first elected to represent Massachusetts in Congress, and 1852, when he left to pursue his main vocation—education—Mann's opposition to the South was expressed fully in a political context. Significantly, however, his concerns about the influence of slavery and the South on the nation had been born in the 1830s and 1840s and derived from his belief in the central importance of education to America's living up to its potential and becoming a successful republic.

Although this study avoids the more extreme abolitionist images of the South, the opinions of a number of radical figures have been examined, including Ralph Waldo Emerson, Charles Sumner, and Theodore Parker. Both Parker and Emerson edited the short-lived *Massachusetts Quarterly Review*, a journal dedicated to the praise of New England at the expense of the South.[46] More importantly, in seeking the roots of the northern critique of the South, one cannot overlook the widespread influence that men like Sumner and Parker had, not just in New England but throughout America. In the 1850s, Parker alone averaged no fewer than 100 lectures and consequently reached about 100,000 people each year. In addition, his lectures were reprinted as pamphlets and widely distributed, and the newspapers often carried reports on his speeches.[47] Parker also sustained a widespread and comprehensive correspondence with many other influential individuals, including William Herndon, who was Abraham Lincoln's law partner. Many of the dominant ideas regarding the South that came to the fore in the North in the antebellum period can be traced to Parker, including the concept of the slave power, which he came up with in 1845. More significantly, Parker's formulation of what he termed "the American idea . . . a government of all the people, by all the people, for all the people," not only achieved a permanent position in American ideology via Lincoln's Gettysburg Address but also expressed what had become, by the 1850s, the fundamental core of northern nationalist thought.[48]

This study is divided into six chapters plus an epilogue. The first three chapters examine northern views of the South and reactions to that section in a broad context; the last three chapters focus on specific examples that illustrate some of the general points made in earlier chapters.

Chapter 1 examines the background of the northern reaction to the South in the antebellum period and argues that many of the current theories that prevail concerning European nationalism can be equally applied to the American case. The reluctance of scholars to apply such theories to American nationalism has limited our understanding of the process of national development in nineteenth-century America, and this chapter seeks to show how a broader approach to the subject may reveal hitherto unrecognized aspects of American national construction. Chapter 2 examines the images of the South that prevailed in the North between 1820 and 1860. It uncovers the background of the northern critique of the South and shows that this, ironically, had its origins in a national outlook that, over time, became entrenched in a sectional ideology. By turning to the nation's past to clarify the concerns of its present, nineteenth-century northerners developed a new nationalist ideology that was not national at all but was predicated on opposition to the South. Chapter 3 examines the emergence of a much more vociferous northern critique of the South, showing how and why this grew in force during the 1840s in response to the Mexican War and to northern ideas about the slave power of the South. Northern fears over southern influence in the nation—a persistent theme throughout the antebellum period—became more focused in this decade and more dangerously sectional in expression, and this chapter assesses the reasons for this shift. Chapter 4 examines how northerners who had visited the South reacted to the region and traces the development of northern nationalist ideology through the writings of William Cullen Bryant and Frederick Law Olmsted. Chapter 5 looks in depth at the brief political career of Horace Mann, whose vision of the ideal republic clashed fairly dramatically with his own image of the South and led him to develop a theory of republican government that made few allowances for the South's role in the nation. Chapter 6 concentrates on the years 1854 to 1856, to show how the violence both in Kansas and in Congress served to exacerbate northern fears of the South and, in the process, consolidate the destructive phenomenon of northern nationalism. The epilogue examines the period after 1856 and looks, briefly, at the impact of the Civil War on northern nationalist thought. It shows how the northern nationalism of the antebellum period, presented with the long-desired opportunity to make its own ideals truly national, ultimately failed to do so.

The decision to take the story up to the Civil War derived from the fact that the whole question of North-South interaction in the antebellum period is dominated by the war that began in 1861. Without becoming too involved in a discussion of the causes of the American Civil War, it is worth making the point that historians generally regard the northern position as reactive and the southern position as proactive in their discussions of the issues. Certainly it was the South that seceded, and some historians have attributed this to the development, from 1830 onward, of "southern nationalism."[49] The construction of the argument, at its most simplistic, is that northerners consistently supported the Union, whereas a small but increasingly influential group in the South did not. Eventually this group of extremists, led by South Carolina, left the Union, and the North took up arms in order to hold the nation together.

Devotion to the Union, then, plain and simple, was what motivated the North to fight. The outcome we all know. The North won, the slaves were freed, and a new era of American history was inaugurated. Southern nationalism had proved itself insufficient to the task at hand. It was, therefore, not a "true" nationalism but an aberration, a myth, an ideology too weak to keep men in the field by 1865. American nationalism, the "real" nationalism, triumphed. This nationalism, however, as this study shows, relied on the South for definition and was in fact far from national.

Via its image of the antebellum South, the North increasingly came to regard the South as a world apart from but not necessarily a threat to its own. The North's attempt to define a national ideal was not, in and of itself, a destructive or wholly exclusive impulse, but over time it became so. This is the crux of the matter as far as the ideological and political changes of the mid-nineteenth century are concerned, but it is a point that is too often overlooked. The Republican Party in 1856 and again in 1860 promoted itself as the party of the Union, the party of the nation, but it was not. It was a sectional party with a sectional ideology, an ideology, as Foner has shown, that was predicated on opposition to the South, to the economic, social, and political reality of that section. The South was necessary to the development and refinement of this ideology. I will not go so far as to say that if the South had not existed the North would have invented it—although some do argue that the North "invented" the South—but the South played an important role in the development of what became American nationalism. And to a degree, that was the role of scapegoat.[50]

This point was made by C. Vann Woodward, who argued that "[t]he South has long served the nation in ways still in great demand. It has been a moral lightning rod, a deflector of national guilt . . . a floor under self-esteem."[51] He expanded on this observation in his assessment of the antislavery "myth," which he described as "the legend that the Mason and Dixon Line not only divided slavery from freedom in antebellum America, but that it also set apart racial inhumanity in the South from benevolence, liberality and tolerance in the North. . . . Looking back through the haze of passing years that obscured historical realities," he argued, "the myth-makers credited the North with the realization in its own society of all the war aims for which it fought (or eventually proclaimed)."[52] To a great extent, it was the Whig-Republicans in the 1850s who began this process. The Republicans expanded the portrayal of the South as a section antithetical to the North to one antithetical to the nation. The success of the Republican strategy, of course, only revealed itself in 1865. The outcome of the war validated what might have been an equally transient phenomenon—that of northern nationalism. The northern ideology survived—albeit in a changed form—and because it survived, it has been ignored. It is too obvious, it is all-pervasive, it is America. Southern nationalism did not survive, at least not in any valid form. It remains forever at Appomattox Courthouse, frozen in time, like a fly in amber.

༺✿༻

ONE

Myths and Memories

The Idea of the South and
the Development of American Nationalism

Now the truth is that American nationality . . . is a thing of ideas solely,
and not a thing of races. It is neither English nor Irish, nor Dutch, nor French:
it is not Puritan nor Cavalier; it is not North or South; our nationality is our
self-government, our system of popular liberty and equal law. . . . Aside from
the identity of our national principles we have no national identity, nor
shall we for centuries.
— *New York Daily Tribune*, 7 November 1854

The question of how the North viewed the South in the years before the
American Civil War is a crucial one, yet it has been only partially addressed.
A fuller understanding of the complexities of the North's position vis-à-vis
the South in the antebellum period is essential, for two main reasons. First,
without this understanding, the historical assessment of a central topic in
American history, the Civil War of 1861–1865, and specifically its origins, will
continue to be unbalanced. The North is too frequently portrayed as more
sinned against than sinning, but this is a misleading picture. It is not necessary to be an apologist for the antebellum South to recognize that northern
attitudes toward the South did little to foster North-South understanding and
in fact frequently exacerbated sectional tensions rather than defusing them.
Second, American history in general, and the development of America as a
nation in particular, is seen as wholly distinct from the broader world experience, but especially from the European experience. Yet in many cases, the
similarities between the United States and other nations are more striking
than the differences. Much work remains to be done on this topic, particularly
in relation to the process of national construction in America. However, a
close study of how northerners viewed the part of their nation against which
they eventually fought a horrifying war reveals a lot about how they saw the

process of national construction and why their attitudes did more to undermine national harmony than to consolidate it.

On the whole, most antebellum northerners did not understand the South.
Certainly they were inclined to adopt a monolithic view of it. Through either
ignorance or inclination, northerners were frequently incapable of recogniz-
ing the variations of southern life and used the term "the South" to refer
equally to Kentucky and to South Carolina, to Tennessee and to Florida,
without acknowledging that there might be differences between these states.
This was the case throughout the antebellum period, and by the mid to late
1850s, northerners were too accustomed, perhaps, to the familiar strains of
Stephen Foster's "My Old Kentucky Home" to question the accuracy of their
essentially undifferentiated view of the South.

Northern opposition to the South developed, in part, out of this blanket
view of a complex and varied region; certainly it was not wholly a product
of the increasing sectional tension of the antebellum period. Rather, it was
rooted in images of the region below the Mason-Dixon line that had been
common currency for some time. Not all these images were negative, and
some were extremely positive. In essence, these images remained, even in the
turbulent 1850s, fairly static. However, the cumulative effect of years of misunderstanding between North and South combined with political, demographic, and geographic changes to produce a situation in which the North's
view of the South became destructive of national cohesion. Northerners had,
by and large, always seen the South as different from the North. In the highly
charged sectional climate of the 1850s, however, the region that had always
seemed alien came to be seen as threatening. Although southern behavior, in
particular the growing desire to protect slavery, contributed to northern concerns, it was by no means the sole cause of northern hostility. Rather, northerners' fear for their own position within the Union, and their more general
concerns about the future of the nation as a whole, encouraged them to view
the South less as a partner in the republican experiment and more as an enemy
within that sought to undermine it.

Ultimately, the northern view of the American nation sought to be inclusive, but at a price. That price was the acceptance of a specifically northern
outlook and ideology, and it was one that the South proved reluctant to pay.
Southern nationalism was, historians contend, essentially a defensive ideology. Unable to reconcile the ideals of freedom, which many northerners
invoked as the nation's heritage, with the reality of slavery, southerners
gradually moved away from a Union that no longer appeared to protect their
interests. By identifying the North as a separate society that was not only

different from but also actively hostile to the South, southerners were able to create and sustain a coherent sense of their own uniquely southern identity.

However, the South was not alone in feeling defensive. Northern reactions to the South throughout the antebellum period reveal the development of a specifically northern nationalism that culminated, in 1856, with the emergence of a northern political party, the Republicans. The Republican Party was engaged in, and was itself partly the result of, a process whereby the American national idea became associated with the North in general and with the Republican Party in particular. Drawing on what was by then a well-established northern critique of the South, the Republicans succeeded in establishing themselves as the national group, even though their ideology was almost wholly sectional. There is no doubt that northern nationalism, although formed in a similar way to its southern counterpart, was ultimately more ambitious in nature and more protective of the Union than the southern variant. Northerners, in the main, did not envisage seceding from the Union. Instead, the North looked forward to a future in which its influence would dominate in both the South and the West, to a time when the nation would reflect all that was best in northern society. The construction of northern nationalism was the first and most crucial step toward this future.

Only one year after the last northern troops left the South and the United States seemed to be leaving the destruction of the Civil War and Reconstruction years behind, Henry James commented that "nothing could be well more characteristic of [American] nationality than the sight of a group of persons more or less earnestly discussing it."[1] One hundred years later, Walker Connor suggested that the topic that James had identified as being of such interest was, in some respects, redundant. Lacking a common origin, he argued, Americans were unable to "appreciate instinctively the idea of the nation in the same dimension and with the same poignant clarity" as many other nations. Indeed, Connor concluded, the American people "are not a nation in the pristine sense of the word," and a tendency to equate the American citizenry with the American nation has "seduced scholars into erroneous analogies."[2]

Certainly the idea of the nation is not instinctive in the American case, but this does not mean that America is not a nation. Indeed, as many nationalism scholars have pointed out, very few nationalisms can be described as instinctive. Although it remains on the sidelines in studies of nationalism, the American experience of nation building in the nineteenth century was hardly different from that of many other nations. It is necessary to define what is meant, in this context, by the idea of a nation, or nationalism. As virtually all scholars of the subject agree, nationalism is a difficult concept to pin down. It has been defined as "primarily a political principle, which holds that the political and the national unit should be congruent"—in other words, as "a theory of political legitimacy"—and, in Benedict Anderson's phrase, as "an imagined political community," fulfilling psychological as well as economic imperatives.[3] No imagined community, however, emerges without effort. As Anthony Smith has pointed out, the creation of a nation is "a recurrent activity, which has to be renewed periodically."[4] The process of defining a nation and establishing a national identity is, he argued, "one that involves ceaseless re-interpretations, rediscoveries and reconstructions; each generation must re-fashion national institutions and stratification systems in the light of the myths, memories, values and symbols of the 'past.'" There is more to the idea of nation than myths and memories, but these are integral to the concept of a nation, since "there can be no identity without memory (albeit selective) [and] no collective purpose without myth."[5]

America, however, does not offer the clearest model for those seeking to identify the myths and memories by which, once a geographic area is settled, the idea of a nation is invoked and a sense of national pride and identity formed. For this reason, the process of national construction being undertaken by the northern states in the mid-nineteenth century has been overlooked. Yet the American experience exemplifies, in many ways, the development of nationalist sentiment and national consciousness as this process has been described by scholars of the subject. Although America is not the subject of his study, an accurate interpretation of the American experience can be found in Peter Alter's description of what he terms the "rather inscrutable process of nation-building." Alter sees this process as engineered by intellectual minorities but "directed at the social group as a whole." Like Smith, Alter stresses that national construction is "an extremely drawn-out process of social and political integration" that "can never be deemed complete, even after a nation has gained its own independent state."[6] This is an important point to bear in mind when studying the political upheavals of antebellum America, particularly when one recalls Ernst Gellner's contention that nationalism, far from being "the awakening of nations to self-consciousness," rather "invents nations where they do not exist."[7]

Besides requiring constant reassessment, nation building frequently relies, as Smith has shown, on "myths of origins and descent, of liberation and migration, of the golden age and its heroes and sages, perhaps of the chosen people now to be reborn after its long sleep of decay and/or exile." Together,

Smith argues, such "myth-motifs can be formed into a composite nationalist mythology and salvation drama."[8] Writing specifically about the Romantic nationalists, Josep Llobera likewise stresses the importance of a mythical past, which for the Romantics "embodied the loftiest and most worthy ideals." For such nationalists, "nostalgia for the past took the form of looking back to a period in the history of the nation when it achieved literary fame, political success, or had flourished culturally."[9] At first glance, this particular foundation of nationhood would seem not to apply to America. Indeed, Theodore Parker argued that America was "one of the few great nations which can trace their history back to certain beginnings; there is no fabulous period in our annals, no mythical centuries."[10] Both historians and nationalism scholars have generally concurred with Parker's assessment and have chosen to consider America, if they consider it at all, as sui generis as far as the process of national construction is concerned.

This is at best shortsighted. Parker ought to have known better than to reach the conclusion he did, since he did so much to draw northerners' attention to the nation's past and specifically to the ideals that he considered the legitimate bequest of the Founding Fathers to the nation they had created. Even a brief consideration of the American variant of those elements that Smith identified as important to a nationalist mythology reveals the applicability of this essentially European pattern to the American case. Although in theory the proximity of the past might be deemed to set American nationalism apart, in practice the distinctiveness of this aspect of the American case was muted by the reverential and quasi-mythical manner in which many antebellum Americans approached their nation's past. The myth of origins and descent, for example, has served America in many contradictory ways. Some of these myths continue to resonate today. The myth of separate origins for North and South is one pertinent example, a myth that developed into the stereotypes of Cavalier and Yankee. Myths of liberation and migration are central to the American nation, founded on the ideals of life, liberty, and the pursuit of happiness and peopled mainly by migrants from other lands. Indeed, the arrival of the Pilgrims on the *Mayflower* and the "great migration" of the Puritans in the seventeenth century were clearly construed as foundation myths of the American nation.[11] In addition, America has never suffered from a shortage of heroes to inspire its population. In the nineteenth century the Founding Fathers fulfilled this function, and many figures have been added to the national pantheon since. Over time, the Puritans' "errand into the wilderness" worked with the republican vision of the Founding Fathers to create the idea of America as a nation with a clear historical mission and of Americans as a uniquely chosen people, charged with the salvation of

humankind.[12] The Civil War threatened this vision by destroying, albeit tem-
porarily, the nation that Abraham Lincoln described as the "last, best hope of
earth." The Civil War—or, more accurately, the American response to it—
represents the final component that Smith identified: the myth of the rebirth
of the chosen people. As Lincoln uttered at Gettysburg: "this nation, under
God, shall have a new birth of freedom—and that government of the people,
by the people, for the people, shall not perish from the earth."

No less than Europeans, nineteenth-century Americans sought to rediscover their past and reinterpret it to give meaning to their present and direction to their future. Like the European Romantic nationalists, antebellum
Americans turned to their past to justify their national claims and support
their national ambitions. Yet there was, from the outset, a distinct tendency to
portray relatively recent history in mythical terms, in particular to modify its
less savory elements and to stress its ideals. History was studied not for its
own sake but to remind Americans of their obligation to the ideals of the
nation's past. In this vein, one New England minister invoked the past to remind his congregation

> how dearly the Fathers prized the right of free discussion. It was for this one
> purpose mainly that they left their native land, and pitched their tents in an
> untrodden wilderness. It was on this one point more than all others that they
> took issue with the despots of the old world. Authority and prescription could
> not bind their conscience. The decrees of Synods and Popes could not control
> their mind. The edicts of aristocracies and oligarchies could not manacle their
> opinions. They held to free speech and a free press. . . . Free thought and free
> speech are fundamental to this Republic. Our whole scheme of government
> and religion is built upon them.[13]

This was a rather rosy view of America's colonial past, but it was typical of
the time. Antebellum "Americans were remarkably attuned to history" and
used it to "reinforce the sense of America's mission as the 'hope of mankind,'
the culmination of millennia of human yearning and struggle."[14]

For antebellum Americans, the colonial past was not the only focus of
interest. The Revolution was even more important in the construction of national identity. Here, too, the tendency was to stress the end rather than the
means. As John Shy noted, the "ink was barely dry on the Treaty of Paris
before myth and reality about the Revolutionary War were becoming en-
twined."[15] The need to downplay the harsh realities of the Revolution led to
its outcome being portrayed not as the fruit of military victory over both
internal and external foes but rather as the logical product of an Enlightenment philosophy that found its fullest expression in the new, democratic re-

public that America represented.[16] This was the beginning of a process whereby Americans sought to justify the Revolution by transforming it into the bedrock of a unifying national mythology. The Revolution soon took its place alongside the foundation myths of the arrival of the Pilgrims and later the Puritans in a fast-developing sense of American historical achievement and a "still inchoate national tradition."[17] By the antebellum period, Americans looked back to the Revolution not only as the foundation of their nation but also as a time when the American national idea was most fully expressed. For them, the Revolution had created not only the American nation but also American nationalism by providing the symbols, history, and myths by which nationhood is expressed.[18]

The problem for the American nation was that the experience of revolution had bequeathed a divisive legacy. The Revolutionary War had pitted the colonists against each other as much as against the imperial power. In the aftermath of the Revolution, the Loyalists had, for the most part, fled to Nova Scotia or New Brunswick, Canada, or back to Britain, but the revolutionary generation could hardly forget the existence of Loyalist sentiment or its implications. The Union's position was, from any angle, a precarious one. America represented an experiment in a new form of government, and not everyone expected this experiment to succeed. During the early years of the Republic, the prediction that the Union would not last was so common as to be "a standard conversational gambit." Indeed, as Linda Kerber reminds us, "it was the persistence of union which excited surprise rather than recurring secessionist sentiment." From the outset, it seemed clear that if the Union were to come apart, it would do so because of the essential differences between the North and the plantation South.[19] There was little real unity in the early Union. Local and sectional loyalties always threatened to subvert the developing sense of national mission and destiny. In the American case, it has been argued, "the fears of Montesquieu and older political theorists were not without foundation. If a single great republic was to survive here, it would have to find a way of stemming the secessionist tide."[20]

One way that national consolidation was attempted was through celebratory rites focused on the Revolution, such as Fourth of July festivities. Also accomplished was elevation of the war's supporting documents—the Declaration of Independence and the Constitution—and the conflict's military leader and America's first president, George Washington, to the status of national symbols. Over the years, additional symbols were added, most notably the Great Seal, with its classical allusion *novus ordo seclorum* and the motto *e pluribus unum*. Both phrases were, however, more expressive of future hopes than of contemporary realities. Before the Civil War, the American nation seemed to be strong only in the face of an external threat. Great Britain played that role once again at the start of the nineteenth century in the so-called second war for independence, the War of 1812. At the conclusion of the conflict, American diplomat and Secretary of the Treasury Albert Gallatin felt enthused enough to observe that the war had "renewed and reinstated the national feelings which the Revolution had given and which were daily lessened. The people have now more general objects of attachment with which their pride and political opinions are connected. They are more American; they feel and act more like a nation; and I hope that the permanency of the Union is thereby better secured."[21]

Gallatin's optimism was premature. The upsurge of nationalism induced by the War of 1812 was somewhat soured by the image of New England Federalist extremists advocating secession from the Union in 1814. In the years following, overconfidence in the American democratic experiment and in the strength of the Union went hand in hand with deep-rooted fears over the national character and the nation's future. It has been argued that "American nationalism was not based upon language, nor upon any external symbols; it was founded upon an idea."[22] By the antebellum period, however, North and South interpreted that idea in very different ways. If the Founding Fathers were all too conscious that the Union represented at best a "perilous political experiment," antebellum Americans were hardly more confident.[23] In the antebellum period, American opinion on the meaning and the future of their nation was clearly mixed. In 1853 Massachusetts senator Caleb Cushing exuberantly described his country as "that colossus of power, that colossus of liberty, that colossus of the spirit of nations."[24] The following year, however, New York lawyer and diarist George Templeton Strong sounded a more cautious note when he confided to his diary that Americans "are so young a people that we feel the want of nationality, and delight in whatever asserts our national 'American' existence. We have not, like England and France, centuries of achievements and calamities to look back on; we have no *record* of Americanism and we feel its want."[25]

As William Brock argued, "since the Revolution, Americans had been conscious of their reputation in the world. They knew that their political experiment had no precedent in history, expected admiration, and were acutely sensitive to criticism." To a great extent, he concluded, the "American character had been negatively defined. Americans were not monarchists, had no hereditary aristocracy, and were not subject to the constraints of Europeans. The Old World, and especially England, was a 'negative reference point' which helped Americans to define their own positive qualities."[26] As far as national construction is concerned, this process is typical. The growth of any nationalist sentiment, the impulse toward a coherent national identity, is sustained by reference to an external threat or by feelings of inferiority. In the case of America, it was both.[27] In the middle decades of the nineteenth century, America was facing, not for the first time, what Seymour Martin Lipset defined as the "crisis of legitimacy." This was a "basic problem faced by all new nations," Lipset argued. "The old order has been abolished. . . . The imperialist ogre upon whom all ills were blamed has now disappeared, and there has been a slackening of the great unifying force, nationalism, under whose banner private, ethnic, sectional, and other differences were submerged."[28] Lipset was, of course, referring to the years immediately following the Revolution. However, the middle decades of the nineteenth century, much more than the colonial or revolutionary period, was a time when Americans felt most threatened, on two distinct fronts.

First, as far as their culture was concerned, many Americans concurred with Margaret Fuller's complaint that "although we have an independent political existence, our position toward Europe, as to Literature and the Arts, is still that of a colony."[29] It was even earlier, in 1820, that Sydney Smith posed his now famous query in the *Edinburgh Review:* "in the four quarters of the globe, who reads an American book? Or goes to an American play? Or looks at an American picture or statue?"[30] Many Americans were painfully aware of the fact that their culture, in the early nineteenth century, remained essentially derivative; in the words of John Clive and Bernard Bailyn, it was a province, "cultural as well as political and economic, of the English-speaking world whose center was London." All too aware that "they lived on the periphery of a greater world," Americans experienced a "sense of inferiority" as early as the eighteenth century.[31]

Little had changed by the nineteenth century. It was in response to such cultural uncertainty that Ralph Waldo Emerson adumbrated his plans for a native American culture in his "American Scholar" address. "Our day of dependence, our long apprenticeship to the learning of other lands, draws to a close," he declared. Americans would, in the future, "walk with our own feet; we will work with our own hands; we will speak our own minds."[32] Emerson was reiterating a message that Noah Webster had attempted to drum into Americans some fifty years earlier. "Unshackle your minds and act like independent beings," he urged them. "You have been children long enough, subject to the control and subservient to the interest of a haughty parent. You now have an interest of your own to augment and defend—and a national character to establish and extend by your wisdom and judgment."[33] It was not until the nineteenth century, however, that Webster's message finally struck a chord, and not until 1855 that the *New York (Daily) Times* identified "the sudden development of an intense yearning for a nationality and a literature which shall be wholly American."[34] In short, nineteenth-century Americans seemed to be a people who felt "culturally at a disadvantage."[35]

Second, nineteenth-century America was a country in upheaval, but the winds of change blew hardest in the northern states, where the effects of industrialization, immigration, and urbanization were making themselves felt. Because these cultural and social concerns occurred at the same time as, and were exacerbated by, a geographic and demographic expansion, the search for an American identity took on a new urgency. By the antebellum period, the efficacy of America's revolutionary myths and symbols in creating a unified concept of the nation was being undermined by sectional tensions. Although Americans continued to refer to the Revolution, using biography, history, oratory, art, and fiction to create a compelling mythos around it, this proved insufficient for national stability.[36] From the Revolution that they had in common, North and South constructed separate, contradictory ideologies increasingly at odds with each other. In time, North and South came to see in the other a threat to the American national ideal. Each side accused the other of betraying the legacy of the Founding Fathers and denying the sacrifice of the revolutionary generation. It need not have been so. Michael Kammen, for example, noted that the antebellum desire to honor America's revolutionary heroes "may have had a sectional emphasis, but it was genuinely a national gesture."[37] Unfortunately, it was not a successful one. Far from being a unifying part of the national past, the Revolution became a bone of contention over the national future.

In the course of his famous reply to Robert Hayne in the Senate in 1830, Daniel Webster had drawn his audience's attention to the fact that Massachusetts and South Carolina had marched shoulder to shoulder in the Revolution, and "hand in hand they stood round the administration of Washington. . . . The past, at least," Webster declared, "is secure."[38] His certainty on this point was misplaced. Nineteenth-century northerners rarely missed an opportunity to make sectional capital out of the national past. As the *New York Tribune* argued, from "the origin of our National history, the North has been steadily loyal and devoted to the Union, while every formidable opposition to it has derived its impulse and power from the South." Naturally inclined toward Loyalist, Tory politics, the *Tribune* asserted, the South had proved a hindrance rather than a help to the revolutionary cause.[39] There was, however, an apparently insurmountable difficulty here. Southerners had played a central role in the creation of the American nation. Indeed, a "large, perhaps disproportionate, share of early American patriot heroes were Southerners," from presidents Washington through Jefferson, Madison, and Monroe to spokesmen and leaders such as Richard Henry Lee and Patrick Henry.[40]

Northerners responded to this discomfiting fact in one of two ways. Sometimes they acknowledged it and used it as support for their argument that the South had always enjoyed more than its fair share of power in the nation. Alternatively, they took issue with it and argued that southerners had not shared the burden of the revolutionary struggle equally with northerners; Theodore Parker, for one, argued that it was "Massachusetts that took the initiative in the great strife of the eighteenth century," rather than the South.[41] Southerners reacted strongly against both interpretations. They were particularly dismayed at the efforts of George Bancroft, the nation's first historian and a northerner, to "glorify the deeds of the heroes of their own section" and concluded, not without reason, that "southerners could not entrust to northerners the responsibility of recording something so important as the South's role in the American Revolution." The South, of course, was equally guilty of highlighting its role at the expense of the North. Here, as John Hope Franklin noted, "was a strange spectacle indeed. Here were two sections virtually at war with each other in the 1850s, not merely over the current problems that beset them but also over their comparative strengths and weaknesses during the war for independence."[42]

Although it seems unusual that North and South should have used their common past as a means of establishing sectional differences, the fact that they did so is extremely revealing as far as American national construction is concerned. As nationalism scholars have frequently pointed out, the construction of any national identity is a process involving discussion and debate. It is also a process that each generation must go through, either to reaffirm or to question the nationalist position established by previous generations. In this context, it is worth reminding ourselves of the process whereby nations are created.

Anthony Smith identified three routes that lead to the formation of a nation. In the case of what he termed the "civic" nation, the type with which Europeans are most familiar, membership depends on residence in the homeland, or *patria,* and comprises a "community of common laws." "Ethnic" nations, by contrast, are genealogically defined; collective ties of descent, albeit often fictitious, are the unifying feature. In the "plural" nation, however, "residence and ethnic descent are subordinated, at least in theory, to an overarching civic religion."[43] In the case of the plural nation, of which America is the prime example, it is clearly of paramount importance that this civic religion be overarching. More than most, members of a plural nation need to develop a clear idea of what the nation is and what it stands for and to hold on to that idea.

For Abraham Lincoln, as for many of his contemporaries, the fundamental core of American nationalism was represented by the ideals set out in the
Declaration of Independence. In the course of the famous Lincoln-Douglas
debates in 1858, Lincoln addressed the question of American nationality and
the role of the Revolution and the Declaration of Independence in this. For
Lincoln, the Declaration of Independence offered the only valid means to
nationhood for a people comprising many different ethnic groups. "We are
now a mighty nation," he confidently declared in 1858, but he was conscious
that national ties were not necessarily obvious in a nation whose people lacked
a common history. Many Americans, he knew, could not trace their connec-
tions to the nation's past "by blood" and could not "carry themselves back
into that glorious epoch and make themselves feel" a part of a nation in which
their ancestors had not been born. Yet they could establish American nationality through the Declaration of Independence, since, Lincoln argued, they
had "a right to claim it as though they were blood of the blood, and flesh of
the flesh" of those who wrote it. The moral sentiment of the Declaration
of Independence, Lincoln averred, constituted an "electric cord" that linked
the nation together.[44] For Lincoln, the Declaration of Independence defined
"the spirit of collective American identity . . . and it reminded succeeding
generations of the obligation to preserve and extend the founding's legacy of
freedom."[45]

In assessing the Civil War generation's fascination with the Revolution's
legacy, Reid Mitchell described what amounted to almost a cult of ancestor
worship in America. Americans, he argued, "thought of the nation as a community of the living and the dead. The American family extended in time.
The dead remained part of the American nation; they still made claims upon
the living and they could find fulfillment in the nation's destiny."[46] Mitchell's
description fits almost exactly with David Miller's definition of the nation as
a "community of obligation," although, again, this is not an idea that is com-
monly applied to America in studies of nationalism.[47] American historians,
however, have long recognized the nineteenth century's sense of obligation to
the Founding Fathers and their legacy, in particular to Thomas Jefferson and
the Declaration of Independence. This sense was perhaps best expressed by
Lincoln when, in 1854, he sought to alert Americans to the dangers of stray-
ing from the past and from the founders' legacy of freedom by allowing slavery to expand across the nation. "Our republican robe is soiled, and trailed in
the dust," Lincoln averred. "Let us repurify it. Let us turn and wash it white,
in the spirit if not the blood of the Revolution. . . . Let us readopt the Declaration of Independence, and with it the practices and policy which harmonize
with it."[48]

In the midst of the secession crisis in 1861, Lincoln was moved to consider "what great principle or idea it was that kept this Confederacy so long together." The answer he arrived at was that the sentiments enunciated in the Declaration of Independence offered "liberty not alone to the people of this country, but hope to the world for all future time."[49] The Declaration of Independence, as Lincoln interpreted it, provided a basis both for ideological unity and, by extrapolation, for political union, but not everyone saw it that way. Indeed, its precepts were a major source of disagreement for Lincoln's generation. Theodore Parker, like Lincoln, stressed the role of the Declaration of Independence in American national identity. For both, the Declaration represented the foundation and focus of the "American idea," which was best summed up in the "triple refrain describing government of, by, and for the people" that both employed.[50] Where Parker differed from Lincoln was in his identification of the South as a section opposed to this American idea. Unlike Lincoln, Parker used the Declaration of Independence not as a means of reinforcing ideological unity between North and South but as a stick to beat the South with.

The conflict, for Parker, was not between geographic regions but between value systems. As he saw it, the North represented democracy, and the South represented despotism; the North was free, and the South was enslaved. Parker reiterated this theme time and again. In a speech entitled "The Nebraska Question," he emphasized the need for the North to use its superior economic and intellectual strength to crush slavery. Only then, he averred, would "the blessing of Almighty God . . . come down upon the noblest people the world ever saw—who have triumphed over Theocracy, Monarchy, Aristocracy, Despotocracy, and have girt a Democracy—a government of all, for all, and by all—a Church without a Bishop, a State without a King, a Community without a Lord, and a Family without a Slave."[51] Parker was undoubtedly more radical—not to mention less tactful—in his assessment of North-South differences than Lincoln. He was also more representative of a growing body of opinion in the North. However, the opportunity to create a viable and sustainable civic religion for the American nation at this time was severely undermined not just by the extremist rhetoric of men such as Parker but also by the fact that there was some validity to the argument that North and South held very different ideas about America's national identity.

The North came increasingly to interpret the Declaration of Independence as the nation's "mission statement" and used it to justify an expansive and outward-looking philosophy that drew on America's revolutionary heritage to both define and encourage a growing sense of what would, in the 1840s, be termed Manifest Destiny. Building on the eighteenth-century belief that America represented the new Israel and its populace God's new chosen people, many Americans regarded it as their divinely inspired right to expand across the continent. When Lincoln argued in his First Inaugural that the North and South could not physically separate, he was expressing a belief in geographic predestination that informed America's expansionist aims.[52] This was not solely a northern perspective. The South was equally, if not more, keen on expansion in the years prior to the Civil War. However, the fact that it saw this as a means to consolidate the peculiar institution of slavery rather than as an opportunity to spread the benefits of liberty placed it at odds with the sense of national mission that Lincoln invoked in both 1858 and 1861. From a European perspective, Lincoln's argument was hardly watertight. It may have been undesirable, but it was certainly not inconceivable that the United States should split into two separate countries, as many in the South advocated in 1861. For the South, the Declaration of Independence came to represent less a mission statement than an insurance policy against the encroachments of centralized power. The argument that a people had the right to "alter or abolish" a government that no longer guaranteed their "safety and happiness" became more important to southerners than the "life, liberty, and the pursuit of happiness" philosophy that, Lincoln argued, informed America's national doctrine.

Rush Welter argued that antebellum Americans saw themselves as "heirs of all the ages" and their nation as the fulfillment of "the progressive dreams of mankind."[53] Heirs of the ages they might have been, but nineteenth-century Americans could never forget that they were more directly heirs of the revolutionary generation and that their challenge was to live up to the ideals enunciated in the Declaration of Independence. In effect, they felt—indeed, they welcomed—a sense of responsibility to "create the excellence which the revolutionaries had demanded."[54] This was a tall order, and, in a sense, Americans were not equal to the task. Although conscious of an imbalance between their new nation's professed ideals—most notably its devotion to liberty—and the reality of a Union in which slave states coexisted with free states, the revolutionaries' progeny failed to grasp the political and moral nettle of slavery and sought compromise rather than closure on this divisive issue. As Charles Francis Adams put it, no "man can have watched the course of events in this Union for the past fifty years, without perceiving that the great prosperity of the free States has gradually diminished and deteriorated that love of freedom which was bequeathed to them by the founders of the Republic."[55]

One did not have to be an abolitionist to realize that there was a fundamental difference in outlook between the North and the South (although it helped) and that as time passed the difference was becoming more rather than less pronounced. Americans of the North and South had much in common: a shared history, however brief, based on migration and the Revolution; shared heroes, notably Washington and Jefferson; a shared political system, albeit one prone to change; a shared way of life, in the main; a shared belief in the merits of popular government; and a shared commitment to the ideals of liberty. Yet the national consensus that had emerged from the revolutionary experience had, by the antebellum period, virtually disintegrated. North and South held increasingly disparate views of America's purpose and destiny, and by the 1850s, there was no truly national sense of the American nation.

In his study of the similarities between the antebellum North and South, Edward Pessen made the point that the terms "North" and "South" themselves "distort and oversimplify a complex reality, implying homogeneity in geographical sections that, in fact, were highly variegated."[56] Recent scholarship has done much to develop Pessen's conclusions, and it is now clear that North and South had more in common than historians once supposed. This fact was not apparent to antebellum Americans, however, and Pessen's comment sums up the prevalent impression held by northerners and southerners on the eve of the Civil War. As William Taylor indicated, by 1860, "most Americans had come to look upon their society and culture as divided between a North and a South, a democratic, commercial civilization and an aristocratic, agrarian one."[57] This is not to suggest that North and South held fixed images of the other, but when northerners did picture the South, the tendency was to exaggerate certain elements and play down others. Those who were sympathetic to the South tended to stress only the positive aspects of southern life, whereas those hostile to the slaveholding states pictured a society of corruption and decay. This is understandable, since both views often relied on stereotypical images that, by their nature, exaggerated certain aspects of the subject at the expense of its subtleties and variations. The element of bias in many northern views of the South is also unavoidable, as some northerners deliberately played up only one side of southern life. Those who were concerned about the social effects of the North's increasing democratization looked to the South for evidence of a conservative, stable society rooted in traditional English values. Those who welcomed progress and who sought to create a society sustained by American, as opposed to Old World, values regarded the southern way of life with suspicion and tried to show how essentially backward it was. If America's "moral legitimacy" was, as Fred Somkin has argued, "critically related to its secular progress," then the image of a South held back by slavery was clearly un-American, an affront to every-thing the nation was believed to stand for.[58] The abolitionists and other like-minded reformers of the period had even more cause to play up the negative side of southern life, focusing on the suffering it caused not only to the slaves but also to the nonslaveholding white majority.

Politicians used the South in a variety of ways. By the 1850s, the newly formed Republican Party was promulgating the idea of the South as both an affront and a threat to its free-labor ideology. The Democrats, in contrast, by their support for the southern way of life—in particular their support for the southern response to the problem of race (or, in Bruce Collins's phrase, their "moral laissez-faire")—indicated their commitment to both the ideals of a white, Anglo-Saxon republic and the need for a Union that accepted both cultural pluralism and regional diversity.[59] With the collapse of the Second Party System and the subsequent party and political upheavals of the 1850s, some politicians' attitudes toward the South prompted them to change party affiliation. Jean H. Baker cited the case of Hannibal Hamlin, who joined the Republicans and became vocal in defending the North against what he saw as southern "political complicity and collusion to seize the executive."[60] Indeed, much of the impetus for the formation of the Republican Party can be found in the increasing northern hostility toward the South. As the political alignment shifted from a national to a sectional basis, many northerners closed ranks against what they perceived as a negative culture.[61]

In almost all cases, however, the apparently opposing views held by different groups of northerners relied on the same image of the South. The two contrasting views of the plantation, as both pastoral idyll and stagnant backwater, seem to be mutually exclusive only at first glance. They were, of course, the same view seen from different angles. The images supporting the idea of a distinctive southern culture tended to be, in C. Vann Woodward's phrase, "Janus-faced," comprising both positive and negative aspects.[62] In the mind of a hostile northerner, the ideals of southern chivalry became examples of southern arrogance; southern paternalism and concern for the slave were transmuted into racism; the plantation idyll became a stagnant society entrenched in the past; honor became, through the practice of dueling, violence; and the leisurely lifestyle that slavery seemed to allow became an example of southern laziness. This provides a clue to the construction of northern nationalism in the antebellum period. Both those northerners who admired the South and those who were critical of it portrayed the region as a world apart from the antebellum North. This was not a problem in itself. In the context of the search for a viable American national identity, however, it became one. As a world apart from the North, the South was ideally placed to supplant Europe as the essential negative reference point in American national con-

struction. Again, this point was made by Woodward, who argued that North
and South "have used each other, or various images and stereotypes of each
other, for many purposes. They have occasionally used each other in the way
Americans have historically used Europe—not only to define their identity
and to say what they are *not*, but to escape in fantasy from what they *are*."[63]

The achievement of national identity in antebellum America, as in many
European nations, was a complex and drawn-out process. For Americans, the
problem was compounded by the presence of so many different ethnic groups
and by the sectional forces that operated against the construction of a viable
national identity from the very beginning. The sectional theme has been a
persistent one throughout American history. From the outset of the nation's
life, there was a distinct tendency on the part of many Americans "to exter-
nalize inner conflicts by focusing on the South as a deviating section." The
South, indeed, has always been a region that nonsoutherners regarded as distinct and separate from the nation as a whole, "as aberrant in attitude and
defiant in mood, and as differentiated in some mysterious and irrational way
from the national experience and the national ideals."[64] It is one thing, however, to regard a region as separate from the rest of a country, and quite another to see it as removed from supposedly national ideals and experience.
That the South came to be seen in this way derives directly from the process
of American national construction in the antebellum period, a process that
involved the construction of a distinctive northern nationalism that became
national in time but certainly did not start out that way.

By the eve of the Civil War, even those events that the North and South
had in common—in particular their history—had become yet another bone of
contention between them, as each side tried to show that it had fought harder
in the war against Britain and was therefore the true inheritor and upholder
of the revolutionary heritage. Two "imagined communities" were created,
each dependent on the other to sustain it. Northern nationalism, although
clearly differing from southern nationalism in several respects, developed in
much the same way. It represented the first stage in a process that attempted
to redefine the American nation and American nationalism in the face of the
potentially destructive political, economic, and social changes of the early
nineteenth century. In effect, nineteenth-century northerners, in an attempt
to realize what they regarded as the legacy of the Founding Fathers, increasingly used the South as a negative reference point against which to measure
northern and, by extrapolation, American nationalism. But the victory of the
northern variant of American nationalist ideology has obscured the process
of national construction in nineteenth-century America and hindered our appreciation of the central role that the image of the South played in the construction of American nationalism.

In his presidential address to the Southern Historical Association, Carl
Degler touched on the reasons for this. "The contours of the nation's history," he argued, "have been defined by the present: the story of America has
been perceived as the triumph of freedom, national unity, and equality, the
acquisition of wealth, the growth of great urban centers, and the ethnic diversification of the population. The present, as epitomized by those activities
and values," he concluded, "is obviously northern in character; the North and
America have been made synonymous."[65] Degler was arguing that the South
was the victim of the Whig interpretation of history, an argument designed
to highlight the reasons for the South's image as an outsider in the American
nation. However, it is not only the South that has fallen victim to this type of
interpretation. Degler's comments shed some light on the difficulties encountered when one turns to the subject of American nationalism and the role of
North-South interaction in this. They help explain why this topic, even in the
present climate of renewed interest in the subject of nationalism, seems to
defy analysis.

To grasp fully the subtleties of the northern view of the South in the early
to mid-nineteenth century, it is essential that one try to ignore hindsight—a
dubious ally for historians—and focus on contemporary opinion. This is easier said than done, of course, especially when the period under assessment is
revealingly termed "antebellum." Yet the northern critique of the South had
its origins in the decades prior to the 1850s, when it became fully and destruc-
tively developed; obviously it was not constructed in the shadow of the Civil
War to come. Both northerners and southerners often talked a good fight long
before they had to put such talk into practice, but it is unlikely that the majority of Americans—northerners and southerners—ever believed that a war
costing over 600,000 lives would result. Nevertheless, the gradual buildup of
hostility toward the South in the northern states undermined the possibility
of compromise between the sections and went some way toward ensuring
that any accommodations reached between nonslaveholding and slaveholding
states would prove to be tenuous and short-lived.

Ironically, northern reverence for the Union and the North's more idealistic interpretation of America's national mission proved to be, in the short
term, destructive of American nationality. Only by approaching the American case in the context of studies of both nationalism in general and the antebellum period in particular can we begin to unravel the complexities of the
process of American national construction. Specifically, through an assessment of the northern image of the South in the nineteenth century, we
can trace with some clarity the origins and development of an outlook that
equated the North with America and northern ideals with national ones.

※※※

TWO

A World Apart

The Romance and Reality of the South

The Cavaliers who emigrated to Virginia and the Puritans who planted
themselves in New-England, may be regarded as presenting the most
marked dissimilarities of character of the whole bulk of those who first
populated America. And yet between those two parties there were no permanent and enduring differences, such as are engraved by race and language,
or even religion. Transient causes had divided them in England, and they
would inevitably have mingled in a homogeneous body had not the acciden-
tal institution of Slavery deepened and confirmed their differences.
— *New York Times*, 25 July 1855

In the nineteenth century, the image of the antebellum South as an agrarian,
quasi-feudal society was contrasted with that of the North as a commercial,
successful, forward-looking society. The North represented the democratic
future; the South the aristocratic past. The other side of that aristocratic image, however, was the view of the South as backward. Southern deficiencies
in manufacturing and transportation were regarded as indicative of a society
that was stagnating in the past. Both images drew their inspiration from, and
centered on, the southern plantation.

The myth of the South as a land of opulent plantations has long since been
exploded, but the plantation image was, and remains, a dominant one. The
plantation was the backdrop to the southern gentleman and his belle, to hundreds of happy and contented slaves, and to a pastoral way of life far removed
from the commercial bustle and urban squalor of the northern city. Even in
the antebellum period, the southern plantation was regarded by many northerners as symbolic of a lost Golden Age. The plantation image contained
many elements that appealed to nineteenth-century Americans. It was a place
"rich in both the pageantry and the psychology of feudalism." The plantation
represented a simplified social hierarchy where everyone, but especially African Americans, knew their place. On the one hand, there was "hereditary
authority, exercised with the graciousness of condescending mercy," and on

the other hand, "a comic inferiority and a devoted concurrence in the scheme of government."[1] As a place of order and stability in a century characterized by rapid change and development, the southern plantation supposedly appealed to those northerners who looked nostalgically to a past their nation never had, to a people they never were.

Throughout the antebellum period, however, the press, periodicals, pulpits, and politicians of the North presented a very different picture of the slaveholding South. In the 1830s and 1840s, this picture was neither wholly negative nor overtly hostile. By the 1850s, however, it was both. By then, an increasing number of northerners had developed a coherent northern nationalist ideology that relied more on the reality than on the romance of the South for definition. This ideology was predicated not on the belief that the South was really a world apart but on the recognition that it, and its labor system, was integral to the national world that both North and South had created and inhabited. Paradoxically, the recognition that slavery was a national issue with national implications failed to draw North and South closer together. Instead, it drove them even further apart. From what was clearly a national perspective in the 1830s and 1840s, northerners managed, by the 1850s, to create a sectional ideology that portrayed the South as a world apart not just from the North but also from the nation.

I n several respects, the agrarian nature of the plantation drew on Thomas Jefferson's vision of America as a New World rural arcadia, far removed from the corruption of the Old World. The general understanding of the town-country divide was summed up by Joseph Green Cogswell, professor of mineralogy and geology and librarian at Harvard in 1821. American towns and cities, Cogswell argued, were much like those in Europe; they had "all the luxury and vice of an advanced civilization." By contrast, those "who lead an agricultural life, enjoy all that happiness which is preserved from the exercise of the social virtues in their primitive purity. Their affections are constant; felicity crowns the conjugal union; respect for paternal authority is sacred; infidelity on the part of the wife is almost unknown; crime is rare; mendacity and theft uncommon."[2] As the nineteenth century progressed, this town-country split was transmuted into the North-South divide. The North represented the corruption that accompanied progress; the South represented the agrarian ideals of the past and was the repository of all the social virtues Cogswell had listed. Indeed, the contrast between a bucolic Golden Age and a corrupt urban environment had been a common motif in Elizabethan literature. Its reemergence in mid-nineteenth-century America was, in Leo Marx's words, "a native version of an ancient hope."[3]

Central to this image of the pastoral ideal was the figure of the southern gentleman, who was a very different breed from the northern Yankee. The former, according to one northerner, lived in a "baronial state, an autocrat among his slaves, a nobleman among his peers," while the latter spent "his days in bustling activity among men and ships, and his nights in sober calculation over his ledger and day-book."[4] One of the North's most famous statesmen, Edward Everett, similarly believed that southerners had traditionally "lived in great splendor and luxury, imitating the mode of life of the English aristocracy, and by natural association inclined to their principles."[5] Lorman Ratner, in his analysis of antiabolitionist sentiment, isolated the image of the southern gentleman for particular comment and argued that many northerners regarded the planter as a superior being. This, he concluded, "was a national myth with a national connotation." For northerners, the southern planter, "living close to nature and at the same time displaying all the social graces," seemed to be "the ideal citizen of a republic of virtue."[6]

However, as William R. Taylor noted, the figure of the southern gentleman "masked a whole complex of fears and anxieties about the consequences of changes then taking place in American life."[7] For some northerners, the South's gentlemen planters seemed to represent a conservative, ordered way of life that the North no longer provided. For others, they became dangerously subversive aristocrats who had no valid place in any democratic nation. Still others rejected the whole idea of the Cavalier-Yankee paradigm. Henry De Forest, for one, objected to the manner in which southerners laid "claim to all the generosity & all the 'chivalry' in the nation . . . while the Yankee is a mere money making machine."[8]

Nineteenth-century literature, as Taylor and others have shown, certainly drew on and influenced a positive response to the South. The figure of the refined and relaxed planter was a clear counterimage to that of the hardworking, acquisitive Yankee. Washington Irving's Rip Van Winkle is a case in point. The lazy Rip is certainly no hero, but the real villain of the piece, David Bertelson argued, is Rip's wife, "whose demands for labor in the name of civilization finally reduce poor Rip almost to despair." Southern idleness, in contrast, was not regarded as laziness but was reformulated as an aristocratic pursuit of leisure, the "Aristotelian meaning of freedom from the necessity of having to engage in manual labor."[9] By crafting the image of the southern planter in the mold of the English country gentleman, northerners portrayed a lifestyle that, unlike their own, did not encompass material gain as the ultimate goal. The literature of the day—by both northerners and southerners—reinforced this image. The figure of the English country squire in Washington Irving's *Bracebridge Hall* (1822) was one example. Similarly, both John Pendleton Kennedy in *Swallow Barn* (1832) and James Kirke Paulding

in *Westward Ho!* (1832) and *The Puritan and His Daughter* (1849) gave their
readers a "traditional" view of southern plantation life. The literary representation of the plantation idyll, Taylor argued, was not a southern image
"concocted to propagandize the North" but was the dominant national image
at the time.[10]

Yet one of the most widely read women's magazines of the nineteenth
century, *Godey's Lady's Book,* which otherwise tended to concentrate on domestic advice and sewing patterns of devilish complexity, frequently carried
articles and short stories that focused on the South and exploded the luxurious
plantation image. Indeed, the magazine took great pains to dispel any lingering remnant of the myth of the South. With this in mind, *Godey's* published
the reminiscences of a northern tutor who had found work during the 1840s
on a plantation in Mississippi. The tutor acknowledged that the reality of
southern life was very different from what she had expected. Initially she was
pleased with the prospect of life on a plantation, because in her "imagination
a Southern planter held a sort of middle place between a baron in the old
feudal times of Europe, and a Northern farmer." She admitted that visions
"of magnificence, of boundless liberality and hospitality, rose before me
whenever my thoughts turned to my future home."[11] She found the reality to
be quite different. The plantation itself was far from luxurious and lacked the
amenities—including furniture, pictures, and books—of northern life. The
people, however, were far kinder than she had anticipated and much more
hardworking than she had been led to believe. Only the planter himself came
across as a stereotype in her description, as a man who was fond of "a mint-
julep and a good cigar" and who sustained "an intense dislike of Yankees."[12]
The plantation's mistress, in contrast, was unlike the stereotypical southern
belle and was described as far more practical than the majority of northern
women.

In general, throughout the antebellum period, northern publications did
more to debunk the plantation myth than to support it. The short stories that
Godey's published supported the image of the South provided by the
nonfiction articles. These were frequently devoted to the subject of northern
women marrying southerners. The stress was usually on the amount of hard
work and sheer physical effort that such women's lives were likely to involve.
All "Southerners are rich . . . and Southern ladies, every one knows, never do
anything, but sit still all day and have a servant to dress their hair, and bring
them even their pocket-handkerchiefs," one writer wryly noted, before describing the disillusionment her subject experienced on meeting her new husband's family. "You know we are plain farm people," the bride is told. "Further South, on rice and sugar plantations, where the heat is greater, and wealth

is in proportion to the number of hands and acres, you might have realized this paradise of indolence; but, as far as society goes, you would be still worse off," since women there were truly "domestic," which meant that they remained at home and had few opportunities for social contact.[13]

In direct contradiction of the image of the lazy southerner reclining on his veranda, *Godey's* more often stressed that southerners were extremely hard workers. It was the northerner in the South, the magazine noted, who played at being the wealthy, lazy aristocrat. If the romance of the South was ever acknowledged, it was in conjunction with decay. Descriptions of "the mould and the rust, the results of the dampness of the climate, that imported air of remote antiquity to the buildings," went hand in hand with admiration for "the striking romance of the scenery" and criticisms of the barrenness of much of the countryside. To one writer, the South seemed "like the solemn ruins of a temple of nature, still consecrated and unpolluted," as remote in place and time from the antebellum North as the ruins of ancient Greece or Rome.[14]

The image of the South as a land of decaying splendor was typical by the 1840s. The press, periodicals, and politicians of the North were already fairly fixed in the habit of drawing comparisons between the free and the slave states, to the detriment of the latter. "If we compare South Carolina and Massachusetts," one paper argued, "we shall find that one is a large and fertile State, in a mild climate, with slave labor, and free trade philosophers to rule it; and the other a small and barren State, in a rigorous climate, but with free white men to do the work." The result, it concluded, "is that South Carolina is now growing old and poor, is deficient in roads . . . and almost wholly destitute of the local markets of towns and factories necessary to support in prosperity her farmers."[15]

The crux of much northern criticism was how little the South had achieved since the Revolution, in contrast to the growth and expansion sustained by the North. "It is the peculiarity of the State of Virginia," wrote one reviewer, "that it is at once old and yet undeveloped. Rich in resources, she is yet poor; rich in memories of the past, yet falling behind many a younger State in her influence upon the present, and failing to fulfil the high promise of her youth."[16] Such sentiments reinforced northern feelings of superiority by portraying the South as a region that remained at the frontier stage of social and economic development while the North was already exhibiting all the trappings of a forward-looking, modern civilization. They found an echo in a letter that Free-Soil sympathizer John P. Hale sent to his wife from the South. "Here I am at the Capital of the old famous State of Virginia," he wrote, "famous rather for what she has been and what she has done and the men she has produced, than for any particular eminence which pertains to her at the present in any respect whatsoever, save that ancestral pride, which the children of broken down families retain to the last, when every other relic of greatness is departed."[17]

It has been argued that in the twentieth century the West has given the United States a past that, in purely historical terms, it was lacking in comparison to Europe.[18] In the mid-nineteenth century, however, when the West was only beginning to be developed, the South increasingly fulfilled this function. The South, as many northerners portrayed it, belonged to the past. As far as northern, and later Republican, ideology was concerned, the South as it was—feudal, aristocratic, backward—had no obvious or desirable place in America's future. The plantation image was a romantic one, but it was the romance of the past, an anachronistic image in the forward-looking society of nineteenth-century America. Most northerners were fully cognizant of the fact that the plantation image was, at best, an idealized one. They may have enjoyed the literary representation of the South and wallowed in the romantic picture it presented, but most were in no way deceived by it. The reality of the South, as many northerners well knew, was rather different from the fictional world.

In contrast to the fictional image of the South, northern newspapers and journals of the period lost little opportunity to portray the South negatively. In the process, of course, they presented the North in a contrasting favorable glow. Indeed, the tendency to use the South as a foil for extensive and frequent praise of the North was already common in the 1820s. In 1821, the *Boston Daily Advertiser* boasted of the "love of correct, well-regulated freedom," which, it argued, was the distinguishing characteristic of Massachusetts, in contrast to the slaveholding South. "Our ancestors came from Europe in an age in which the world was enlightened, and at a moment when the spirit of freedom was warm and unrestrained," the paper argued. This, combined with the inhospitable climate of the North, meant that New Englanders had never been tempted to "form great plantations and to cultivate them by slaves."[19]

The tariff debates of the 1830s, which posited northern (pro-tariff) interests against southern (free-trade) interests, provided an additional excuse for northerners to criticize the South and to shine the harsh light of reality on the plantation romance. The *Albany Evening Journal*'s response to the tariff debates was typical in its scathing critique of the "chivalrous sons" of the South and in the damning contrast it drew between the northern and southern states. In the former were "cultivated fields, fair orchards—industrious, well-clad freemen—prosperous manufactories, good roads, bridges, fences, schoolhouses, churches, and social institutions—convenient and comfortable dwellings—activity, wealth, and enterprise." In the latter there were only "execrable roads," "bridgeless streams," "rickety fences," and "squalid slaves."[20]

This was perhaps the most persistent theme in northern criticisms of the South. The backward nature of southern agricultural and economic development, which many considered to be the reality of plantation culture, greatly concerned northerners. But criticism of the South was seldom expressed without some measure of accompanying praise for the North. As one senator argued, the "Southern planter does not, like the hardy farmer of the North and West, lay his hand to the plough; he neither holds nor drives; the culture of the fields is left to the overseer and the slaves, and their cultivation is without skill and without care."[21] The unwillingness of southerners to engage in hard work, combined with the South's slave-labor force, was considered to have a detrimental effect on every aspect of southern life. It was argued that, in the South,

> the lights of science, and the improvements of art, which vivify and accelerate elsewhere, cannot penetrate, or, if they do, penetrate with dilatory inefficiency, among its operatives. A disrelish for humbler and hardy occupation; a pride adverse to drudgery and toil; a dread that to partake in the employment allotted to color, may be accompanied also by its degradation, are natural and inevitable. The high and lofty qualities which, in other scenes and for other purposes, characterize and adorn our Southern brethren, are fatal to the enduring patience, the corporeal exertion, and the pains-taking simplicity, by which only a successful yeomanry can be founded.[22]

Businessman and northern representative Nathan Appleton, who was admittedly biased, as he had a vested interest in seeing the protective tariff system adopted, linked southern backwardness to "the general or political character of society. All industry is set in motion by capital," he argued, "and [the tariff system] seeks to induce capital to devote itself to the employment of domestic industry; because, by adding to the means of comfort and happiness in the laboring classes, their character and standing in society is elevated, and they are better fitted to discharge the duties of good citizens." Appleton purported to wonder "whether this cheap slave labor does not paralyze the industry of the whites? Whether idleness is not the greatest of their evils?"[23] It was a rhetorical question. Appleton, like so many northerners, saw the South as a real hindrance to the nation's future economic success.

The debates over the tariff were not trivial or subsidiary to northerners, and they went to the heart of northern concerns over the nation's future. As a representative from Pennsylvania put it, labor "is the foundation of national prosperity; it is the great parent of all production. Depress labor and you depress the nation. Labor would prosper or decline precisely as you increase or diminish protection."[24] America's future commercial success was an issue that exercised many northerners throughout the antebellum period. Successful commercial development, one writer argued, "requires the possession of civil and political liberty: the freest countries are always the most strongly commercial, and the most barbarous and enslaved the least. In the former we find an extraordinary degree of intelligence, and a freedom from restraint discernible only in connexion with rational and well-defined liberty."[25] Another writer agreed: "Of the connexion that has, from the earliest ages, subsisted between commerce and intellectual improvement," he stated, "the records of the human race bear ample and constant evidence."[26]

From a northern perspective, commerce and industry were integral to America's national character. "Were it to be asked," declared one writer, "what is the most distinguishing feature which marks our republic, a ready answer might be given: —it is the productive enterprise of the people."[27] In a similar vein, a northern minister reminded his audience that the "American character is strongly commercial. Habits of trading are here formed almost from the cradle." Nothing, he argued, "so stimulates the growth of a nation as this very spirit of trade." The American nation, he concluded, although still in its youth, was "now forming the chart of its future voyage on the sea of existence"[28] Of course, the iceberg in nineteenth-century America's particular sea of existence seemed to be the South. There it floated, resolutely reluctant to join the rest of the nation in the uninhibited pursuit of profit, and unwilling to develop its impressive natural resources to this end.

Northerners were encouraged in this line of thinking by the fact that many southerners concurred with it. The southern nationalist and anti-tariff spokesman, George McDuffie, was only one of several southerners who supported the negative view of southern development. "The staple-growing states," he argued, "can never be practically independent . . . until the commerce which is funded on their valuable productions, shall be carried on by our own merchants permanently resident among us."[29] Another southerner argued that the South had significant sources of coal and water and "many other elements of prosperity provided by nature," but overall "there is wanting, to bring them into full and active operation, an accession of such an enterprising, active, and industrious class of citizens as exist in New England, and developes her less abundant resources." It was the writer's opinion that such "a population is gradually but slowly forming, but the prevalence of slavery is a bar to its rapid increase. Virginia, like the States south of her, is, in great measure, dependent on the superior industry and enterprise of her eastern brethren."[30]

In general, the belief that southerners knew little about either commerce or agriculture and, worse, cared less predominated in the northern states in the 1830s and 1840s. Far from being ideal citizens of a republic of virtue living in harmony with nature, southerners, it was believed, were poor farmers who knew little about the land. They "cultivate it some years until every particle of nourishment is extracted from it . . . they have no resources for enriching the soil as we have at the north," a northern tutor in the South reported.[31] Northerners were quite well informed, albeit in a negative sense, when it came to the subject of southern agricultural practices. Northern migrants to the South were not slow to express their "wide-spread disdain for Southern farming methods" and to report that they "found native Virginians indolent, ignorant, and unaware of proper farming techniques."[32] The South offered opportunities to those northerners who were prepared to swap "a healthy for a sickly climate" and to live "in a country in every way uncongenial to their feeling and their habits." But as northerners were quick to point out, southerners, being unused to hard work, rarely tried to make their fortune in the North.[33] Such views would have reached a fairly wide audience in the North via the pages of newspapers and various agricultural journals such as the *Cultivator, American Agriculturist, New England Farmer,* and *Country Gentleman,* so it is unlikely that northerners would have been unaware of arguments concerning the backwardness of southern agricultural and commercial practices. Indeed, Amos A. Lawrence observed, somewhat sarcastically, that a commercial publication such as *Hunts' Merchants Magazine* was "appreciated here [New England], but will do more good at the South."[34]

Northerners exploited the propaganda potential offered by northern farmers' success in reclaiming the worn-out lands of the South. For northern reformers, the region's hardworking farmers allowed them plenty of opportunity to support and expand on their argument that northern ways were far superior to those of the South and that slavery had always hampered southern social, cultural, and agricultural development.[35] By the 1850s, northerners were well used to such arguments. In Frederick Law Olmsted's series of letters from the South, he quoted a letter from Thomas Crux of Fairfax County, Virginia, to Thomas Ewbank, the U.S. commissioner of patents, to draw his readers' attention to the noticeable improvement in the land in that county, which he ascribed to the efforts of northern migrants.[36] Another correspondent supported Olmsted's picture. "The surrounding country is rapidly improving. Land has doubled, and in many cases trebled its former price," he argued, since "Northern families have bought a considerable part of the worn-out lands of Fairfax County, and greatly enhanced its worth."[37] For those, like Olmsted, who were so inclined, the success of northern migrants in the South was evidence of both northern superiority and southern backwardness. "The commercial results of the free states is the offspring of their voluntary labor system," Olmsted asserted. "The inability of the Virginians to engage in commerce is the result of their system of involuntary servitude. The condition of the laborers predetermines the condition of the people."[38]

Olmsted never allowed his readers to lose sight of northern success and the "sad contrast between capacity and achievement" that he saw in the South. "With a wide-spread domain, with a kindly soil, with a climate whose sun radiates fertility, and whose very dews distil abundance," Olmsted noted, "we find an inheritance so wasted that the eye aches to behold the prospect."[39] This was a standard picture by the time Olmsted visited the South. By the 1850s, northern images of the South often focused, as they had in the 1830s and 1840s, on what one writer termed the "material decay and disaster" of southern land and on its destitute, barren nature in contrast to the fertility of the northern states. "The very soil of the South is blasted by slavery," another writer concluded.[40]

In assessing such negative images of the South, it is clear that they were predicated on a variety of concerns that prevailed in the North. To those directly involved in the issues raised by the tariff debates, the South's apparent reluctance to encourage American commerce and industry was a major irritant. Yet the fact that the negative image of the South thrown up by such debates was not much different from that expressed by those not engaged in business and trade reveals that there was more involved than questions over land management or business. In opposing what many understood to be the interests not just of the North but of the nation as a whole, the South seemed to be maintaining a sectional position that undermined the success of the American republican experiment. Even an essentially conservative northerner such as Edward Everett read more into the tariff issue than the question of import duties alone. In it, he saw a direct challenge to northern—and specifically New England—influence in the nation. Indeed, Everett's "attempts to preserve New England's power not only submerged his nationalism but often shaped his nationalist ideology" in a distinctly sectional form.[41]

Although Everett defended his support for the protective tariff on the grounds that agricultural and manufacturing strength was required for the stability of the Union, his concerns were more sectional than national. For Everett, a balanced, stable, successful society required three economic branches: commerce, agriculture, and manufacturing. In Everett's view, only

New England sustained all three, and it was to defend New England that he spoke out against the South's position on the tariff. Only New England farmers, Everett later argued, were capable of leaving behind "a posterity competent not only to preserve and assert, but to augment and improve, their heritage."[42] Indeed, for Everett, the ideal American character was clearly the New England Yankee writ large, and the best possible future for the American nation would be achieved if New England values became national ones.[43] Like so many other northerners, Everett had developed a defense of his own section that was predicated, to a great extent, on the shortcomings of the South.

The main cause of southern backwardness, as many northerners saw it, was slavery. Slavery, the *Albany Evening Journal* declared, "is the bane of Virginia. It has made 'waste places' of her fruitful fields, and enervated her people. It sits like an incubus upon her, and has left the impress of decrepitude and decay upon all her interests. Her soil, once as prolific as that of any other State in the Union, is exhausted, and imbecility has become the predominant characteristic of her people."[44] Yet the northern attitude toward slavery was, throughout the antebellum period, ambivalent. Until the late 1840s, the predominant attitude among northern moderates was that slavery was not the fault of the South but an institution that had been forced upon that region. Indeed, the belief that slavery was a curse bequeathed to the South by the nation's Founding Fathers (or by Britain) had been prevalent in the North at least as far back as the Missouri Compromise debates of 1820–1821. Slavery, according to eminent Boston lawyer (later judge) Lemuel Shaw, was "a great and acknowledged evil," yet it remained a necessary one. Despite his strong opposition to the South's peculiar institution, Shaw believed that slavery was "too deeply interwoven in the texture of society to be wholly or speedily eradicated." Sudden emancipation, he believed, "would be productive of greater evils than the continuation of slavery." Ultimately, Shaw concluded, southern society under slavery suffered

> a succession of evils, scarcely less than those it inflicts. A state whose laws and institutions recognize and habitually cherish a disregard to the fundamental principles of natural rights and social duty, cannot be founded upon a safe and stable basis. It possesses within itself sources of corruption, weakness, and degeneracy, which must endanger its safety and finally accelerate its ruin.

Since the North was exempt "from the great moral and political evil entailed" upon the South, Shaw argued, northerners regarded the South's "condition more in sorrow than in anger."[45] This was a fair assessment of attitudes at the time and throughout the following decade. Slavery, according to the *Albany Evening Journal*, was an "unblest inheritance that has been cast upon" the

South. One representative from Ohio similarly argued that since the institution was an "evil, cast upon our Southern brethren, not by their own acts, or of their own choice, but by the cupidity of a foreign nation while we remained her colonies, [it] is one for which they are entitled to any thing rather than reproach and censure."[46]

Significantly, in the 1830s and early 1840s, slavery was regarded not as a sectional matter but as a national one. As the *New York Tribune* reminded its readers, the "whole Country is chargeable with the guilt of American Slavery. It was the East that robbed Africa of her children, and enriched herself by selling them to the South."[47] Northern Congregational minister and reformer Horace Bushnell similarly counseled members of his congregation not to be too harsh in their condemnation of the South, advising them that if "there was ever a people on earth involved in crime, who yet deserved sympathy and gentleness at the hands of the good, it is the slave-holding portion of our country." He asserted, "We are linked with slavery by duties of mutual aid and defense. . . . We also have a common character with the South, we are one nation. If we hold our breath where the honor of our nation is thus deeply concerned, we are not Americans. A man's right hand cannot be a thief's and his left's an honest man. No more can a nation have its honor or its dishonor in single limbs and fragments."[48]

Bushnell's attitude, however, was not as reasonable as it appeared. Indeed, his recognition that slavery was a national problem, with national implications, in no sense modified his essentially negative view of the South. If anything, it exacerbated it. "It ought to be a matter of great weight with us here at the North," Bushnell averred, "that slavery has no agreement with our institutions." The supposed equality of the South, he argued, was "not the equality of citizens, but of so many masterships or slavedoms. The notions bred in them by their education are too often correspondent. They grow up in command, not in concession. In childhood they make the law, not learn subordination to it. They invigorate their will, but not their notions of equal justice. Their organ is power, not reason. And, accordingly, when they come into the Congress of the nation, they too often come with a jealous and imperious spirit, which well nigh disqualifies them for a place in that reasoning and deliberative body."[49]

In his portrayal of the southern gentleman turned tyrant, Bushnell was clearly paraphrasing Thomas Jefferson's argument about the impact of slavery on the slave owner as outlined in his *Notes on Virginia*, an argument that northerners were familiar with and referred to often in the years before the Civil War. But unlike Jefferson, Bushnell was not especially concerned about the impact of slavery on the South or on the slave; his concern was the North.

He also drew on the kind of imagery that Taylor and others identified as inculcating a positive response to the South—namely, the plantation idyll dominated by the southern gentleman planter. Seen in a negative light, the southern gentleman still dominated southern society, but now his patriarchal domain compromised not only slaves but also poor whites, whose suffering he caused by maintaining a system of slave labor. His gentlemanly qualities, in the eyes of a hostile observer, became symptomatic of corruption and decay, and his aristocratic mien was transformed into "haughty self-conceit" and "marble-headed insensibility."[50]

This in itself was of little concern to northerners such as Horace Bushnell. What did concern them was the influence the South was having on the North and on the nation as a whole. Paradoxically, the recognition that slavery was a national and not a sectional issue actually encouraged the development of a northern, predominantly sectional critique of the South. Bushnell himself returned to the issue of the South's impact on national institutions in 1844, when the debate over the proposed annexation of Texas was raging. "Once more," Bushnell declared, "the predominant influence of slavery, in the institutions of our country, is a powerful cause of the result we are deploring. With a population inferior to that of the free states and rapidly decreasing, it is yet demonstrable that slavery has hitherto borne rule in the nation." It was not simply southern political power that concerned Bushnell, but rather the influence of the South on the northern states. "The moral deterioration of which I have complained here at the north," he asserted, "has been visibly due, in no small degree, to the assimilating power of southern influence. Slavery, as such, has no principle—it loosens all the evil passions of human nature." The South, Bushnell warned, "has been steadily traveling northward, bringing its license with it, expelling the ancient time when merit reigned among us, and making us familiar with the lawless spirit of political adventure and rapacity. Our evil communications have corrupted our good manners, till now, the separation of politics from the fear of God, and the constraints of moral obligation is becoming national in our people."[51]

If slavery was national, then its detrimental effects were national. It was a logical conclusion, and Bushnell was not alone in reaching it. Ralph Waldo Emerson, transcendentalist and perhaps New England's most famous philosopher and poet, managed, in the course of the antebellum period, to move from a national to a distinctly sectional position on the matter of slavery and the South. Initially, Emerson advocated an understanding attitude toward the South. In his first address on the slavery issue, he was more concerned with the abstract issue of free speech and with the mote in the eye of the North: "Let our own evils check the bitterness of our condemnation of our brother," he declared, "and whilst we insist on calling things by their right names, let us not reproach the planter, but own that his misfortune is at least as great as his sin."[52] This sympathetic image of the southerner as a man enslaved by slavery was fairly typical in the 1830s and 1840s. It may well have been an expression of genuine understanding. After all, only a fanatic maintains a rigidly hostile view of a subject, with no allowances made. Yet Emerson's general view of the South was far from positive. Sympathy for the South was clearly not the only reason he advocated understanding between the sections.

In common with many northerners, Emerson was concerned about the changes he saw around him in northern society. As he put it, there was a "good deal of character in our abused age. The rights of women, the anti-slavery, temperance, peace, health, and money movements; female speakers, mobs & martyrs, the paradoxes, the antagonism of old & new, the anomalous church, the daring mysticism & the plain prose,—the uneasy relation of domestics," all of which revealed that "life at the heart [was] not yet justly organized at the surface."[53] In the face of the upheaval in northern society, Emerson acknowledged but resented the comparative stability and confidence of southerners: "I am always a fool to these mannered men at the first encounter," he admitted. Yet he made it clear that, overall, he considered northerners far superior to southerners. Addressing an imaginary southerner, he advised him not to "presume on this gay privilege of thine. Yonder simple countryman, on whom you have yet bestowed no smile, strikes down all your glittering & serried points with a wave of his hand. . . . He oversteps with a free strike all your spaces marked with ribbond & etiquettes, for he does not respect them; he is dignified by a higher thought."[54]

Emerson detected his own weakness in the northerners around him. Even the abolitionists, who "vapor at the North and in the streets of Boston with Massachusetts at their back," in the South were "at once hushed by the 'chivalry' which they sneer at, at home." Southerners were "haughty, selfish, willful, & unscrupulous men, who will have their way, & have it. The people of New England with a thousand times more talent, more worth, more ability of every kind, are timid, prudent . . . calculating men who cannot fight until their blood is up, who have consciences & many other obstacles betwixt them & their wishes. The Virginian has none, & so always beats them today, & is steadily beaten by them year by year."[55] In common with Bushnell, Emerson was concerned with southern influence on the North. Out of this concern, both men gradually developed a hostile critique of the South predicated on the superiority of their own section.

Emerson's views on the South derived at least in part from firsthand experience of that region. Emerson first visited the South in 1826 for health reasons and commented favorably on the manners of southern society, particularly among southern African Americans.[56] His praise for southern manners can be read as much as an indication of his racism as a declaration of his admiration for the South. It may well have been both. Certainly Emerson, in common with many northerners, was not sensitive to the reality of slavery in the South. Slavery, for Emerson, was an abstract evil, an institution he used in general terms "when he needed examples of man's inhumanity to man."[57] It was an institution that encouraged men to "use persons as things"—something he thought the North as guilty of as the South.[58] By the time of his second visit to the South in 1843, Emerson's opinions had altered somewhat. By then, Emerson placed far more emphasis on the cultural, social, and economic superiority of the North—specifically New England. There was "nothing very distinctive in the population" of the South, Emerson noted, and "a large proportion of the people in active professions are Yankees." The South, Emerson concluded, was a blighted region that sustained no poets, no libraries, no men of note. "Charles Carroll the signer is dead, and Archbishop Carroll is dead," Emerson declared, "and there is no vision in the land."[59]

The year following this visit, Emerson delivered his first "Emancipation in the British West Indies" address, during which he developed a sustained critique of slavery and slaveholders. Like Bushnell, Emerson portrayed the southerner as a gentleman turned tyrant, a "spoiled child of his unnatural habits" who exhibited a "love of power, the voluptuousness of holding a human being in his absolute control."[60] Yet Emerson's concerns still had little to do with slavery; they were derived purely from his fear of southern influence in the nation. He continued to berate the North's lack of spirit in opposing this influence and attributed this weakness to the combination of southern political power and northern economic greed. Emerson was especially critical of northern manufacturers that maintained close links with the South and believed that the North was compromised by their position. "Cotton thread," he argued, "holds the Union together; unites John C. Calhoun and Abbott Lawrence. Patriotism [is] for holidays and summer evenings, with music and rockets, but cotton thread is the Union." Emerson considered the nation as a whole to be "wanting in the male principle." Although it had "immense resources, land, men, milk, butter, cheese, timber, and iron," America suffered from "a village littleness . . . village squabble and rapacity characterize its policy." This was, Emerson concluded, "a great strength on a basis of weakness."[61]

In time, Emerson became even more hostile toward the South, but it is clear that by 1846, the main outlines of his personal critique were already in place. Although Emerson, like many of the northerners that Taylor identified, expressed concern at the tenor of the times and regarded the South as comparatively stable and well ordered, in the end, this only made him more conscious of the threat the South posed to the North. By 1846, Emerson was already turning away from a Union that, in his opinion, had nothing more substantial than cotton thread to hold it together. Like Edward Everett, Emerson believed that the North, despite its problems, represented the closest approximation to the ideal American society. But the North's influence was undermined and its values threatened by its relationship to the slaveholding society of the South. This was not at all what northerners had expected.

Long used to arguments that the North was much more advanced than the South, many northerners considered their section to be representative of the nation. The South was an aberration in this regard. As the *Albany Evening Journal* argued, the South's lack "of enlightened enterprise, combined with the enervating influence of Slavery, has not only kept them poor, but stripped them of almost all of the distinguishing traits of the American character. They appear like dwarfs by the side of the giants of the North." Five years later, the paper continued to argue that the southern states "follow the Free States not like rivals but like shadows. The ground they are traversing now, the Free States passed over years ago."[62] It was a common notion that the South could achieve its full potential only by adopting "northern implements, northern wages, habits, customs; northern schools and churches; northern industry and economy . . . and northern restlessness and progressive improvement."[63] Northerners frequently boasted that it was "the inevitable destiny of the South to be molded by the North, and be forced by steadily progressive circumstances into practically industrial communities," but by the late 1840s it seemed more likely that any influence was moving in a South-North direction rather than vice versa.[64]

One of the North's foremost Unitarian clergymen and authors, Andrew Preston Peabody, summed up northern concerns in this regard. He noted that "New England men, wherever they go, occupy prominent places, and exert a commanding influence. They are more apt to give than to receive law;—to control the current of opinion than to yield to it." However, when a New Englander moved to the South, a transformation took place. These "adopted citizens of the South are, for the most part, among the strongest and least tolerant advocates of slavery," Peabody asserted.[65] That the worst southerners were northerners would become a northern cliché. It was one that Harriet Beecher Stowe invoked in her creation of Simon Legree, the evil overseer from Vermont. It revealed an underlying concern about New Englanders' capacity to influence the rest of the North, let alone the nation, in any kind of beneficial way. If "the northern man, born on the battle-ground of freedom, goes to the South and becomes the most tyrannical of slavedrivers," then southern influence was clearly a force to be reckoned with.[66] The danger for the North was, as Theodore Parker observed, that "the idea which allows Slavery in South Carolina will establish it also in New England."[67]

There was clearly more to the construction of the northern critique of the South than assertions of northern superiority. The fact that northerners were so determined to stress their section's superiority, and to uncover evidence of it at every opportunity, was indicative of uncertainty about their own position. Theodore Parker had observed that the "people of New England, as much from taste & constitution as from necessity, have devoted their chief energies to production & accumulation & have finally come to think this the chief end of man."[68] Parker was more extreme than many northerners in his emphasis on the moral and spiritual dimensions of life, but his argument—that to some degree the North had been spoiled by its own success—struck a chord. Many northerners would have readily taken the point made in the *Newark Daily Advertiser* regarding Yankee influence. "We may laugh at the Yankees," the paper observed, "but they are the most thriving people in the world." Puritan influence accounted for this, the paper argued, and it acknowledged the prevalent view that New Englanders' influence in the nation was widespread. However, it continued, it "remains to be seen whether the reflex operation of their influence on other people will make them better or worse; whether commerce will deteriorate the agricultural simplicity; whether the blade may not acquire a wire-edge from overwhetting; and turn awry upon excessive legislation, ever-lasting conflicts about abolition and the like; and whether the inventiveness which has been too keen for all the world, will not wound itself, like a sword which cuts its scabbard."[69]

Emerson had expressed concern about the unsettled nature of northern society, and he was not the only one to do so. Northern pro-Union statesman Caleb Cushing argued that "the state of opinion at the North is fluctuating. . . . Nothing is fixed in religion, in morals, or in politics; but in all these things, the wildest, the meanest, and the falsest delusions are continually arising one after another." This "chronic anarchy of opinion," Cushing averred, "defies all calculations in public affairs." Cushing was not seeking to make any particular sectional point with this observation. Indeed, he approved of the fact that "there is more of healthy conservations in the organization of society at the South than at the North."[70] However, for many northerners, southern stability and, especially, the political power that derived from this undermined the efforts of the North—specifically, New England—to bring the South around to its particular version of the American idea.

Faced with southern reluctance to conform to northern ways, and fearing the effects of southern influence on their own section, northerners moved away from their earlier acceptance of slavery as a national problem and began to portray it as a sectional defect. At the same time, more radical elements in the North began to construct a myth of uncommon descent for northerners and southerners. In time, this myth crossed the line between extremist, essentially abolitionist, rhetoric and became a standard by which to measure and explain North-South differences. The Cavalier-Yankee paradigm was not new, but by the late 1840s it was being invoked in a new and dangerously sectional way.

John Gorham Palfrey, a noted Unitarian clergyman and historian, was one of the first to try to reinterpret the traditional understanding of the differences between the Cavalier and the Yankee, differences he considered to have been constructed solely by the South in an attempt to establish its aristocratic origins. According to Palfrey, it was the "Roundhead founders of Massachusetts" who were actually "of the noble and gentle blood of England" and "persons of fortune and education." The settlers of Virginia, in contrast, "were Cavaliers of that sort which Wildrake, in Scott's novel *Woodstock*, is the type and embodiment. . . . 'Many were poor gentlemen, broken tradesmen, rakes, and libertines, footmen, and such others as were much fitter to spoil and ruin a Commonwealth than to help to raise or maintain one.'"[71] Parker, as one might expect, was even more active in the construction of the myth that more than slavery differentiated North and South. From the earliest days of America's settlement, he argued, the character of the people of the South was different: "their manners, their social and political ideas were unlike those of the North," he asserted. Further,

> the Southern States were mainly colonies of adventurers, rather than establishments of men who for conscience' sake fled to the wilderness. Less pains were taken with education—intellectual, moral, and religious—of the people. Religion never held so prominent a place in the consciousness of the mass as in the sterner and more austere colonies of the North. . . . Slavery easily found a footing at an early day. It was not at all repulsive to the ideas, the institutions and habits of Georgia and South Carolina. . . . Consequences follow causes; it is not easy to avoid the results of a first principle.[72]

Parker was doing more, however, than criticizing the South. The main thesis behind his critique was an attempt to establish a link between northern virtues and national virtues. The northern states, he argued, "in all their constitutions and social structure, consistently and continually tend to Democracy—the government of all, for all, and by all," whereas the southern states, "in their constitutions and social structure, as consistently tend to Oligarchy—the government over all, by a few, and for the sake of that few."[73] To isolate what he saw as the "American idea" in the North, Parker increasingly used his particular version of American history to make the point, and he isolated northern superiority in "the blood of those Puritans who planted themselves on these shores, which," he averred, "gave their descendants a Power of Idea and a Power of Action, such as no people before our time has ever had."[74]

This was a viewpoint that Parker pushed hard in the pages of the short-lived *Massachusetts Quarterly Review,* which he edited with Ralph Waldo Emerson and John Elliot Cabot from the end of 1847 through September 1850. Indeed, both Emerson's concerns about the state of society in the North and Parker's more aggressive criticism of the state of society in the South found expression in this journal. In their inaugural editorial, the editors denounced the lack of moral influence in the nation and indicated, somewhat high-handedly as well as unrealistically, that it was the aim of the *Review* to rectify this defect. In its short life, the *Review* frequently stressed that the "most marked characteristic of the American nation is LOVE OF FREEDOM, OF MAN'S NATURAL RIGHTS." Americans "have a genius for liberty," it argued, "the American idea is freedom."[75] The editors rarely missed a chance to make sectional capital over North-South differences. It was the North, they argued, that fought hardest in and paid for the American Revolution; the North that paid the bulk of the nation's taxes; the North that owned "the mills, the shops, the ships" and wrote "the histories, poems, philosophies, works of science [and] even the sermons and commentaries on the Bible." It was the North alone that educated its children; built schools, colleges, and churches; and "made the nation great, rich, and famous for her ideas and their success all over the world." Northerners, the journal concluded, represented "the American sentiment, the American idea . . . [and] the spirit of the nation is on their side."[76]

There was clearly more than a touch of a specifically New England outlook in the antisouthern outbursts of men like Parker, Emerson, and Palfrey. Certainly the contrast they drew between New England and the South was, by the 1840s, a familiar one. Edward Everett's brother, Alexander, had argued in 1834 that the New England colonies were "the only ones in the whole number, that were not founded with a view to pecuniary profit or any secular advantage." New England's foundation in religion, he believed, "has been the real source, not only of their unparalleled prosperity, but in great measure of the prosperity of the whole country, which has always received, and still receives, its principal impulse from this quarter."[77] Almost identical views were expressed in 1851, when it was argued that "it is impossible to traverse our country in any direction without being convinced, that whatever progressive energy stamps its seal in any department of human pursuit, it has been done in nine cases out of ten by the hand of a native-born New Englander."[78] However, although New Englanders may have been the most outspoken in their use of the national past for essentially sectional ends, they were not alone in doing so, and the arguments they constructed resonated far beyond New England.[79]

Throughout the antebellum period, many northerners turned to evidence from the past—both genuine and fabricated—in an attempt to establish a working basis for an American national identity. This is not unusual. All nations rely on the past, or on some version of the past, for national definition. The country's relatively brief history notwithstanding, nineteenth-century Americans were no different in this regard from many nineteenth-century Europeans. J. V. Matthews, however, stressed that for antebellum Americans in particular, "history became something of a national preoccupation as the generation which had inherited the new nation worked out a conception of its nature and destiny." For a new nation, he argued, "an aesthetically and emotionally satisfying myth of origins is not only a necessary ingredient of an evolving national identity but a prerequisite for a sense of future direction and development."[80]

Unfortunately, as far as national stability was concerned, in the process of constructing an emotionally satisfying myth of origins, northerners managed to exclude the South from their vision of American national identity. Indeed, they came to rely on the South as the essential negative reference point in the construction of that identity. In the search for what one New York minister summed up as "the national idea which will create our national character and social condition," an increasing number of antebellum northerners turned to the South for evidence of everything they did not wish to be. "Virginia and Massachusetts were an extension of the cavalier and Puritan into the Western continent," he argued, yet "one powerful tendency from the first has striven to fuse these diverse masses, has created a national history and is now toiling to form a national character and society . . . *reverence for the individual man.*" This idea, he stressed, "is creating a new order of social affairs." However, in his opinion it was no longer the case that North and South were working together in this regard. Indeed, reverence for the individual seemed, in his view, to be lacking in the South and, by virtue of southern influence, in the nation as a whole. "The national society," he concluded, "is now governed by the two powers of hereditary distinction of races and acquired wealth."[81]

In an article occasioned by the Fourth of July celebration, the *Pittsburgh Daily Gazette* reminded its readers that whereas other nations "have sprung from barbarism, ignorance and superstition," America had developed "from the midst of a refined and intelligent civilization. Other Nations have been established by Military despotisms and to perpetuate tyrannical power. Ours was founded upon the Rock of Civil and Religious Liberty." Reflecting on the nation's future, the paper argued that Americans had an obligation to live up to the ideals of the nation's Founding Fathers, ideals that the South was drawing the nation away from. "It depends upon ourselves, our patriotism, our jealous watchfulness of Power, our careful guardianship of our civil and religious rights," the paper warned, "whether all this shall be perpetuated to our successors." Americans had to "through the past look back to the great and noble" as a guide to the future.[82] Similar arguments were made by another northern minister, who regarded the mid-nineteenth century as a formative period for American national development. The American nation, he declared, "is called to lay the foundation, and fix the institutions of a new empire . . . almost a new world . . . [and] its political and social character will be formed according to the shape it now receives." As he saw it, it was "a question between education and ignorance; between virtue and moral degradation; between generosity and brutality; between piety to God and profane infidelity; between free and protective industry and servile and profitless toil; between civil and religious liberty and an unmitigated despotism." Slavery and republicanism, he concluded, were wholly antithetical to each other: "The one is democracy—the other is absolute monarchy."[83]

The logical conclusion of such arguments was that it was not slavery that separated North and South but fundamental differences that had been present from the outset. Parker had certainly made this point, and by the late 1850s, Samuel Nott had reached a similar conclusion. Slavery did not, in his view, even enter into the reasons for North-South differences. "The North is settled chiefly by the Anglo-Saxon race; whether superior by nature, or not, it is needless to ask," he asserted. "At the time of their emigration, they were, at this present, they are, farther advanced in civilization, more enterprising and persevering, with more science and art, with more skill and capital." The South, Nott concluded, "is a lower civilization" solely by virtue of its "greater barbarism and poverty at the starting-point of emigration."[84]

Throughout the antebellum period, northerners increasingly came to regard the South as a land, and southerners as a people, apart. Rather than constructing a unifying myth of common origins and descent, nineteenth-century Americans were more interested in inventing a myth of *uncommon* descent, a process summed up by the stereotypical images of the southern Cavalier and the northern Yankee. Although it was a fictitious construction—and a destructive one—the idea that North and South had separate origins helped northerners distance themselves from a society that they saw as an affront to American values. It absolved them, too, of any residual share of the guilt in the maintenance of the South's peculiar institution and conveniently ignored the overt racism of northern society.

It is important to bear in mind that when northerners invoked the past to support their ideas about liberty, republicanism, and the American idea, they were constructing a past that was about as realistic as the myth of the South's aristocratic origins. The ideas of liberty, freedom, and republicanism were part of a national creation myth, which became a northern creation myth. By focusing on the religious ideals that supposedly motivated almost all migrants to the North, and downplaying the violence, dissent, and general disorganization of the North's colonial past, nineteenth-century northerners were attempting to set their section apart from the South. At the same time, they were involved, in a genuine way, in the complex process of trying to establish the American national idea when this was far from obvious. As Fred Somkin argued, the antebellum period was one in which "America was engaged in a quest for a definition of self that would give meaning to the American past, present, and future. . . . With the passing of the Revolutionary generation . . . it remained for a generation of Americans born free to discover for themselves in a shifting environment what it meant to be an American and what the destiny of America was."[85]

Americans in this period gave a great deal of thought to their national character and to American national identity. Specifically, the link between the northern critique of the South that Eric Foner identified and the more positive reactions to that section uncovered by William Taylor lies in northern concerns over American national character. James Freeman Clarke, a northerner who had worked for some years in Kentucky, hoped that the American national character might eventually comprise a mix of northern and southern traits. In the 1830s he thought that "the genuine Kentuckyian is the model of what our national character will one day be. He has the enterprise, coolness, sagacity of the north, and the warmth, frankness & generosity of the south."[86] Others, as Taylor argued, thought that southerners might, in many ways, be superior to northerners. "The cavalier spirit, if not carried to excess, certainly has its attractive aspect, its bright side," argued one northerner, "and [has] value as an element of national character; nor, if genuine, is it in any way incompatible with true republicanism."[87] John A. Kasson, who was later active in the formation of the Republican Party, spent part of his earlier life as a tutor on a plantation in Virginia. At that time, he too found much to admire in the South. Although he believed that the region lagged behind the North educationally, he concluded that southern manners more than made up for this defect. Indeed, he suggested that northerners, whose "heads are filled with business and nothing but business," could learn much from the South as far as hospitality and social intercourse were concerned.[88]

Northerners often did not know how to react to the South, whether to praise it or damn it, admire it or fear it. Some managed to do both. James Watson Webb argued that slavery was "a curse to the country where it exists, and utterly demoralizing to the people who tolerate it." This was apparent, he argued, "by the habits and customs, the violence and the habitual disregard of life, and the whole tone of thought and action, among people who are born and educated amidst its influences." Yet after all this, he was able to conclude that the "Southern gentleman and the Southern Lady, are . . . noble specimens of humanity, well calculated to grace and adorn every society in which they may be cast." They were "the aristocracy of the institution" and "the inheritors of all the good it dispenses."[89]

There was little, in the end, that was romantic about the reality of the South as many northerners saw it in the antebellum period. Although the image of the South remained ambiguous, for an increasing number of northerners, this ambiguity was resolved toward the negative. The southern gentleman, a tyrant on his plantation and a despot in his society, sought to control the federal government and impose southern values on the nation. The creation of such a powerful enemy lent cohesion to the conglomeration of disparate forces that composed northern society. It gave northerners a focus for their fears and a scapegoat for their problems. By the 1850s, an identifiable northern nationalism had emerged, predicated on opposition to the South. It was an ambitious nationalism that sought to impose its own values on the South and on the nation. An editorial in the *Albany Evening Journal* made the point clearly, if inadvertently. In a discussion of the Kansas-Nebraska bill, the writer queried what "the North" might do about this. He continued to refer to "the North," then switched to "the United States," and ended up using both terms synonymously. Clearly, for him there was no distinction between the North and the nation.[90] By portraying themselves as the true and sole heirs of the Founding Fathers, northerners left no obvious place in the nation for the South. Instead, the North used the South to define and defend a specifically northern ideology, a northern nationalism that, in time, many hoped would become truly national. The process of constructing this northern nationalism, however, did little to foster the kind of North-South understanding that might have made an American nationalism viable in the antebellum era.

✺

THREE

One and Inseparable?

The North, the South, and the Nation

[T]here is no sectionalism to be found in any part of the country except what is generated by Nationalism. The feeling of loyalty and fidelity to the Union is strong and all pervading. Calhoun and his legatees were and are sectionalists. They call themselves State-rights men, but it was an assumed living to subserve sectional ends, and their constant efforts were to engender strife and hostility between the North and the South.

— Gideon Welles to General Houston, 22 July 1855

"Liberty *and* Union, now and forever, one and inseparable," was the ringing injunction with which Daniel Webster concluded his second reply to Robert Hayne in the Senate of the United States on 27 January 1830.[1] Webster's speech sold over 40,000 copies in three months and was reprinted in many newspapers. In pamphlet form it exceeded 100,000 copies. It was, according to Merrill Peterson, "the triumph of an idea: the supremacy and permanency of the Union." It "raised the idea of Union above contract or expediency and enshrined it in the American heart. Liberty was identified with the Union, the Union with Liberty; together they defined American nationhood."[2]

Even Daniel Webster, however, defined American nationhood from what was essentially a sectional perspective. His speech was one "in which the virtues of New England life and character were pitted against those of the South." Seldom, William Taylor argued, "had the complexities of the national character been so interestingly and so publicly expressed." Whereas Hayne "cast himself as a passionate Cavalier and slipped frequently into military terminology," Webster "was the transcendent Yankee, peaceable, cool and deliberate."[3] In his Senate speech, Webster stressed the importance of union in the face of Hayne's essentially sectional rhetoric. More than that, he portrayed New England and the North as being more strongly devoted to union than the South. The southern outlook, declared Webster, was narrow in contrast to the national outlook of the North. "[W]e narrow-minded people of New England do not reason thus," Webster asserted.

Our notion of things is entirely different. We look upon the states, not as separated, but as united. We love to dwell on that Union, and on the mutual happiness which it has so much prompted, and the common renown which it has
so greatly contributed to acquire. In our contemplation, Carolina and Ohio are
parts of the same country—states united under the same general government,
having interests common, associated, intermingled. . . . We do not impose
geographical limits to our patriotic feeling or regard; we do not follow rivers,
and mountains, and lines of latitude, to find boundaries beyond which public
improvements do not benefit us.[4]

Clearly Webster was a man who knew his audience. If he attributed national
sentiments to the North and sectional sentiments to the South, there must have
been many in Congress and beyond who would have concurred with him.

The sectional theme in American national construction always found its
clearest and most destructive expression via the U.S. Congress. The eventual
emergence of a northern sectional party—the Republicans—brought together a plethora of northern concerns about the South and focused these in
a dangerously partisan way, giving them a momentum they would not otherwise have had. Specifically, although the idea of the "slave power" had
emerged outside Congress, it was predicated on the behavior of southern representatives and senators in the U.S. legislature. The belief that southerners
had always enjoyed, and continued to hold, a disproportionate share of power
in the federal government contributed to northern fears of the slave power
conspiracy, and the violent behavior of several individual southern representatives in Washington in the 1850s reinforced these fears.

The South had, of course, through the agency of the Democratic Party,
been able to exploit the divisions between the factions in the North, so northern concerns in this regard were not wholly unfounded. The basis of the
South's power was deemed to derive from the fact that the region's various
interest groups, unlike those in the North, were able to act in a coherent,
united manner. The institution of slavery was the main reason for the South's
apparent unity, but it was not the only one. Northerners were generally unable
to see the South as a diverse region. Increasingly, they saw it, and reacted to
it, as a single entity. This not only led some northerners to make sweeping
generalizations about the South's exclusively sectional outlook but also encouraged them in their belief that a united South might very well be a threat
to the free-labor society of the North. Consequently, when the slave power
idea became more prevalent, as it did in the later antebellum period, it found
an audience that was already primed to believe in it.

As Webster's speech made clear, as early as 1830 there was a tendency for
northerners to sectionalize the nation's problems. Not only did the antebellum

North attempt to wash its hands of the glaring moral dilemma posed by slavery, but by doing so, it was able to portray itself as the section that adhered most closely to American national ideals as set out in the Declaration of Independence. Webster had declared liberty and union to be one and inseparable, yet liberty, as antebellum northerners continually reminded themselves, was not a national institution. Slavery was not a national institution either, but it was, arguably, a national problem, even though many in the North refused to see it this way. Some northerners tended to take refuge behind a conveniently placed sectional barrier of their own construction, while at the same time attacking the South for being, in their view, too narrowly sectional. But to what extent was Webster playing to the gallery when he chose to juxtapose the exclusive sectionalism of the South with the inclusive nationalism of the North? To answer this question, it is productive to go back a few years and consider how previous generations approached the question of sectionalism in general and the South in particular.

L ong before the notion of the slave power was introduced in the North, both northern and southern congressmen had been preconditioned to think and behave in a sectional way. The terms "section" and "sectional" had, since the third quarter of the eighteenth century, been favored by American congressmen and politicians, even when the rest of the country was still using terms such as "department," "part," and "quarter." Whichever term was used, however, the impulse to "think sectionally" had been reinforced as early as the revolutionary era, when the Atlantic communities were always listed from north to south in the political arena. In the first meeting of Congress on 5 September 1774, the roll call ran from New Hampshire, Massachusetts, Rhode Island, Connecticut, and so on down the eastern seaboard. Listing the colonies geographically had the effect of reinforcing a sectional awareness that had been present even at the outset of the new nation's life.[5]

The Founding Fathers had been aware of the existence of sectional forces. George Washington sought to direct Americans toward the path of successful nationhood in his Farewell Address of 1796. He encouraged them to avoid sectional disagreement and to strive for national unity. Washington's emphasis on Americans as a people bonded not by ethnic or historical ties but by political inclusiveness and through choice found a resonant echo in Abraham Lincoln's invocation of the Declaration of Independence as the only viable means to nationhood for a people comprising so many different ethnicities and histories. During the Constitutional Convention of 1787, George Mason expressed his concern that the government be composed of representatives

from the northern, middle, and southern states "to quiet the minds of the
people and convince them that there will be proper attention paid to their
respective concerns." Similarly, James Madison believed that the greatest
danger to the new government lay in "the great southern and northern interests of the continent being opposed to each other. Look to the votes in Congress," Madison urged, "and most of them stand divided by the geography of
the country, not according to the size of the states." As the years went by,
Madison's fears were confirmed. Gradually the terms "section" and "sectional" became more common in both legislative and popular usage.[6]

By the time of the Missouri Compromise debate, some northerners were
not optimistic about the future of the Union. In 1820, Harrison Gray Otis had
expressed views on the South, and on the behavior of southerners, that would
become standard observations some thirty years later. "In the South," he declared, "party and local interests are combined in one, which is made indissoluble by the common tie of property in slaves," whereas the North was
divided between local and party interests. "Thus have we been always governed and controlled by the South," he concluded; "while Pennsylvania, New
York and the Eastern States are agitated by feuds which appear to be of deadly
malignity . . . the South moves in phalanx upon all great occasions and leaves
us to our brawls . . . to their infinite sport and adventure." Three years after
Webster's reply to Hayne, Otis repeated his concerns to Theodore Sedgwick,
writing that Sedgwick's father had "belonged to a party who forty years ago,
well understood that the negro holders when they ceased to govern us, would
cease to be governed by us. As yet the contingency has not happened. They
govern us effectually thus far, and I believe will effectually blast the prosperity of N. England this very Anno Domini." Two months later, Otis received
a letter from George Harrison, who observed despondently, "[i]f I have a few
years longer . . . I shall witness the dissolution of our Union & I am not one
who will deplore it. I would willingly and cheerfully let the South go."[7]

For northern congressmen, the very fact that they were in Washington
representing their states gave them a stronger regional awareness than existed
in northern society as a whole. On the one hand, as defenders of their section's interests—most notably in the debates over the Missouri Compromise
and later the tariff debates—they had more cause, on a daily basis, to work
up anger against representatives of interests that were opposite and hostile to
their own. The Gag Rule (the 21st rule), which prevented discussion of anti-
slavery petitions in Congress between 1835 and 1844, also had an effect, since
it shaped northern ideas concerning free speech and civil liberties and was not
regarded as a purely slavery-related issue.[8] On the other hand, northern representatives and senators also had more opportunities to get to know southerners personally, to cultivate friendships, and, given Washington's location,

to visit the South with relative ease. Many of them did so, visiting the homes of southern representatives they had befriended. In short, along with the opportunities for intersectional hostility, there were also at least some chances for intersectional understanding and an opportunity to dispel some of the myths and false images of the South.

Yet when northern representatives described the South in their letters home and in their speeches, the same images and themes appeared. Some representatives, especially in the 1820s and 1830s, argued that the South was not to blame for its peculiar institution and were positive about the black experience under slavery. In 1822, Caleb Cushing, for example, defended the South from its critics. He argued that southern planters were "wholly blameless" in the crime of slavery, since the institution was merely their inheritance from the previous generation. Cushing stressed that blacks were happier on southern plantations than they could hope to be elsewhere. And in his opinion, slaves had easier lives than the mass of European peasants. Too many northerners, Cushing averred, were guilty of "misplaced sentimentality" on the subject of slavery.[9]

The image of the aggressive and aristocratic southerner was also standard, even in the letters of those who were essentially supportive of the South. "I am sensible," wrote one of Cushing's correspondents, "that the southern members are violent & too dictatorial, but great allowance is to be made, assailed as they are by the frantic abolitionists & standing as it seems on the crater of a Volcano. I think therefore it is the duty of the northern members to [stamp] upon all attempts at immediate emancipation—indeed at present nothing can be done on the subject except to assert our constitutional principles & these certainly are not to be yielded." Some thought that the North had already yielded too much. One correspondent argued that "[f]it only for *Slaves* are those persons who can sit calmly by their fire-sides in a state of inaction and lethargy, while their dearest rights are trampled underfoot. . . . Tell the haughty Southerners," he advised Cushing, "that they shall not ride roughshod over the necks of New England men—that the spirit which brought the Puritans to the rock of Plymouth, and animated our fathers at Bunker Hill, yet glows . . . in the bosom of their descendants." Still others thought that Cushing had already done much to support the North against southern aggression and wrote to thank him for "the very manly and honorable stand which most of the delegation from Massachusetts . . . have taken in maintaining the rights of the North, and the pure principles of liberty as designed by the formation of our government."[10]

Cushing's correspondents touched on a theme that was prevalent both in and out of Congress throughout the 1830s: southern dominance versus northern submission and the South's use of the Union for its own ends. One northern minister, for example, advised his congregation that northerners were not safe in the southern states and were frequently attacked. He argued that the power of the southerner in Congress only served to diminish the authority of the North. He suggested, too, that southerners generally hated northerners, and whereas the "inhabitants of the non-slaveholding States are generally disposed to be quiet and civil," southerners were rowdy, violent, and sought only to dominate the rest of the nation.[11] As one northern representative put it in 1832, "[w]e of the North and West . . . are tributary—'hewers of wood and drawers of water' for the South. But with all this they are not content; we must be degraded to the condition of abject slaves; and if we object, they will dissolve the Union! Sir, it is the South, and not the North, that is most benefited by the Union."[12] The biblical allusion to the "hewers of wood and drawers of water" was a common one, used by the press, in pamphlets, and in political speeches. Taken from the Book of Joshua, the phrase referred to the punishment inflicted on the inhabitants of Gideon for attempting to deceive the children of Israel. The fact that northerners used it on a fairly regular basis to invoke their relationship with the South spoke volumes—as it was doubtless intended to.[13]

This is not to suggest that southerners were always portrayed in a negative light, but their arrogance and aristocratic bearing were considered detrimental to the North's representatives and to the North as a whole. When serving in Congress, Nathan Appleton received a letter from Amos Lawrence about the ongoing debates over the protective tariff—which Appleton had helped frame—in which Lawrence portrayed southerners as chivalrous bullies. Lawrence was not overtly critical, but he objected to what he saw as the South's superior tone.[14] Even a cursory study of the *Register of Debates* reveals repeated evidence of this theme in both the House and the Senate, particularly when it came to the issue of the tariff. Senator Dickerson of New Jersey argued, "If the cotton planters of the South would, with candid and liberal feelings, consider the immense advantages they enjoy over the North, in consequence of this Union, their deadly hostility to our protective system would cease." Senator Holmes of Maine summed up the prevalent view of the North-South divide when he observed, "Sir, it is not the democracy, it is the aristocracy of the country that is complaining [about the tariff]."[15]

The shortcomings of the South also concerned northerners in the 1830s and 1840s in other ways. They were especially worried about how the existence of slavery was regarded abroad and what it said about their republican experiment. As William Cullen Bryant noted, Americans were particularly sensitive to foreign criticism. "They have this in common with other nations," he observed, "but they have another habit which shows that, with all their national vanity, they are not so confident of their own greatness, or of their own capacity to estimate it properly. . . . They are perpetually asking, what do you think of us in Europe? How are we regarded abroad?"[16] In a letter to Robert Winthrop, William Channing proved Bryant's point. Channing reported a conversation with an Englishman who had been critical of slavery. "How painful and humbling," Channing wrote, "that our country, boasting of its attachment to freedom, should come in conflict with another, because the latter declares that whoever touches her soil is free." Americans, Channing argued, had good reason to be ashamed of their country, and its poor reputation throughout Europe was well deserved. "I fear," he concluded, "that we are to plunge into deeper infamy, are to array ourselves against the principles of justice and humanity which other nations have adopted,—are to throw ourselves in the way of the advancing civilization and Christianity of our age. The free States have been so accustomed to succumb to the arrogance of the South on the subject of slavery that I cannot but fear."[17]

Throughout the 1830s and 1840s, events conspired to persuade a growing number of northerners that the South was not merely an affront to national pride but also a direct and growing threat to the northern states. The expulsion from South Carolina of Massachusetts' emissary Samuel Hoar—who had gone to Charleston to protest the fact that northern African American seamen were routinely imprisoned there while their ships were in dock—provoked intense outrage in Massachusetts and prompted the state senate to inquire hotly whether the "Constitution of the United States [has] the least practical validity or binding force in South Carolina, excepting where she thinks its operation favorable to her? . . . Are the other States of the Union to be regarded as the conquered Provinces of South Carolina?"[18] Ralph Waldo Emerson was equally angered by what he saw as South Carolina's high-handedness, but he was opposed to retaliation. This, he felt, would only bring New England down to South Carolina's level, something he could not envisage. New England culture, Emerson declared, "is not so low. Ours is not a brutal people, but intellectual and mild. Our land is not a jail." In the future, Emerson concluded, northerners should go to South Carolina "in disguise and with pistols in our pockets, leaving our pocketbooks at home, making our wills before we go." He saw the whole event as typical, and it offered further proof that North and South were separated by more than slavery. "It is the inevitable effect of culture to dissolve the animal ties of brute strength, to insulate, to make a country of men; not one strong officer, but a thousand strong men. . . . In all South Carolina there is but one opinion, but one man— Mr. Calhoun. Its citizens are but little Calhouns. In Massachusetts there are many opinions, many men."[19]

Emerson was not alone in his assessment of either South Carolina or John C. Calhoun. As Merrill Peterson noted, Calhoun eventually attained "on a symbolic level the sectional ascendancy he could never attain politically. Among anti-slavery men in the North he already appeared as the evil genius of the Slave Power."[20] Actually, Calhoun, along with the state he represented, had a fairly poor reputation even among moderate northerners. Philip Hone, for example, the famous New York diarist and close friend of William H. Seward, Daniel Webster, Henry Clay, and John Pendleton Kennedy, remained as critical of extremists in the North as he was of those in the South. But even he thought that the South had gone too far over issues such as the Gag Rule and the restrictions placed on mail to the South, which sought to limit if not wholly prevent the dissemination of abolitionist literature south of the Mason-Dixon line. The general tone of southerners in Congress upset him. Like Emerson, he advocated moderation, since in his view, "the remedy [was] worse than the disease." South Carolina, however, worked him up to such an extent that he described South Carolinians as "the most clannish, selfish people in America. They have no affection for anything except South Carolina." South Carolina personified had much the same effect on Hone as it had on Emerson. "I am a Northern man, and a New Yorker," Hone declared, and as such "I can never consent to be ruled by one whose paramount object is one of opposition to the interests and prosperity of this part of the Union. Mr. Calhoun has talents of a superior order. So much the worse, for his enmity is the more effective. The canker of envy, hatred and malice against the Northern and eastern States lies deep in his heart."[21] Hone was not alone in his antipathy for South Carolina. George Templeton Strong, another New York diarist, consistently expressed similar sentiments. South Carolina was described by Strong in 1850 as a "preposterous little state . . . utterly below the city of New York or Boston or Philadelphia in resources, civilization, importance, and everything else." He repeated this view even more strongly later in the decade, after events in Congress had confirmed his earlier assessment.[22]

For many northerners, the threat presented by southern views on the tariff and the Gag Rule and irrational acts such as Hoar's unceremonious expulsion from South Carolina was nothing compared with the threat presented by the annexation of Texas and the Mexican War that broke out as a result. As Edward Everett wrote in dismay to Robert Winthrop, "[w]e have sprung up at once into a nation of Conquerors. Heaven preserve us from the heroes."[23] The historical assessment of the Mexican War has tended to stress its national, rather than its sectional, impact. In his assessment of the war's influence on the American imagination, Robert Johannsen argued strongly that it had the effect of papering over sectional differences and reinvigorating the patriotic sense of the American people. A sufficiently large number of Americans supported the war, Johannsen argued, "to give credence to the popular perception of the war as an important episode in the American quest for national identity."[24] However, when one assesses the response to the Mexican War in the context of northern images of the South, it is clear that both those who supported it and those who opposed it were prompted to reconsider their ideas concerning American patriotism. Ultimately, the Mexican War could be said to have reinforced American patriotism but undermined *national* identity. For many northerners, the patriotism they took into the conflict was not quite the same as the sense of national identity they took away from it.

There is a wealth of evidence that some felt that during the Mexican War the country actually grew closer together. The war was not cited as the cause of this, however. "There is a steady growth of nationality among our people," the *American Review* declared, "a feeling that the States are merged in the Nation, and owe their power, importance and dignity in the eyes of the world to the Union and the General Government." The journal put this down to a general expansion of industry and a reduced reliance on southern products, which "must make the South less peculiar in its interests, less separate in its position, more inclined to compromise or co-operate with the other portions of the Union. . . . To industrial change, bringing about a great community of labor and production," it concluded, "do we confidently look for the gradual dissipation of all sectional prejudices, in every part of the Union, and the growth in their stead of a lasting community of interest and regard." Two years later, the journal was still optimistic concerning the "manners and customs and habits of thought" of Americans, which it believed were "generally alike throughout our country; so much so that it may be said with truth, we think, that a native of any Southern State would scarcely be distinguished . . . the very first day he should be transplanted from his native region to a residence in Boston."[25] There is also, however, a wealth of evidence showing exactly the opposite. As one northern representative declared:

> If there were a defect more prominent than any other in the national character of these United States, it was the very want of nationality. A spirit of common loyalty has not been as successfully cultivated here as among some other nations. . . . A nation derives strength as well as pride from the recollection of its heroic ancestry. It ever looks through the era of achievement, and glories in the simplicity of the dawning of its common origin. . . . What has the rock of Plymouth or the settlement of Jamestown . . . to do with Texas or the Rio del Norte? . . . The effect of annexation in any shape is at variance with the constitution.[26]

The war that resulted in the following year concerned many northerners for several reasons. Many clearly thought that the war was intended to expand

the slaveholding states, which would thereby increase the South's power in
Congress. However, many also saw it as a watershed in American development as a whole. The South, by pushing for the war, was seeking not only the
domination of new lands but also the domination and transformation of
America's republican experiment. Concern over this aspect of southern behavior can be traced to the start of the annexation debate, when the *Pittsburgh
Daily Gazette* warned, somewhat lyrically, that when "this nation goes to war,
its cause should be such as Angels might espouse. . . . When Liberty draws
the sword, Honor should hold the scabbard. The people should be more concerned at the sacrifice of truth than at the approach of an army with ban-
ners. Foreign invaders may be repulsed but what can wipe off a stain upon
the character of the nation?"[27] For northern radicals such as John Gorham
Palfrey, the war offered further evidence—if any were needed—that North
and South were worlds apart in outlook. "Every person in the United States
is the subject of two governments," Palfrey asserted. "We, of this Commonwealth, considered as the people of Massachusetts, are free citizens of an ex-
cellently constituted republic. Considered as people of the United States, we,
with the rest of the so-called free people, both of the free and of the slave
States . . . are subjects of an oligarchy of the most odious possible description; an oligarchy composed of about one hundred thousand owners of men
. . . [who] administer our affairs."[28]

For Horace Bushnell, too, the war represented nothing less than "the
influence of slavery, as it enters into our American social state, and imparts
its moral type of barbarism, through emigration to the new west . . . which
has its beginning and birth in what I have called the bowie-knife style of
civilization—a war in the nineteenth century, which, if it was not purposely
begun, many are visibly determined shall be, a war for the extension of slavery."[29] Bushnell was not alone in his views. All over New England, ministers
took it upon themselves to warn their congregations of the dangers posed to
American democracy by the annexation of Texas and the designs of the slave
power. The Reverend George Allen, for one, declared that the annexation of
Texas was designed specifically to "fortify, extend and perpetuate the slaveholding power" and could have only a bad effect on the nation.[30] The *New York
Tribune* concurred with such views, especially once the war had broken out.
"We do not believe it possible," the paper argued, "that our country *can* be
prosperous in such a War as this. It may be victorious; it may acquire immense
accessions of territory; but these victories, these acquisitions, will prove fearful calamities, by sapping the morals of our people, inflating them with pride
and corrupting them with the lust of conquest and of gold."[31]

The Mexican War had the effect of forcing northerners, in particular, to reconsider the foundations of their nation's success as well as its future direction. Again, the past played a role in northern assessments of the nation's future. Greek democracy and the early, virtuous Roman republic rather than the later Rome of the Caesars held a continued fascination for antebellum Americans, representing, as they did, the basis of so much American political theory.[32] The Mexican War, however, brought the country uncomfortably closer to the Rome of the Caesars than it had ever expected to go. The *New York Tribune* did not allow its readers to ignore this fact. "The analogy between the character of the Roman Republic and our own becomes more striking each day of our national existence," the paper warned, "[as] wars of conquest and colonization vex us now as formerly them; we equally 'annex' whole countries and extend to the conquered population full citizenship, in servile imitation of Roman example." The *Tribune* ended by reminding its readers that the "analogy may become still more complete, and more fatal," since slavery had been the real source of the Roman Empire's downfall.[33]

For northerners opposed to the war, its outbreak represented the culmination of a series of events that offered proof positive that the South constituted a tangible threat to American national success and stability and, indeed, to American national character. Under slavery, one northern minister argued, "pride is engendered, indolence is encouraged, and profligacy, intemperance, licentiousness, cruelty, revenge, murder, assassination, and all manner of evils are very prevalent."[34] In editorials that covered the history of the previous decade and beyond, the northern press emphasized that the South had dominated, was dominating, and would doubtless continue to dominate the affairs of the nation. The *New York Tribune* was the most outspoken of all the northern papers but was not alone in its sentiments. For years, the *Tribune* declared, "a spirit has been rampant in our public affairs, styling itself 'the South,' and demanding that the whole nation should fall down and worship whatever graven images it chooses to set up." Citing the tariff debates, internal improvements, the use of public funds, the Gag Rule, and the annexation of Texas as evidence, the paper concluded, "in short, 'the South' must be allowed to do everything they please, and make the North do likewise."[35] A few months later, the paper asked, "how can any man who pretends to be a Republican . . . look on these proceedings without apprehension and abhorrence. . . . Who does not see that they are undermining all the settled and salutary standards of popular judgement—exalting Might above Right—and teaching our Youth to look to superior force rather than to Law as the guide of their aspiring steps? Has the world ever known a Republic which extended its boundaries by the subjugation of diverse and hostile races without undermining thereby its own liberties?"[36]

One of the most outspoken opponents of the war was William Jay, who argued that in light of "the bitter sectional feelings already engendered by the question respecting the extension of slavery over these regions . . . and the perpetual struggle for mastery which must prevail between a powerful yeomanry, depending on their own industry, and a landed aristocracy supported by some millions of serfs, surely we have cause to apprehend much irritation, civil dissensions, and the ultimate disruption of the Union."[37] Even Johannsen, who dismissed Jay's work as irrelevant to "popular perceptions of the war," acknowledged that it "used language that was all too familiar to Americans in the 1840s."[38] Certainly, Jay's criticism of the aristocracy of the South, the threat he saw in that section, the military spirit that attended it, and the dangers this posed to American democracy were familiar themes for Americans in the 1840s. His criticism of the Mexican War, indeed, summed up the concerns of many in the North and went straight to the heart of how northerners understood their national identity in this period. Patriotism is not something that can only be created and defended in a positive way. Indeed, it is more likely to be successfully defined against opposition, either to a military opponent or to those within the same culture holding alternative views.

By its actions with regard to Texas annexation and the resultant conflict, many northerners believed that the nation had betrayed, not confirmed, its revolutionary past. This did not mean that they felt less patriotic toward the nation, however. If anything, it intensified their belief in and support for the American republican experiment. Northerners would not have expressed concern over the fact that the Mexican War had, in their view, "dyed the garments of the Nation in blood" if they had not felt a strong sense of attachment to that nation.[39] Unfortunately for American national stability, the fact that opposition to and support for the war were frequently couched in sectional terms meant that although many northerners came away from the conflict with a heightened sense of obligation to the nation, it was an obligation that expressed itself in opposition to the South, and so was no longer truly national. The nation's apparent deviation from its own founding principles prompted an upsurge of nationalist sentiment predicated on the belief that only one section—the North—continued to hold to these principles.

The Mexican War was clearly a turning point for the construction of northern nationalism. Although the debate over the rights and wrongs of the conflict did not produce any new images of the South, it provided a focus for many of the most negative ideas about the South and encouraged the development of a nationalist sentiment that was, in virtually all aspects, sectional. The full impact of the conflict, however, was not felt until the 1850s. The concept of the South as a threat to American values intensified, but did not alter, the negative imagery surrounding the slave states and prompted a re-affirmation of sectional sentiment that had always been one aspect of the northern mind. By the 1850s, however, this sectional sentiment had in many cases been translated into national concerns. The image of the South as back-ward had been acceptable to northerners for much of the early nineteenth century. Indeed, as a suitable foil that highlighted the comparative success of the North, the image of the blighted South often said more about the North's self-image than it did about the reality of the South. It was expected that slavery, the supposed cause of much of the South's backwardness, would die a natural death in time, at which point the South would come to resemble the North in both the ideological and the practical sense. Until that time came, however, many northerners would have concurred with John Hale, who in 1850 declared himself willing to compare the free laboring of the North "with the population of the South, leaving the slaves out of the comparison alto-gether, and taking the masters; and then see on which side of the scale the intellect, the intelligence, and all the virtues which adorn the human character will be found."[40] Hale's audience would have had no doubt that the northern laborer would come out best in such a comparison. The North's superiority was something that many northerners took for granted by 1850, even if they purported to believe that it would not necessarily last.

Once northerners understood that the South was prepared not only to defend its peculiar institution but also to attempt to extend it into the West, they became concerned. As Theodore Parker put it, "the North is like New England . . . essentially so. The West is our own daughter."[41] Southern in-fluence could not be permitted to dominate the new territories. In this context, southern society came to be perceived as increasingly antithetical to northern concepts of freedom and democracy, and when that society seemed to be im-posing its values on the North and potentially the West, the problem became a national one. Essentially, this type of view was indicative of northern con-cerns about the future of the nation. How could America sustain the ideal of Manifest Destiny and be the nation of the future if the South, and its system of slave labor, held the country back not just economically but ideologically as well? Slavery was fast becoming an anachronism in the nineteenth century, and northerners were all too aware of that fact. Seen from this angle, the South was perceived as a moral and physical blight on the nation. This hostile image of the South drew its impulse from the same background as the be-nevolent image of the plantation South. Proponents of this negative view— even if they expressed concern over the economic development and increasing social mobility of the northern states—welcomed what they viewed as progress and resented what they perceived as southern attempts to restrict the nation's future potential.

This view was an intrinsic element in the Republican political outlook. As far as the Republicans were concerned, the South represented "a society which seemed to violate all the cherished values of the free labor ideology, and seemed to pose a threat to the very survival of what Republicans called their 'free-labor' civilization."[42] This free-labor ideology not only defined the Republican model of the good society but also provided a standard against which to measure other social systems. However, it was in the 1850s, when the political upheavals that attended the passage of the revised Fugitive Slave Law, the repeal of the Missouri Compromise in the Kansas-Nebraska Act of 1854, and the *Dred Scott* decision of 1857 seemed to validate northern fears of southern unity and premeditation in the political arena, that the idea of the slave power conspiracy gained momentum. It was in this highly charged political climate that the most extreme image of the southerner-as-threat was defined.

Daniel Webster's notorious speech of 7 March 1850 evinced a more obviously national position than had his 1830 speech, which many believed had consecrated the Union. "Mr. President," Webster declared in 1850, "I wish to speak to-day, not as a Massachusetts man, nor as a northern man, but as an American. . . . I speak today for the preservation of the Union. 'Hear me for my cause.'" Ironically, the effect of Webster's pro-Union speech was to increase sectional disagreement, certainly between New England and the South. One of John Hale's correspondents summed up the reaction of many New Englanders to Webster's speech when he wrote: "Webster feels not at all. His speech falls upon N.E. like a cold North east wind from the icebergs."[43] Yet although Webster was considered a traitor to the cause of freedom by the more radical element among the New England Whigs, even moderate politicians could see that the Compromise of 1850, which he supported, had the potential to disrupt rather than consolidate the Union. Robert Winthrop, for one, had long since seen this coming. He wrote to John Pendleton Kennedy: "I hate controversy, & most of all sectional controversy. . . . I trust we are to have peace at last upon this Negro question, but the Fugitive Slave Law will be a terrible bone of contention. The South has over-reached itself for such a law. They will get no runaways under it, in this part of the country, & as to Congress, it will be another 21 rule in the way of agitation & inflammation. It has given free-soilism a fresh base & I fear a long one. They would have died else. I am by no means sure that Massachusetts Whiggery will survive the shock, which this [among] other things, have given it." Writing to Kennedy the following year, Winthrop assessed the impact of the Fugitive Slave Law: "I believe it to be not only as law wholly at variance with our most cherished principles of justice, but I believe its passage will have done more to weaken the bonds of Union than all other measures since '89. If it is executed, it rouses up indignation in the North; if it fails of execution, it rouses up indignation in the South."[44]

Winthrop had summed up the matter succinctly. The Union in 1850 was in a no-win position as far as slavery was concerned, and clearly there were elements in New England society that no longer considered the North and the South to be one and inseparable. Equally, there were those who continued to view the South in a more benevolent fashion. One of Caleb Cushing's correspondents advised Cushing that one "thing displeases me in the consideration of our New England character, & that is candor, 'the pretence of conscience.' This of late years seems to be in the ascendant, it pervades all the parties." The North, he argued, "is the aggressor, & always has been interfering with Southern rights & Southern interests."[45] By the 1850s, however, there were many more in the North who took the opposite view. For those so inclined, the compromise became yet another stick to beat the South with. The northern press, in particular, got as much mileage as possible out of the matter. The *Albany Evening Journal,* for one, argued that as far as the Compromise of 1850 was concerned, "with the exception of the admission of California . . . the North has gained nothing while the South has carried every point for which it contended." Prompted by the Kansas-Nebraska Act of 1854, the paper returned to the same theme that year and refused to drop it. "In all the conflicts between Slavery and Freedom," the *Journal* asserted, "from the Compromise of 1821 to that of 1850, Freedom has yielded most. Indeed Freedom has yielded all that Slavery demanded."[46] The *New York Times* concurred and argued that the "slaveholding interest . . . has for years controlled . . . every department of the national Government."[47]

Although the political climate of the 1850s gave added impetus to the negative image of the South, it is important to stress that northern concerns over the nature and degree of southern influence in the nation did not arise as a result of the Compromise of 1850. In highlighting what many saw as the compromise's defects, the northern press was merely reiterating arguments that northerners had been using for several decades. The effect of the compromise, however, and later the Kansas-Nebraska Act, was to intensify rather than to radically alter the northern critique of the South. Echoing concerns that were already common currency in the North in the 1840s, one minister argued in 1854 that the South had always appropriated more than its share of "the national treasury, which has been gorged to repletion by taxes imposed on the free and industrious North" simply "to provide herself with troops and hounds for hunting down and exterminating a few hundreds of Red-men in the swamps and everglades of Florida." Harking back to the Mexican War of a decade earlier, he concluded that worse still was the fact that "slavery infuses a love of carnage and conquest into the heart of this great nation, whose essential mission is one of peace."[48]

There was, however, more than a slight element of contradiction in northern reactions to the South in the 1850s. Northern views of the South frequently fell into neither the "Republican critique" camp identified by Eric Foner nor the "plantation ideal" camp that William Taylor described. Rather, they swung between the two. It was not simply a case of some northerners becoming more overtly hostile toward the South as a consequence of the political upheavals of the decade while others were pushing for a more conciliatory, pro-Union line. It was more a case of the overt praise of the North that often accompanied (or was the real motive behind) criticism of the South becoming tempered by a note of criticism for the North. The *New York Tribune* considered the North to be weak and argued that it had yielded too frequently to the South. "Have the northern states and the northern people no individuality?" the paper asked; "is the example of the South one which the North is too timorous to follow?"[49] Again, the *Tribune*'s position was echoed by others in the North. In response to the violence in Kansas in 1855 and the attack on Massachusetts senator Charles Sumner by southern representative Preston Brooks the following year, one northerner asserted that it was "enough to make the blood of a true patriot tingle to his fingers' ends to behold the indifference and subserviency of even liberty-loving men to the aggressions of the Slave Power."[50]

Some in the North clearly did not know which way to turn and alternated extreme and sustained criticism of the South and southern behavior with a defense of that region against the fanaticism of certain northerners. Only a few months before it accused the South of consistently controlling the federal government, the *New York Times* positioned itself as the South's defender against the extremist rhetoric of northern radical Theodore Parker. Parker's speech on the "Nebraska question," the *Times* suggested, was likely to make southerners justifiably angry. "It imputes motives to them which they never cherished," the paper declared. "It charges them with opinions and purposes they hold in abhorrence. It recognizes no palliation for the evils that exist among them. . . . It is a stern, wholesale, undiscriminating, uncharitable, malignant denunciation of the South—attributing to it the worst motives and the basest schemes, and summoning the North to meet it as an enemy which must be crushed in self-defense."[51] In the same period, the *Times* also argued that the railways were "social ties—nationalizing powers—bonds of love and peace. Every mile of them is a new argument for union." It professed itself especially keen "to see North and South brought more and more together, that we may correct each other's prejudices and strengthen each other's hands in the good work of fraternal affection."[52]

Such contradictions went to the heart of northern concerns about southern influence in the nation and specifically in the North. Long used to arguments about how backward the South was in comparison to the North, northerners became adept at criticizing southern "*arrogance,* or an insolent assumption of superiority." Yet, paradoxically, it was believed that southerners could control only "those that are shallow in judgement or weak in courage."[53] This rather revealing contradiction was evident in the arguments of many northerners throughout the antebellum period, but it came to a head in the 1850s. The South was, according to some, a section that was intellectually and materially stunted, yet at the same time it posed a real and tangible threat to the North. There would have been no contradiction here if northerners had not placed so much emphasis on the glories of their own society, if they had not expounded at length on the learning and the intelligence of the North, on the number of professors and judges and men of science and literature that existed above Mason and Dixon's line. If northern society were truly blessed with such an array of intellect, why were its politicians so fallible, and why was the South able to control the federal government so effectively?

This apparent confusion stemmed from northerners' uncertainty about their country and their place in it. There was, in the antebellum period, a "sharp increase in confusion over social roles," which the North sought to resolve in its image of the slave power. This enabled northerners to bring together "all the contradictions between appearance and reality in American society . . . between the image of benign plantation life and the backstage brutalities of slavery," and it provided them with "a means of conceptualizing and attacking all the threatening illusions of American life."[54] In theory, at least, the notion of the slave power also allowed northerners to attack one part of the South—its apparent aristocracy—while sparing the majority of southerners from criticism. For John Gorham Palfrey, the slave power simply signified "that control in and over the government of the United States which is exercised by a comparatively small number of persons . . . bound together in a common interest, by being owners of slaves."[55] But the emphasis on the control the slave power exercised over both nonslaveholding white southerners and the federal government undermined the efficacy of the critique of only one element in the South. The *New York Times* genuinely may have wished to extend the hand of fraternal affection toward the South. It may also have identified a distinction between the South and the slave power. Yet the overarching authority this power was deemed to hold in the South and in the nation, together with northern criticisms of the South, made such a distinction increasingly difficult to sustain.

Significantly, the belief that southerners controlled the federal government was not confined to the more radical elements in the North or to New England. Pro-Union moderates such as Edward Everett had expressed concern over southern political power in the 1830s and developed a defense of their own section in response. "The real interests of New England require that the South not be permitted (as she has done systematically since 1801) to play off our factions against each other," Everett had advised his brother in 1830.[56] Although they might have agreed on little else, the belief that the South had consistently undermined the authority of New England and of the North brought together such diverse northerners as Edward Everett and Theodore Parker, Ralph Waldo Emerson and Philip Hone. None of these individuals was active in the formation of the Republican Party in the 1850s. All of them were, however, active in the creation of a northern critique of the South that the Republicans seized on and developed in the run-up to the election of 1856.

Too often in discussions of ideology there is a marked tendency to distance the outward expressions of the ideology from the social, religious, political, and economic realities that gave rise to it in the first place. In this context, it is important to remember that northern nationalist ideology, and the later Republican ideology that it clearly influenced, did not consist of a set of random notions pulled from the air but was firmly rooted in concern for the white laborer of the North and, by extension, for the American republican experiment. Northerners' confidence in Manifest Destiny was undermined by their concerns over the expansion of slavery and its effect on the North and the West. By the late 1840s, they were far from optimistic that slavery would disappear in the face of free-labor competition. The South was, and remained, the focus of their concern—both the South as it was and the influence it threatened to have in the future. The fears of America's Founding Fathers had, unfortunately, been realized by the 1850s. Northerners, no less than southerners, were unable to escape from the tendency to think sectionally.

I t is clear that the negative image of the South, like the positive, had its origins in the self-image of the North. Concern for the future of America, and both a belief in and a fear of progress, created a level of hostility toward the South that intensified up to the outbreak of the Civil War. The image of the threatening South did not, however, emerge full-blown from the northern mind. It developed gradually and increased, along with sectional animosity, until the 1850s, by which time events such as the revised Fugitive Slave Act, the Kansas-Nebraska Act of 1854, and the *Dred Scott* decision of 1857, combined with abolitionist rhetoric, had made a rational response to the South all but impossible. Among more moderate northerners, reactions to the South can be divided into two camps: benevolent and hostile. Those in the North who feared the social upheaval of abolitionism and the threat it presented to the Union regarded the South in a critical but indulgent fashion. One reason for this moderate tone was devotion to the Union and fears for its continued survival. As William Taylor noted, both Adams and Jefferson had "expressed doubts about the capacity of the Union to endure," and there were many in the North who were unwilling to rock the boat by being overtly hostile to the South.[57] It is important to stress, however, that concern for the Union in no way altered the negative image of the South. Northerners such as Philip Hone were critical of the South in many ways but preferred to adopt a moderate approach to both it and slavery.

Although the abolition movement necessarily maintained an overtly negative and critical image of the South from the 1830s onward, by the 1850s, much of the moderate sentiment in the North as a whole had given way to a far more hostile approach; consequently, a more negative image of the South began to dominate the northern mind. More ominously, the confidence that many northerners had expressed in the link between liberty and union as described by Daniel Webster in his 1830 reply to Robert Hayne had been severely undermined by the events of the following two decades, in particular the Mexican War. In any case, Webster's "idea of a supreme and permanent Union was still something of a novelty in 1830."[58] By the 1850s, it had become obvious that liberty and union were not, from a southern perspective, inseparable. And for an increasing number of northerners, the idea of a Union without liberty enshrined as its central tenet was equally unacceptable. Northerners continued to stress their allegiance to the Union and to question southern devotion to it. Long used to southern threats to dissolve the national body, by the 1850s, northerners no longer took such threats seriously. Yet paradoxically, at a time when northerners felt most secure about the viability of the Union, their own sectional ideology was working against the Union's survival. Between Webster's 1830 reply to Hayne and his speech in 1850, there had been a gradual buildup of antisouthern sentiment that worked as much against the Union as did the South's states' rights doctrine.

By the 1850s, northern devotion to the Union was couched in such sectional terms that a truly national outlook encompassing both North and South proved impossible to sustain. This is not to suggest that northerners were deliberately disingenuous in their professions of national sentiment and devotion to the federal Union. Northerners such as Daniel Webster were genuine in their attempts to foster an inclusive nationalism focused on the Union. Yet the contrast that men like Webster drew between a national North and a sectional South was hardly designed to bolster the kind of inclusive national sentiment the North desired. The continual repetition of arguments that praised the North at the expense of the South, along with accusations that the South dominated the federal government, was not the most constructive way to persuade southerners to adopt a more national position or to convince the North that it continued to have common cause with the South. Instead, the arguments used by Webster and others to try to inculcate a truly national outlook only further alienated the South and reinforced northern nationalist sentiments. Although it was designed to draw North and South together, northern nationalist ideology only drove the sections further apart.

Ultimately, for many northerners, the nation they revered was not one in which the South was particularly welcome, as the Republicans' antisouthern rhetoric made clear. "Underneath the reassuring gloss provided by such phrases as 'our southern brethren,'" Robert Cook argued, "lay a profound unwillingness to mend sectional fences on Southern terms."[59] Daniel Webster himself recognized as much. In addition to the pro-Union speeches for which he is best remembered, Webster made an equally powerful pronouncement on the status and the future of the Union that he had devoted so much of his life to supporting. Speaking to his neighbors at Marshfield in 1848, Webster declared, "We talk of the North, but up to the recent session of Congress there has been no north, no geographical section of the country, in which there has been found a strong, conscientious, and *united* opposition to slavery. No such North has existed." Webster believed, however, that this was about to change. "I think the North star is at last discovered," he told his audience, "I think there will be a North."[60]

❧✶❧

FOUR

Firsthand Impressions

Northern Travelers in the South

The more the Southerners and Northerners see of each other, the less
will the former suspect the latter of cold-blooded selfishness and the latter
charge the former with unreasonable heat and disaffection.
— *American Review*, March 1845

The tendency for some northerners to downplay the varieties of southern life
in favor of an undifferentiated and frequently negative view of the region
came down, in part, to a lack of firsthand knowledge. But even those who had
visited the South were inclined to fall back on the national North versus sectional South paradigm. A quarter of a century after Daniel Webster had contrasted the inclusive nationalism of the North with the exclusive sectionalism
of the South, Frederick Law Olmsted echoed Webster's arguments in one of
the letters he sent back to the *New York Times*. Southerners were guilty, in
Olmsted's opinion, of "absurd state and sectional pride." South Carolinians,
in particular, exhibited a "profound contempt for everything foreign except
despotism" and a "scornful hatred especially for all honestly democratic
States." Venting his spleen against all things South Carolinian, Olmsted
averred that "the ridiculous cockerel-like manner in which they swell, strut,
bluster, and bully" afforded clear "evidence of a decayed and stultified
people."[1]

Olmsted returned to the subject of the South's sectional focus in his second series of letters to the *Times*, first published in 1854. In a diatribe concerned as much with showing the North in a good light as with showing the
South in a bad one, Olmsted argued that patriotism "at the North is much
more generous and national in its application than it is in the South." The
patriotism of the South, he suggested, "centers between a man's heels," in
contrast to the "broad and generous" and, more importantly, national outlook
of the North. "The North feels towards the South as if it were part of itself,"
Olmsted concluded, whereas the South remained sectional in its sentiments,
backward in its thinking, and out of touch with the nation as a whole.[2]

Antebellum southerners might have been forgiven for failing to appreciate the fraternal sentiments professed by northerners such as Olmsted, especially since these were often accompanied by an unremitting criticism of all things southern. Between 1830 and 1850, praise of the North came too frequently at the expense of the South, and after 1850, northern criticism of the South gathered a momentum that made a more balanced view of the region all but impossible. By 1850, northerners were long used to comparing their own hardworking, free-labor society with what they saw as the backwardness of the slave-supported system of the South. In the contrast between southern aristocracy and northern democracy, between southern feudalism and northern republicanism, northerners had discovered what they believed was irrefutable evidence of the benefits offered by their own society in terms of its economic base, its social opportunities, and its ideological outlook.

As it became increasingly apparent that southerners did not share the North's vision of the good society, the tone of much northern criticism became more vituperative. In the context of events such as the Kansas-Nebraska Act of 1854 and the subsequent violence in Kansas, northerners became increasingly concerned at the extent and nature of southern influence on the nation. The South as many northerners saw it—aristocratic, traditional, feudal—did not alter after 1850, but northerners' ability to see these aspects of the South in any kind of positive light diminished considerably. Indeed, based on the evidence provided by northern travelers' reports, the *American Review*'s optimism that increased contact between the sections would draw them together was somewhat misplaced. From what was undoubtedly a genuinely national perspective, northerners managed to create a sectional critique that served only to drive North and South even further apart.

For many nineteenth-century northerners, the South seemed very much like a foreign country that few had any direct experience of. Northerners were forced to rely on reports sent back to periodicals and newspapers from correspondents in the South. Increasingly, such reports were supported by a range of books detailing life and travel below the Mason-Dixon line. Many of these had a hidden—and in some cases blatant—abolitionist agenda. Some were not genuine travel accounts at all, although they purported to be. Nevertheless, as sectional tensions increased, so did the importance of travel literature for Americans. Despite its biases, such literature provided an opportunity to bridge a distance that had become ideological as well as physical.[3]

From the earliest accounts, it was apparent that the physical experience of travel in the United States was a source of concern to most writers. Facilities for traveling were not especially good anywhere in the country, but they were particularly bad in the South. No traveler had anything good to say about the state of southern roads, which always seemed to be blocked by fallen trees, flooded, or entirely nonexistent. Southern railways were little better, and northerners were generally bemused by southerners' complete lack of concern about the slow and sometimes dangerous state of their public transport. Southerners shrugged off such events as the cars running off the tracks, rails coming up through the floors of carriages, and "other amusements of the kind calculated to make one's hair stand on end."[4]

After braving the hazardous journey south, many visitors were disappointed at what they encountered. Having expected luxurious plantation mansions, the modest wooden constructions they found seemed poor recompense. Southern furniture was of especially bad quality, and there was not much of it. What offended many northern visitors most of all, however, was the lack of books in southern homes, a lack that seemed to confirm northern suspicions that the South remained educationally stunted. Visitors were also dismayed by the reality of southern hospitality.[5] Northerners had been encouraged to believe that southern hospitality was "in the highest degree generous and elegant." Southerners, they were advised, were willing to "devote themselves to you—take you about the city, show you the lions, are ready to go any where with you, send their friends to call on you to help occupy your time agreeably, and take you to their houses where they make you really welcome and at home."[6] Many visitors experienced a rude awakening. In general, they found southerners to be unhelpful and southern hotels to be neglected, damp, and infested with every imaginable—and some quite unimaginable—insect. Southern food, too, got its share of complaints. Twenty-one-year-old Henry Benjamin Whipple, who later became famous for his missionary activities among the Chippewa and Sioux in Minnesota, complained that southerners had "a way . . . of serving up ants with the dishes that is quite annoying to the uninitiated."[7] Whipple was to experience far worse than that in his life, both during the Civil War and later on the frontier in Minnesota, but to his youthful self, the culinary disappointments of the South were bad enough.

Some visitors, of course, were impressed by what they found. New Orleans, in particular, attracted much praise for its enterprise and commercial activity.[8] In 1844, the *Boston Daily Evening Transcript* ran a series entitled "Traits of Home Travel," whose author also found much to admire in New Orleans. There, it was noted, the "people are very hospitable and social, and freer than usual from that selfishness which is observable in most every community."[9] Charleston, too, attracted the attention of many northern visitors, but not always to its benefit. Although one visitor reported that "in a taste and knowledge of the Fine Arts," Charlestonians were far superior to northerners, he went on to criticize the lack of furniture, carpets, and bathing facilities in Charleston homes.[10] Another visitor reported that Charleston was a pleasant city, but one "of more show than solidity, more words than deeds." There "is not a place in the Union whose people have so high an opinion of themselves and their city," he concluded, "and there certainly are none who have less to be proud of."[11]

In the 1830s and 1840s, most northern travelers to the South exhibited, and helped promulgate, an essentially ambivalent attitude toward that region. On the one hand, southern society was genteel, mannered, refined, and in some ways superior to that in the North; on the other hand, the South's social, economic, and cultural defects placed it far behind the North and out of step with nineteenth-century progress in general. In common with other northerners, travelers in the South regarded slavery as more of a strain on white society than anything else. Samuel Bowles, editor of the *Springfield Republican,* saw slavery firsthand on a winter tour of the South in 1844–1845 and argued that "the owners are generally much more the objects of pity and sympathy than the slaves; they suffer from its blighted curse greatly and sensibly."[12] Northerners believed, however, that southerners were aware of the problem. "The South are not blind to the evils of slavery," one visitor argued, "they can see its bad effects as well as the most sharp-sighted abolitionists."[13]

In time, it was expected, slavery would die a natural death. When that happened, the South would readily adopt a free-labor ideology that would bring its society in line with that of the forward-looking, democratic North. This belief permitted a sympathetic approach to southerners to coexist alongside an essentially hostile critique of the South. Whipple, for example, admired southern manners, contrasting them favorably with "that base selfishness so striking a characteristic of one portion of our restless Yankee brethren," and he reinforced northern stereotypes in his description of the southern gentleman. The southern gentleman, according to Whipple,

> is different from the northerner in many striking particulars. He is more chivalrous . . . he has more of that old English-feeling common in the days of the feudal system & crusades. He is liberal in his feelings, high-minded, a warm & generous friend but a malignant and bitter enemy. . . . He is generous to a fault with his property, is fond of gaiety and pleasure & generally dislikes the routine of business. His habits are those of genteel idleness or of the man of leisure.

Yet these habits of leisure were, in Whipple's view, ultimately detrimental to the South. He regarded it as "a matter of deep regret" that slavery had made the notion of industry "if not dishonorable, at least of doubtful gentility." The "energies of the South," Whipple concluded, "are crippled by the incubus of slavery," and southern society as a whole was one in which "no people can live and prosper."[14]

Whipple's attitude was fairly typical. The reaction of many northern visitors to the South prior to 1850 reveals that they expected to find a society of cultivated gentlemen, beautiful belles, graceful manners, and impressive plantation houses. If such expectations were not fully realized, it was a disappointment but not a cause for concern. If the South seemed less democratic than the North, less forward-looking, and less commercial or industrialized, northern visitors responded to this discovery with praise for their own section rather than any sustained criticism of southern backwardness. For some northerners, the obvious superiority of the North—as they saw it—was something they welcomed. Amos A. Lawrence, for example, while traveling through the South on business for his father, reported that southerners

> cannot manage as well as we can & never will. We must excel in wealth & in consequence in learning & refinement the South; this we say we do now, but they will not acknowledge it. In a few years the diversity will be too great to allow a doubt of our superiority. Their climate is unfavourable to industry as ours is impelling to it & their indolence more than outweighs the disadvantages we labour under in being forced to provide for an unproductive & consuming winter.[15]

Lawrence was impressed by Kentucky, although he noted that the dominance of wealthy planters in that state had forced many of their competitors out. Tennessee impressed him less favorably. "What we call comfort does not exist here," he complained. "It does not ever occur that an open door or a broken pane of glass can be cold, as long as a good fire is burning on the hearth . . . consequently the doors are never shut & the windows never are mended."[16] Here, as elsewhere, the young Lawrence (he was twenty-two at the time) expressed surprise at the fact that southerners did not concur with his view that the North was far and away superior to the South. Only "among the enlightened people" did Lawrence "hear high opinions of N. England & particularly of Boston."[17]

Overall, Lawrence's reactions offer a valuable insight into certain aspects of the northern image of the South at this time. Notably, his apparent belief that Kentucky and Tennessee were representative of the South as a whole reveals that he, along with many other northerners, had a fairly one-dimensional view of the region. Where Lawrence differed was in his assessment of the economic impact of the South on the nation as a whole and on the North specifically. In future years, northern critics of the South—who were not drawn from the commercial class, by and large—would portray the South as a great drain on the economy of the nation. Many of their arguments would be derived in part from the tariff debates of the early 1830s. Yet the South as Lawrence experienced it only a few years after these debates seemed to offer no threat in this direction. In common with other northern industrialists, Lawrence did not regard the South as a potential threat to the North. He saw the two sections as complementary to each other: the South produced the raw materials essential for northern manufacturing success. Southern industrial backwardness represented only opportunity to him.[18] In 1836, Lawrence took the South very much as he found it, an attitude that he would retain throughout the next two decades and would ultimately lead him to oppose the sectional, antisouthern rhetoric of the Republican Party.

The reasons for Lawrence's visit to the South made him a rather unusual traveler. Certainly his opinions, like Whipple's, although revealing, would not have reached a wide audience or influenced northern thinking to any great extent. However, in the same year that Whipple set out on his tour of the South, a well-known and ultimately extremely influential northerner— William Cullen Bryant—traveled South to visit a friend, author William Gilmore Simms. By the time he made this trip, Bryant was already an established figure. He had published widely in the *North American Review* and other journals, edited both the *New York Review* and the *United States Review*, and was editor in chief of the *New York Evening Post*. This was not his first trip South, nor would it be his last. In 1832 Bryant had traveled through Kentucky, Virginia, and Maryland, and in 1849 he visited Charleston before moving on to Cuba. During both his 1843 and his 1849 visits, Bryant sent back a series of impressions of the South that were published in the *New York Evening Post*.[19]

Bryant's letters, unlike those of his friend Frederick Law Olmsted, have not stood the test of time well. When they were first published, however, they proved extremely popular and were reprinted in other papers.[20] Indeed, it can be argued that Bryant's view of the South had the greater impact in the North as a whole. As both a Free-Soil activist and an editor of an influential newspaper, Bryant had access to a far wider audience than Olmsted did, and for a longer period. In addition, Bryant was active in the creation of the Republican Party in the 1850s, and particularly in the refinement of its ideology. Despite this, Bryant's reactions to the South, his integration of the reality of that section with his Free-Soil sentiments, and the image of the South that he conveyed to his northern audience have not been adequately assessed. Historians too readily treat Bryant like two separate individuals: either a Free-Soil radical or a literary figure. Yet the focus of Bryant's attention, both in his letters and in his politics, was the South. Although there are distinctions, there is no real difference between Bryant's apparently moderate portrayal of the South in his letters and the more extreme views presented in his editorials, which have been described as "the Northern viewpoint at its best."[21]

It has been argued that Bryant approached the South with as open a mind as possible in a period of growing sectional mistrust. Bryant in no way underestimated the South's socioeconomic difficulties, and he did not expect slavery to die an easy or a natural death. Up to a point, southern life and manners suited Bryant, but it is doubtful that the hospitality he enjoyed actually "tempered his critical acumen." Certainly some of Bryant's comments on the South were moderate to the point of blandness, but the overall image of the region he conveyed to his readers was more informed by his Free-Soil beliefs than restrained by natural politeness. Although Bryant knew very well that the South was not a homogeneous region, this did not prevent him from presenting quite the opposite view in his letters. The fact that Bryant approached the South "from a point of view that was national in its scope" precluded any attempts at objectivity. Like Olmsted, Bryant's national viewpoint revealed a concern for the American republican experiment that prevented him from portraying the South in a favorable light.[22]

Much of Bryant's criticism of the South was focused on slavery. However, he did not express any sympathy for slaves. In common with many northerners, Bryant was more concerned with the effects of slavery on white society. His description of a corn-shucking is a case in point. Bryant described, without any obvious sense of irony, the singing slaves and even repeated for his readers the words of the song: "De speculator bought me, I'm sold for silver dollars . . . I'm goin' away to Georgia, Boys, good-bye for ever." Bryant concluded that the slaves were "a cheerful, careless, dirty race, not hard worked, and in many cases indulgently treated."[23] The following month, Bryant had occasion to visit a sugar plantation farther south, where he found the slaves to be "well-clad young men, of a very respectable appearance," who seemed to be "well-treated."[24] Bryant's descriptions of slaves, particularly on his second (1849) visit to the South, are much like his descriptions of orange groves and riverbanks. In short, to him, the slaves seemed to be little more than part of the southern scenery.

Bryant's was a fairly typical response. The journalist and poet Nathaniel Parker Willis described the overseers and slaves of the South in similarly picturesque terms as *"tableaux vivants."*[25] Many northern visitors to the South—even those who supposedly had abolitionist sympathies—portrayed the South's "peculiar institution" in this way. Whipple reached conclusions similar to Bryant's when he visited the South in 1843. The slaves he encountered seemed well fed and clothed, idle, lazy, and generally contented. Slavery, Whipple decided, "does not appear a yoke to many of them."[26] On a visit to friends in Richmond, Virginia, the northern novelist Catherine Maria Sedgwick reported to her sister that there was nothing "offensive in slavery as we see it . . . the slaves that I see about the streets and in the country look to me downcast or surly, but this may be fancy."[27] Similarly, Bowles concluded that southern slaves were "more contented, better fed and clothed, than the free blacks either at the North or South."[28] Travelers were not the only ones to portray slavery so positively. New York diarist George Templeton Strong believed that slaves in the South were far better off than blacks in the North. The fact that slaves were "more kindly dealt with by their owners than servants are by Northern masters" was not, in Strong's view, open to doubt. The "expediency of slave-holding" was, however, a different matter.[29]

In his attitudes toward slavery, therefore, Bryant revealed himself to be of a mind with many Democrats, Democratic-Republicans, and northerners in general; concerned with the future of white America, they were not especially worried about the plight of African Americans.[30] It is hardly surprising that Bryant shared the racial prejudices of his day, although his close contact with his father's black laborers might have modified his views.[31] Ultimately, what connected Bryant's Free-Soil sentiments with his later hostility to slavery was a growing concern for the American republican experiment, but only insofar as white Americans were concerned.

In the period between his 1843 visit to Simms and his trip to the South in 1849, Bryant spoke out against the proposed annexation of Texas. Indeed, his forceful editorials on the subject were "instrumental in arousing northern anti-slavery men against the measure."[32] In a letter written in 1844, Bryant declared that "they err, who think that the annexation of Texas will not increase slavery and the number of slaves. The annexation is pressed upon us by a portion of the South as a new source of prosperity for slave industry, and a new guarantee for their institutions."[33] This was a view that Bryant promulgated through the *Evening Post* and in his private correspondence. He became increasingly vehement on this subject as a result of the Mexican War of 1846–1848. On the subject of the territories he was clear: they should be spared "the curse of slavery." "It is grossly unjust," he argued, "to claim for a handful of slave holders, to the prejudice of their less opulent brethren among whom they dwell, half the territory for which the great mass of the community are obliged to pay, some with money and others their lives."[34]

Again, Bryant's argument was constructed solely on behalf of white

America. He made his position clear in an 1848 editorial in which he declared that the "question involved in the restriction of slavery in the new territory is . . . not one which particularly concerns the slave, but one which concerns the white man." Ultimately, for Bryant, it came down to the question of whether "the principle of our government be aristocratic; if it be instituted for the sole benefits of the class of slaveholders . . . if it be the intention of the constitution that our federal legislation should be so shaped as to promote their convenience or obey their caprices."[35] Bryant's hostility to aristocracy was in line with northern Free-Soil sentiment and, for him personally, was not new. A visit to Florence in 1834 had set him to thinking about the differences between American and European government. "I think I shall return to America even a better patriot than when I left it," he wrote. "A citizen traveling on the continent of Europe, finds the contrast between a government of power and a government of opinion forced upon him at every step. He sees the many retained in a state of hopeless dependence and poverty, the effect of institutions forged by the ruling class to accumulate wealth in their own hands."[36]

Bryant's antipathy for anything resembling aristocracy is revealed by a striking omission in his letters. Unlike many visitors to the South who clearly found much to admire in the figure of the southern gentleman, Bryant expressed no admiration for—and in fact hardly mentioned—the planter class. He provided his wife with a rather cursory assessment of some Virginians he encountered on an 1832 visit, describing them as "gentlemanly in their manners" and with a "tendency to metaphysical speculation which I have heard mentioned as characteristic of the Virginians."[37] Otherwise, Bryant did not mention the southern gentleman at all. From his first visit to the South, Bryant's interest in the region was based solely on the negative impact of slavery on society.

In one of his last letters from the South, written on the eve of the Compromise of 1850, Bryant commented on the conditions experienced by poor whites of that region. He concluded that the introduction of manufacturing and the replication of northern social and economic practices were the best possible remedy for the South's problems.[38] Ultimately, a South that conformed to northern ideals was the only sort of South that Bryant was prepared to accept. Anything else not only held back the South but also potentially threatened the North and, more importantly, the West. Bryant may have promulgated a more benevolent image of the South than some, but in virtually all its aspects it was a backward image that closely paralleled the views later expressed by Olmsted.

In effect, just as for historians there are two Bryants, for Bryant there were two Souths: the physical and the ideological. One he visited personally as a traveler; the other he considered more objectively as a northerner. In the first instance he was looking only at the view; in the second he was considering the implications of southern ideals and values for the American nation. Throughout the period 1832 to 1856, the image of southern society, as opposed to southern landscape, that Bryant presented through his letters and in the pages of the *Evening Post* was consistently negative, even at its most reasonable. In the end, the reality of the South as Bryant experienced it did nothing to alter his Free-Soil sentiments, even if he found much in individual southerners and individual southern cities to admire.

Bryant certainly regarded the "children of the West" as a possible "living bulwark against the advances of Slavery," but he harbored serious doubts about the effectiveness of such a bulwark.[39] In his letters to his family, particularly, Bryant made it clear that he regarded the majority of the population of the western states as "ignorant" and on a par with the nonslaveholding whites of the slave states, which was where many of the western settlers had originated.[40] Such people were, in Bryant's opinion, exploited and generally incapable of standing up to the slaveholding elite. Again, this thinking reveals him to be of a mind with Free-Soilers, for whom the institution of slavery, with its aristocratic and antirepublican overtones, represented a clear threat to America's white population.

Bryant, in common with many northerners, recognized that the physical extension of slavery was not really the issue. Even if they did not bring slavery with them, many of the settlers in the new territories were the products of a slave society. As such, they suffered from the educational, intellectual, and political limitations that such a society imposed on its members. Their values would remain, even if their geographic location altered. A physical barrier against slavery could not be expected to work against essentially abstract forces: ideological, intellectual, and moral. This was the root of the problem for many northerners concerned about the success of America's democratic experiment.

Bryant's South was a society that had a certain charm. Charleston, in particular, impressed him because its inhabitants appeared to possess "the most polished and agreeable manners of all the American cities."[41] Bryant concurred, however, with the sentiment expressed in a contemporary traveler's account of that city. Charleston's charm had a decaying aspect about it, requiring only "an owl to hoot from the custom-house . . . to make it an antiquity."[42] Charleston's Old World quaintness in no way compensated for the essential backwardness of its social and economic development.

Bryant's letters to the *Evening Post* cut through, to a great extent, the variety of life in the South to focus on the backwardness of southern economic development and on the destitute nature of the society that slavery sustained. With Bryant, this tendency to portray the South in a monolithic, undifferentiated manner both reflected and informed the reaction of many northerners to the South. Indeed, Bryant's description of the South was particularly one-dimensional in some respects. In other reports from this period, one finds many of the standard images of the South that were common currency in the North: the aristocratic southern gentleman, the genteel nature of southern society, the grace of southern women, the comparative lack of religious sentiment, and the propensity toward violence. In Bryant's letters, none of these images appears: scenery and slavery were the only aspects of the South that seemed to interest Bryant and were the only ones he chose to convey to his readers.

In this context, it is important to reflect that Bryant the editor, Bryant the Free-Soil Democratic-Republican, and Bryant the poet were one and the same person, and by 1856, he had abandoned his former political allegiances and was giving his wholehearted support, and that of his paper, to the Republicans. Indeed, the *Evening Post* has been described as "a powerful factor in getting the Republican party off to a good start in its first presidential race."[43] Consequently, it is essential that historians take full account of Bryant's work, not just his editorials or his political speeches. Above all, William Cullen Bryant was a man who regarded his country as a land of limitless opportunity, where "the free spirit of mankind, at length / Throws its last fetters off." And who, he asked, "shall place / A limit to the giant's unchained strength, / Or curb his swiftness in the forward race?"[44] Many years before it became a fundamental part of Republican ideology, Bryant had already concluded that the South might, if unchecked, "place a limit to the giant's unchained strength." Long before many northerners came around to the idea, Bryant had discovered in the South a real threat to the republican ideal. In his letters and editorials he laid at least some of the groundwork necessary for his belief to become more widespread.

Although Bryant's reactions to the South reveal part of the background to the northern critique, northerners were never exposed solely to a negative portrayal of the South, nor did they express consistently hostile sentiments toward it. Much of the positive imagery of the South that appeared in travel accounts represented a continuation and a development of ideas that had been common for many years. In many ways, the positive and negative images of the South were nothing more than inversions of each other. Both were structured around similar themes—slavery, aristocracy, manners, society, and culture—and both presented the South as being very different in most essential respects from the North. Whether this difference was regarded in a positive or a negative light depended on the perspective of the writer.

Slavery, in fact, proved to be of far greater interest to those inclined to view the South in a positive light. However, even those who responded positively to the South's "peculiar institution" advanced only stereotypical images of the slaves themselves. Partly, this was because the northern image of blacks in the South was distorted both by the lens of minstrelsy in northern culture and by the pseudoscientific arguments of the day concerning black inferiority. Caricatures of the southern black male derived from minstrelsy— Uncle Tom, Uncle Ned, Jim Crow, Zip Coon, Sambo—allowed northerners to establish concrete versions of their abstract ideas about blacks. In part, too, such images defrayed any guilt northerners might feel over racism. The image of the politically and economically incompetent slave lent credence to the view that blacks were better off in the closed society of the slave South than blacks and poor whites were in the free market of the northern states. Willis was not alone in his praise of "negro comfort well distributed" in the plantation South "instead of white wretchedness filthy in a heap" on the streets of northern cities. Another visitor to the South concurred and argued that southern slaves experienced "a freedom from care and anxiety which a poor white man never knows."[45] A corollary to this assessment of southern race relations was that slaves needed to be seen as cheerful and contented. Willis's belief that "you would scarce find in the world a class of laborers who are as habitually cheerful as these blacks" was a common one.[46]

More fundamentally, in their praise of southern slavery, northerners revealed their fears over the future of America as a whole. George Fredrickson detailed how the stereotypical images of blacks were derived from northern fears over nineteenth-century progress and the concomitant depreciation of traditional moral and religious values in northern society. The image of the benign black slave became, he argued, a forensic tool, "a vehicle for romantic social criticism."[47] In their obvious appreciation of southern race relations and the southern system of racial control, northern supporters of the South made explicit their concerns for northern and, by extension, American society. In contrast to what he considered the disruptive nature of northern society, Thomas Nichols—doctor, journalist, and editor—expressed his approval for "the appropriateness of everything on these plantations . . . the negroes, male and female, seem made on purpose for their masters." He asked, "Do they not all alike enjoy this paradise—this scene of plenty and enchantment?"[48]

For many white northerners, keeping African Americans within the confines of a plantation—preferably one in the South—was better than having free blacks living in northern society. This attitude was derived in part from the fact that the northern image of the free black as a social threat became more sharply focused throughout the nineteenth century. Certainly the perceived danger arising from the social position of free blacks in the North was an issue that several northern travelers focused on.[49] Consequently, they looked to the southern plantation as a possible solution to the problem of free blacks in American society. The argument was often made that blacks in the slave system were not only better off but also more manageable and better behaved than free blacks. Nichols considered that "there cannot be found anywhere a more perfect manner than among the better class of Southern negroes; but why the manners of the Southern slaves should be superior to those of the free negroes of the North, I will leave it to others to determine."[50]

In some cases, of course, concerns over northern society went hand in hand with basic racism, as evidenced by Nichols's praise for the manner in which the superiority of the white race was "asserted and acknowledged" in the South.[51] In other cases, the positive view of southern race relations was aimed at both abolitionists and foreign critics of America. One traveler's assertion that the "slaveholding states have no starving poor . . . no poor taxes . . . no workhouses" was clearly influenced by his belief that it was for "British fame, and for British gold, the abolitionist writes, and preaches and sings."[52] A *New York Times* correspondent argued that if "fanatical New-Englanders would but take to a Virginia diet, I am bound to believe that they would be less incursive on the supposed evils of Southern civilization."[53] A desire to counter the extreme arguments of the abolitionists, however, was by no means the only influence on the positive view of the South.

Although some northerners in the 1850s still believed that in the South "the bondage of the white to the negro . . . has been very much severer than the bondage of the negro to the white," by this time a very different viewpoint had emerged.[54] In direct contradiction of Bryant's concerns, the southern system of race relations was deemed by many travelers to be as beneficial for white society as it apparently was for slaves. Whatever "evils have been connected with Slavery," one traveler argued, "it has performed a great incidental work in the formation and elevation of Southern character."[55] Nichols, for one, believed that "the habitual deference of the negro to the white, and the corresponding condescension of the white gentleman or lady to the negro, produces a kind of courtliness of behaviour which is not seen in the free communities of the Northern states." "It is notorious," he added, "that the shrinking antipathy of the whites to the black race does not exist in the same degree in the slave as in the free states." Contact with blacks from birth, he concluded, prevented the "colour-phobia, that horror of a black man because he is black," that prevailed in the North.[56]

Again, this view was fairly typical. Olmsted similarly argued that in the South "the alleged natural antipathy of the white race to associate with the black is lost."[57] However, it was not simply the proximity of black and white that, in the opinion of many travelers, prompted such behavior. "The nature of the Southern man," one visitor argued, "fits him to befriend the negro. It is impulsive, free, open, generous." This was due, the writer concluded, to the fact that home "gives character to the South—not business, as at the North. . . . The home is the great civilizer."[58] The North was regarded as lacking in this regard. Northerners, it was argued, did not enjoy the domestic stability of the South and were consequently less inclined to behave in a civilized manner. This was especially noticeable when they moved to the South. "It is notorious," Nichols asserted, "that the worst Southerners are Northerners. They are the most immoral in their habits, and the hardest masters to their slaves." Southern masters were "easy and indulgent," whereas northern slave owners were "hard and exacting." All this derived directly, in Nichols's view, from the fact that in the North "the ties of family are so often broken that they are loosely held."[59] The South, by contrast, sustained the kind of extended kinship networks that were essential for a stable and civilized society.

The southern family, in effect, was regarded by many travelers as a conservative institution in an age of radical change. It seemed to be a repository of moral and religious values in an increasingly materialist and secular world. On his visit to Charleston, Willis concluded that southern values derived directly from "the plantation conservatism of family," from the southern "custom of sending sons to Europe for education," and from the "prevailing tone of courtesy and chivalry handed down from a superior class of first inhabitants."[60] Central to this positive image of southern family life was the figure of the southern gentleman planter, a chivalrous blend of Old World charm and honor. The planter was, according to Nichols, a member of "a higher class; a recognized, though untitled aristocracy" whose influence was essentially conservative.[61] For Willis, the southern planter was

> a gentleman by every influence of education and climate. With a slight touch of the tetrarch in his manner, perhaps, the constant habit of authority had made it sit gracefully upon him, and it impregnates his whole bearing with that indescribable air of conscious superiority which can never be assumed, but which is prized above all other traits by the high-born in Europe.[62]

The difference between Willis's description of the planter and the strikingly similar one put forward by Whipple a decade earlier lies in the fact that, unlike Whipple, Willis did not combine praise for the southern gentleman with criticism of the system that had produced him. Indeed, those who responded favorably to the southern planter regarded his environment as one that was in many ways superior to that of the North.

Clearly, many northern travelers exhibited an "uneasiness about Yankee values" in their praise of the South.[63] As the repository of domestic stability, racial control, and aristocratic values, the benign plantation South was a powerful image for northerners concerned about the rate and the direction of change in their own section. Indeed, some argued that in certain respects the South held more closely to genuine American values than the North did in this period. One visitor mused on the question of "whether we had not a truer and higher type of *American* life and character in the South than in the North, arising from the fact that comparatively few foreigners are there, and that amalgamation of the different races exists to a very limited extent."[64] Another writer considered that southerners possessed a conflation of northern and southern characteristics—namely, "cavalier boldness, as well as Puritan character."[65]

Overall, whether or not the South was more American than the North, it certainly seemed to many visitors to be more stable socially. "Street brawls and conflict between two races of laboring people, or the ignorant and more excitable portions of different religious denominations," Nehemiah Adams argued, "are mostly unknown within the bounds of slavery."[66] Willis believed that the slave system prevented both the violence and the urban squalor that plagued northern cities such as Boston and New York. Nichols went even further and portrayed southern society as a veritable socialist utopia. Paradise, he argued, existed on the banks of the Mississippi, and the "nearest approach to the realization of the schemes of Fourier is on our Southern plantations."[67]

Not all travelers, of course, heaped such fulsome praise on southern society. Some of the pre-1850s travelers, although generally impressed by what they found in the South, expressed reservations. One visitor suggested that the image of southern wealth and refinement was "over-estimated." Although there were rich planters, the majority enjoyed "moderate circumstances." Overall, he concluded, slavery was not "conducive either to the happiness or prosperity of the whites."[68] Others, too, decided that much of southern life was little more than show for visitors. Although southerners had "beautiful parlors and everything for company," in fact "their every-day life is mean and miserable."[69] By the 1850s, however, such moderate criticism was unusual. In general, the ambivalence of the travel accounts of the 1830s and 1840s had given way to views that were fixed. By the 1850s, northern travelers were either in favor of the South or against it: there was little middle ground left.

Some of the most hostile travel accounts from the 1850s were clearly fabricated works, designed specifically to criticize the South.[70] Yet despite their dubious credentials, such accounts were—in common with genuine travel works—frequently no more than distorted mirror images of works that portrayed the South in a positive light. Praise for southern domesticity became transmuted into praise for northern domesticity. "There is not that substantial family discipline maintained, and the salutary home influence in the South," one writer argued, "that are every where seen in New England."[71] The southern domestic environment, in negative accounts, was portrayed as "strange and unnatural. . . . The life of mental and physical inactivity that southern women lead renders them incapable of a judicious training of their children." Slavery, it was asserted, "has no gentle teachings of self-control and self-sacrifice . . . it forms no habits of industry and self-reliance. . . . Indolence and imbecility are its inevitable results."[72]

Southerners themselves were portrayed as being far from the aristocratic ideal. Travel accounts increasingly focused on southern stupidity, laziness, overindulgence in alcohol, gambling, hunting for sport, and all other gentlemanly pursuits that had seemed so appealing when viewed in a positive light. Slaveholders, it was asserted, spent "much of their time in amusements. . . . No business is so important at any time as to prevent them from attending the horse race, the cock-fight, or any other kind of sport."[73] Time and again it was emphasized that "the most prolific source of the drunkenness, licentiousness, and crime which abound in the South, is in the idleness of the slaveholding class."[74] Slave owning, it was argued, made the southerner insensible to the suffering not only of blacks but also of southern society as a whole. The slave owner still exhibited "a certain patrician bearing, a consciousness of his own superiority," which lent him an air of "manliness and dignity." However, in a negative light, these qualities degenerated into arrogance and rudeness, and the slave owner, "habituated to play the tyrant at home, unshackled regent and despotic lord upon his own plantation," no longer seemed so attractive a character.[75]

Many of the negative travel accounts emphasized northern superiority on the pretext of ascertaining what it was that held the South back. The answer was not slavery directly, but rather southern laziness—a consequence of slavery. Parsons, for example, argued that northern success was predicated on "the superior physical education of the North—the practical knowledge, and the advantages derived from the various kinds of labor to which her whole people are devoted." As he saw it, North-South differences came down to the fact that northerners adhered to the *mens sana in corpore sano* dictum: the "superior intellectual character of the people of New England," Parsons suggested, "is to be attributed mainly to their early habits of industry, which give them athletic physical systems for vigorous minds to work in."[76]

Again, the image of the stunted South was no more than a skewed reflection of the image of the South as a land of plenty. Nichols had presented the South as a land of milk and honey, where the soil was fertile "and the climate so soft that people can sleep under the trees the year round," where flowers "cover the earth, grapes and delicious fruits grow spontaneously, while the country was stocked with deer, wild turkeys, horses and cattle."[77] John Stevens Cabot Abbot simply inverted such images when he described a South in which the "fields are worn out by wasteful culture" and the "plantation houses, deserted by their former inmates, are tumbling into ruins; and the negro cabins, hardly superior to ordinary pens for pigs, in their rottenness and desolation, harmonize with the whole aspect of decay." Massachusetts, Abbot argued, "occupying a region comparatively cold, bleak, and barren, is a cultivated garden in contrast with South Carolina."[78] Northern critics of the South pushed this comparison as far as they could, and at length. It was via the image of the blasted South that some northerners managed to translate sectional sentiment into national concern. As Abbot argued:

> This poverty, ignorance, and debasement, are not merely sectional. They constitute a national calamity, an element of impoverishment, a running sore in the body politic. The whole Union is weakened by it; and though a vastly greater calamity to the South than to the North, it is certainly of such magnitude, that the whole nation is affected by it, and by the whole nation it must be deplored.[79]

The negative image of the South that many travelers portrayed by the 1850s was inspired less by the reality of the South than by northern concerns for the nation as a whole. The fact that several travel accounts were not genuine travel reports at all reveals a growing tendency in the North to sectionalize national problems. This tendency can be identified in the writings of Bryant and other travelers in the 1830s and 1840s, but by the 1850s, it had become a persistent theme in northern accounts of the South—both genuine and contrived. The latter could not have argued the line they did—nor would they have been inclined to—had genuine visitors to the South not pointed them in this direction. The increased focus of 1850s travel accounts on southern backwardness reveals that northerners wanted to show that American expansion and affluence were not merely the result of immigration combined with the country's natural resources, but rather represented "the fruit of free institutions."[80] The desire to prove this beyond a reasonable doubt certainly motivated the South's most famous visitor, Frederick Law Olmsted.

Although Olmsted's influence on northern views of the South has been described as "overpowering," both in his own day and in ours, the plethora of works on the South makes this seem unlikely.[81] By the time Olmsted's letters from the South were published, northerners had been reading about the South for quite some time in a wide variety of publications: newspapers, periodicals, trade journals, and books—both fictional and factual. Indeed, when *A Journey in the Seaboard Slave States* first appeared, it floundered in a market already oversupplied with similar books. Despite favorable reviews, Olmsted's work sold slowly: the first print run of 2,000 in January 1856 was supplemented by an additional 5,000 copies by April of that year, but more than two months later, the publisher still had some 2,000 of these in stock.[82]

When Olmsted suggested that "northern men have, at present, too little information about the South that has not come to them in a very inexact, or in a very suspicious form," he was being somewhat disingenuous.[83] This was little more than a publicity statement designed to make his work stand out in a market already full to bursting with newspaper reports, travel works, pamphlets, novels, and political and religious tracts devoted to the South. Historians have, however, been too quick to take Olmsted's statement at face value and to extract those parts of his work that best suit their particular purposes. Objectivity is what Olmsted claimed to be offering at the time, and objectivity is what historians have relied on him for.[84] Paradoxically, there is also general recognition that Olmsted's New England background predisposed him to find the South lacking in several crucial respects.[85] Objectivity may have been what Olmsted was expected to deliver, but it seems clear that, for a variety of reasons, he could not deliver it.[86]

In his introduction to the *Times'* new series on the South, the paper's editor, Henry J. Raymond, argued that "nearly everything written concerning the South hitherto has been written to sustain some 'foregone conclusion,'" and he presented Olmsted's letters as a fresh perspective on a region "more talked about than understood."[87] Southern papers were, unsurprisingly, immediately suspicious of both Olmsted's and Raymond's motives. The *Savannah Republican,* for one, believed that Olmsted's "early education, his prejudices, [and] the prevailing opinions at the North" all made him "totally unfit to judge impartially."[88] Oddly enough, the *Times* itself lent credence to southern fears only a few months after it began publishing Olmsted's reports. Addressing the South directly, the paper asked,

> do you believe . . . a man can travel from the Northern to the Southern States with as little prejudice as one from the South to the North. . . . Especially since he has followed poor "Uncle Tom" with his co-sufferers, and listened with tearful eye to his last escaping breath, as he lay lacerated upon the cabin floor of the distant plantation. . . . With these things before him, think you that a Northerner's mind is like a blank sheet going to press, when he travels South?[89]

For Olmsted to have approached the South in an unbiased manner, he would have to have been unusually disengaged from the society around him. With the best will in the world, Olmsted's response to the South was both informed and circumscribed by his own concerns for the future of America's republican experiment. Olmsted, in common with many northerners, saw the South as a direct threat to the success of this experiment. Olmsted and Raymond may genuinely have wished to place themselves above the biases of their time by adopting an empirical approach to the question of slavery and southern backwardness. Their attempt to do so, however, was doomed from the start. Olmsted undoubtedly felt that, as a detached observer, he could provide a distinctive angle on the South and its problems for *Times* readers.[90] Yet from the outset, both he and Raymond knew what they were looking for. Their own foregone conclusion was that slavery had a debilitating effect both on southern agriculture and on the region's social and cultural development, and that this hindered America's development. In this context, it is revealing that, though supposedly traveling without preconceptions, Olmsted did not take a long time to develop his thesis. Less than two weeks after arriving in the South, he was able to advise Charles Loring Brace that he was confident of being "able to show conclusively . . . that free labor is cheaper than slave."[91]

In light of his letter to Brace, it is plausible to question Olmsted's assertion, made in his seventh letter from the South, that "I did not intend when I commenced writing these letters to give much attention to the subject of Slavery." In particular, it is unlikely that the conviction that slavery was "universally ruinous" had been forced on him "to a degree entirely unanticipated."[92] This is almost certainly window dressing: an attempt on Olmsted's part to make his conclusions appear to be the result of empirical research. Yet the evidence that Olmsted used to support his conclusions was hardly drawn from his own experiences in the South. Most of it came from the census of 1850, a document that many northerners would have been familiar with. Too often Olmsted is credited with being the only northerner to examine slavery from an economic rather than a humanitarian perspective.[93] Yet when Olmsted first traveled south, and certainly by the time *Seaboard Slave States* appeared in 1856, such economic evidence for southern backwardness was commonplace. Newspaper reports, pamphlets, other travel works, and political speeches were frequently based on the North-South differences revealed by the 1850 census. Olmsted did not need to travel south to reach the conclusions he did, and there is no evidence in his work that he deliberately sought to measure the census's conclusions against his own firsthand experience.

On arriving in the South in 1852, Olmsted got straight to the heart of the matter. In his second letter to the *Times*, he, like so many commentators before him, offered a critique of Richmond, Virginia. Although Richmond had more natural advantages than either New York or Glasgow, he argued, it lagged far behind both in terms of its development. Richmond was, he stressed, an active commercial center but was not making the best of its potential. Here one can already see the outlines of Olmsted's main thesis, but combined with an acknowledgment of southern commercial and economic development that was missing from other accounts of the South.[94] Where Olmsted also differed from other commentators was in his criticism of the *lack* of aristocratic features in Richmond, a criticism that reveals much about his expectations regarding the South.

Olmsted's comparisons of the free states and the slave states continued throughout his early letters. In particular, and in common with Bryant, he was critical of the unproductive nature of master-slave relations. In his seventh letter, he described how the slaves had to be bullied into working at all. By his ninth letter, he was convinced that slavery as a system relied on "the very low and degraded condition of the mass" of white southerners. Southern educational backwardness in general struck him as a serious problem. "From their want of intelligence," he argued, the majority of white southerners "are duped, frightened, excited, prejudiced and made to destroy their most direct and evident interests by the more cultivated and talented spendthrift and unprincipled of the wealthy class."[95]

Although many historians emphasize Olmsted's conclusions about the detrimental impact slavery had on the South's white population, it is important to bear in mind that his arguments on this subject were not new. Olmsted was reiterating a problem identified as early as 1820 by Ralph Waldo Emerson, and one that a variety of northerners—from Bryant to educational reformer Horace Mann—had focused on since then. In common with an increasing number of northern intellectuals in the antebellum period, Olmsted revealed himself to be predisposed to finding the South lacking in all the aspects of what was considered a civilized life. The values that Olmsted held most dear—a belief in community, stability, service, civilization, and the importance of education—seemed to him to be wholly absent in the South and, to some extent, in the North as well.

Charles Beveridge has argued that throughout Olmsted's life, he "had always before him an image of the society that America should become. . . . The millennium he hoped to achieve was an American society in which people of all classes had the opportunity to acquire the 'mental & moral capital of gentlemen' and did so." The South, with its dominant minority of wealthy landowners and its mass of illiterate poor—both black and white—was anathema. For Olmsted and his peers, northern society was the Puritans' "city on a hill" made manifest. Indeed, John Winthrop's declaration to his flock on a ship bound for the New World in 1630 that their purpose was, in the words of the Sermon on the Mount, to create a society that would be "the light of the world. A city . . . set on a hill" for all to see and, more importantly, to emulate had particular resonance for northerners such as Olmsted. Believing in America's "historic mission" to influence humankind for the better, they were acutely sensitive to—and embarrassed by—the fact that slavery remained an integral part of the nation. In their view, only northern society, with its free-labor system that held the promise of opportunity for all, came close to Winthrop's vision of America's future, and only northern values were worthy of emulation. Consequently, when Olmsted traveled south in 1852, it was with the deliberate intention of proving that free labor was superior to slavery, thereby vindicating the North's version of the American republican experiment.[96]

In Olmsted's earliest letters, he made it clear that it was slavery as a system rather than the southerner per se that was hampering the South's development. In 1853, Olmsted decided that the fact that southerners seemed to be "less enterprising, energetic and sensible in the conduct of their affairs" derived "not from the blood but from the education they have received; from the institutions and circumstances they have inherited. . . . Give Virginia blood fair play," he concluded, "remove it from the atmosphere of Slavery, and it shows no lack of energy and good sense."[97] By 1856, however, Olmsted seemed less convinced that the South's difficulties sprang not from blood but from education. South Carolina in particular struck him as a state lacking in all accomplishment. This Olmsted put down to the fact that it was, in his view, "almost from the start distinguished as the worst governed, most insubordinate, and most licentious and immoral of all the English settlements in America." Despite boasting several "men of learning," the state had achieved little in the way of "valuable inventions and discoveries, or designs in art, or literary compositions of a high rank, or anything else, contrived or executed for the good of the whole community, or the world at large."[98]

Certainly, between the appearance of Olmsted's letters in the *Times* and the publication of his books on the South, a great deal had changed in terms of North-South interaction. By the time *A Journey in the Seaboard Slave States* was published in 1856, for example, the main elements of the Republican critique of the South were already in place. Republican propagandists were in the process of fine-tuning this critique and adding supporting evidence, but its essential elements had already been established. Olmsted may have been influenced by this. What is certain is that he chose to alter several of his letters before they appeared in his books. Consequently, the image that Olmsted conveyed to the northern public in 1853 and 1854 was different from that presented after 1856. Beveridge puts this down to an unwillingness on Olmsted's part to "emphasize those aspects of Southern society that he had found to be better than traditional wisdom in the North held them to be." In particular, he avoided making "those pleas to Northerners for understanding and forbearance toward their Southern brethren that he had made repeatedly in his newspaper letters."[99]

Olmsted's pleas for forbearance, however, require closer examination. It is not simply the case that Olmsted showed some sympathy for the South in 1853 but by 1856 had become overtly hostile. In 1853, he advised his readers that a "proper estimation of the difficulties that embarrass the people of the South in connection with the subject of Slavery . . . would do more to restore friendly feeling and confidence between the two great sections of our country, than all the compromise measures that could be contrived." At this point, Olmsted, like Bryant, argued that slaves were "in the majority of instances . . . happier, intellectually, morally and physically in Slavery than in what passes at the North under the name of Freedom."[100] In his later books, Olmsted was less considerate of the problems that slavery caused the South and more inclined to regard these as self-inflicted. He was also less willing to repeat his favorable estimations of the institution of slavery itself. Here, in fact, he was prepared to alter what he had written. In November 1853, for example, Olmsted described the punishment of a slave that he claimed to have witnessed. He expressed surprise that the slave did not seem "to suffer the intense pain that I supposed she would." When this letter reappeared in *A Journey in the Back Country* in 1860, Olmsted denied having witnessed the event in question and portrayed it as involving more cruelty and eliciting "screaming yells" and "sobbing, spasmodic groans."[101]

In assessing why Olmsted chose to alter his report of this incident, various factors must be considered. It is unlikely that, between 1853 and 1856, Olmsted's views on slavery had undergone any dramatic change. Indeed, Olmsted was no particular fan of the kind of abolitionist rhetoric that *Uncle Tom's Cabin* exemplified. He initially considered slavery to be a problem that the South had inherited from the colonial past and the nation's Founding Fathers. As an early biographer put it, in the early 1850s, Olmsted regarded the South "less as the criminal than as the patient."[102] By the time his books appeared, Olmsted had become much more hostile. As to the cause of this change, historians isolate the Kansas-Nebraska Act of 1854 as the crucial turning point for Olmsted, the straw that broke the camel's back.[103] For Olmsted, the Kansas-Nebraska Act indicated that the North was incapable of holding to its own principles and was too willing to accede to southern pressure. Consequently, by the late 1850s, Olmsted was less inclined to offer the hand of friendship to the South or even to make allowances for its problems. For that reason, he saw fit to present the South in a more negative light, to play up incidents of cruelty that he had downplayed before.

Ultimately, what prompted Olmsted to intensify his criticism of the South was an increase in his concern for the North and for America as a whole. Given that Olmsted had traveled South with his agenda firmly in place, his firsthand experiences had merely confirmed, rather than altered, his suspicions about that region. Olmsted found the South to be a society lacking in many of the benefits of civilization as he understood them. This was no surprise to him. What was surprising, however, was the fact that the South was not unique in this regard. Olmsted's initial intention had been to prove, beyond doubt, that the North's free-labor society was both superior to and more efficient than the South's "peculiar institution." Like so many northerners, Olmsted had sought in the South confirmation of the superiority of the North. What he actually found was an exaggerated version of the nation's—indeed, the world's—problems. This is evident in the tirade aimed at the North that concluded his tenth letter:

> Oh, God! Who are we that condemn our brother? No slave ever killed its own offspring in cold calculation of saving money by it, as do English free women. No slave is forced to eat of corruption, as are Irish tenants. No slave freezes to death for want of habitation and fuel, as have men in Boston. No slave reels off into the abyss of God, from want of work that shall bring it food, as do men and women in New-York. Remember that, Mrs. Stowe. Remember that, indignant sympathizers. Oh, Christian capitalists, free traders in labor, there is somewhat to be built up, as well as somewhat to be abolished before we repose in the millennium.[104]

It proved impossible, in the end, for Olmsted to separate his concerns for civilization as a whole from his specific criticisms of the South. He was offended by the fact that southerners enjoyed no "lyceum or public libraries, no public gardens, no galleries of art . . . no public resorts of healthful and refining amusements, no place better than a filthy tobacco-impregnated barroom or a licentious dance-cellar."[105] Yet Olmsted did not think that there were enough outward signs of civilized life in the North, either. In one of the final letters in his first series, he argued that government in general ought to encourage parks, gardens, and galleries to curb "the excessive materialism of purpose in which we are, as a people, so curiously absorbed."[106] Here is the voice of the landscape architect and designer of Central Park that Olmsted was to become. In the context of his views on the South, Olmsted's sentiments on civilization in general serve as a reminder that he was, above all, a man with an integrated vision of the ideal society. His beliefs regarding the importance of civilization were a constant in his life, whether in 1854 or much later in his career. What he found in the South only strengthened his conviction that the lack of any outward trappings of civilization condemned America as a whole, not just the South, to an inferior kind of existence.

In particular, and in common with Bryant and other northern visitors, Olmsted was critical of the enervating influence of the South's landed class on civilization as a whole. Unlike many northerners, Olmsted seemed not to oppose the notion of aristocracy per se, but he was certainly opposed to the version of it he encountered in the South. His initial impressions had been disappointing. Having expected clear signs of an aristocratic lifestyle, he was dismayed to find none. Increasingly, he devoted more attention to this subject and eventually concluded that an aristocracy did exist in the South, but in a corrupted form. True Southern gentlemen were, according to Olmsted, "the nearest approach to the English aristocracy which America has ever possessed, not only in their follies and views, but in their virtues and excellence." Unfortunately, they were no longer to be found. They had been supplanted by men who were "invariably politicians, and they generally rule in all political conventions. . . . If they were not dependent on the price of cotton for the means of their idleness, they would have the country incessantly at war. . . . Call them what you will," he concluded, "they are a mischievous class—the dangerous class at present of the United States. They are not the legitimate offspring of Democracy . . . but of slavery under a Democracy."[107]

Olmsted's meeting in November 1853 with Samuel Perkins Allison, a planter from Tennessee who had been a classmate of Olmsted's brother John at Yale, went some way toward confirming Olmsted's fears regarding the South's ruling class. This meeting persuaded Olmsted that there was an unbridgeable distance between the intellectual class of the North and the ruling elite of the South. The encounter with Allison dispelled Olmsted's hope that he would find the South's elite to be cultured and refined. Clearly his conversation with Allison had a significant impact, since immediately afterward Olmsted penned his forty-sixth letter in which he held forth on civilization and aristocracy, subjects that were obviously linked in his mind. After this meeting, Beveridge argued, Olmsted "saw more clearly than before the urgency of creating in the North a state of society that elevated all classes and gave the lie to proslavery apologists and their mudsill theory of society."[108] Writing again to Charles Loring Brace, Olmsted advised him that southern aristocrats such as Allison "do not seem to have a fundamental sense of right. Their moving power and the only motives which they can comprehend are materialistic."[109]

The subject of aristocracy was one that Olmsted pursued throughout his later letters and in his books, particularly in *A Journey in the Seaboard Slave States* and *A Journey through Texas*. Aristocracy, he warned his readers, "or an established superior class, necessitates inferiority, or a subject class, at whose expense . . . the aristocracy is supported." In the South in general, he concluded, the "Democratic theory of the social organization is everywhere ridiculed and rejected, in public as well as in private, in the forum as well as the newspapers."[110] Charleston struck Olmsted as a town full of character that was "much more metropolitan and convenient than any other Southern town," but even Charleston seemed to him "to have adopted the requirements of modern luxury with an ill grace, and to be yielding to the demands of commerce and the increasing mobility of civilized men slowly and reluctantly."[111] Aristocracy was the cause of this state of affairs, Olmsted asserted. "The greater the class distinctions," he argued, "the more general will be the habit of lazy contemplation and reflection—of dilettantism—and the less of practical industry and the capacity for personal observation and invention."[112]

In the years between Olmsted's tour of the South and the publication of his books, sectional tension between North and South erupted into violence, both in the territories and in Washington. Such events caused Olmsted great concern. Writing to the *Times* from Edinburgh during a European tour he undertook in 1856, Olmsted expressed his fears for the future of America's republican experiment. "When a great nation thus departs from its fundamental principles," he cautioned, "common sense as well as history assure us that either a speedy reaction must set in, or that the political system must fall into ruin and dissolution."[113] The following year, in the introduction to *A Journey through Texas*, Olmsted warned that "the character and reputation of the nation, and with it the character, the social claims, and the principles, of every individual citizen, have been seriously compromised in the eyes of the civilized world, by recent transactions growing out of the unsettled state of our policy with regard to slavery extension."[114] In a similar vein, in the introduction to *The Englishman in Kansas,* Olmsted queried whether northern "charity has not been carried too far." Had northerners "so habituated themselves to defend the South that they have become as blind to the essential evils and dangers of despotism as if they were themselves directly subject to its influence?"[115]

By 1857, Olmsted had come a long way from the confident northerner who had traveled south to prove that slave labor was more expensive and less efficient than free labor. Events in Washington and Kansas, together with his own experiences in the southern states, had convinced him that the issue went far beyond the benefits or drawbacks of a labor system. Slavery not only held the South back in economic terms but also informed every aspect of its daily existence and supported an aristocracy whose values stood in direct contradiction to those of the "republic of virtue" in which Olmsted believed. For Olmsted, the struggle in the 1850s was one between "the divergent forces of idealism and materialism." Both were "contending for the ultimate character of the American nation, although he cast the struggle more in terms of the two 'strains' he saw in the American democracy—a strain toward civilization and a strain toward barbarism."[116] Before he visited the South, it is unlikely that Olmsted had associated either of these forces with one particular section. By 1857, however, the forces of idealism and materialism were represented, in his mind, by North and South, respectively.

It is revealing that, in contrast to many other northern visitors to the South who regarded the region as an effective counterforce to the rampant materialism of the northern states, Olmsted reached precisely the opposite conclusion. The course of political events since Olmsted first traveled south in 1852 did much to undermine his initial assumption that the reality of the South would do no more than confirm the superiority of northern society. Having approached the South with the belief that it was inferior to the North, Olmsted initially concluded that North and South had more in common than he had supposed. In effect, his experiences in the South prompted Olmsted to approach the subjects of slave versus free labor, aristocracy versus democracy, and materialism versus idealism within a national context. Yet ironically, Olmsted's recognition that the South's problems had national implications served to reinvigorate, rather than diminish, his earlier sectional position, which, in the wake of the Kansas-Nebraska Act, returned with a vengeance. If overconfidence in the superiority of the North had defined Olmsted's sectionalism in 1852, underconfidence in the ability of his own section to withstand the negative impact of southern institutions defined it in 1857. In the South, Olmsted found confirmation not just of southern backwardness but also of his worst fears for the future of America.

In the end, Olmsted could find little that was positive about the South. His direct experience of it forced him to conclude that even the apparent traditionalism of the South was hardly a benefit, either to southerners or to Americans in general. Olmsted found that the forces of materialism that reigned in the South condemned it to a way of life that, in his opinion, belonged to the Dark Ages. Not only did slavery educate southerners "in habits which, at the North, belong only to bullies and ruffians," but it made an effective prison of southern society. The apparent stability of the South came at a high price, Olmsted asserted. Again, he turned to Charleston for evidence. There, he argued, one encountered "police machinery, such as you never find in towns under free government: citadels, sentries, passports, grape-shotted cannon, and daily public whippings." In Charleston, Olmsted had witnessed "more direct expression of tyranny in a single day and night" than he had seen in Naples in a week. The South as a whole, he believed, was "a people divided against itself, of which one faction has conquered, and has to maintain its supremacy." The military methods employed in this process were "those of the feudal ages, or of savage warriors." By 1857, the only remaining question for Olmsted was what the North ought to do "to guard against the sinister influences upon our own politics and society, of contiguous States, under the laws of which there is still the liability of such an explosion of constitutional barbarism."[117]

Olmsted's firsthand experience of the South ultimately served to make him more aware of the dangers that its slave society posed to the nation. Whether he managed to convey his growing sense of alarm to his readers is a different issue. One reviewer of *A Journey in the Seaboard Slave States* regarded Olmsted as intrinsically hostile both to slavery and, by extension, to the South as a whole. Olmsted's thesis, the reviewer noted, had much in common with that of George Melville Weston, one of the Republican Party's more extreme propagandists who published a series of pamphlets on slavery and southern backwardness the same year that Olmsted's first book appeared.[118] However, another reviewer of *A Journey in the Back Country* was fulsome in his praise of Olmsted's "kind, conciliatory tone" and his "rigid impartiality." Here was a work, the reviewer declared (somewhat late in the day, as things turned out), "admirably adapted to rebuke and allay both Northern and Southern fanaticism."[119]

It is unlikely that Olmsted's last book could have done much to allay either northern or southern fanaticism. By the time *A Journey in the Back Country* appeared, the nation was on the brink of civil war. In any case, Olmsted's work, along with that of many others, had done more to fan the flames of sectional antagonism than to quench them. And if Olmsted appeared to some readers to be impartial and conciliatory, that would have given his critique of the South even more validity in northern eyes. The fact remains, however, that Olmsted's work intensified rather than contradicted the negative image of the South that had been introduced by William Cullen Bryant and others in the 1840s. His emphasis on the problems that slavery caused white society and on the backward nature of southern agricultural, economic, and social development; his portrayal of the South as belonging more properly to the nation's past than to its future; and his concern for the American republican experiment revealed Olmsted to be of a mind with Bryant and a growing element in the North.

Between 1830 and 1860, certain distinctive elements in northern travelers' reports from the South can be identified. Both the positive and the negative responses to the South were constructed around the themes of slavery, aristocracy, the southern class system, southern economic backwardness, social stability, and the figure of the plantation owner—the southern gentleman. How these various themes were articulated, however, depended on the biases of the individual traveler and on the political context in which they were written. Although many northerners traveled extensively in the South between 1830 and 1860, their encounters south of the Mason-Dixon line did little to alleviate sectional mistrust and misunderstanding. Too frequently, those northerners who traveled South did not approach the region with an open mind. Instead, they went south with a preconceived idea of what they would find and, unsurprisingly, found it. By the 1850s, the desire to prove the superiority of the North's free-labor society informed many of the travel accounts, including those by the supposedly objective Frederick Law Olmsted. This was a development of sorts. William Cullen Bryant had definitely not approached the South with this in mind. His negative reactions to the region, however, fed into and ultimately influenced not only the northern critique of the South in general but also the specific responses of other travelers—including Olmsted—who followed in his footsteps.

The northern critique of the South did not, however, rely on negative reports alone. Indeed, the tone of the positive accounts of the South that appeared in the antebellum period offers a valuable clue to the construction of the northern critique of the South and the concomitant development of a northern nationalist ideology. The positive reports, for all their praise of the

South, too closely paralleled the negative accounts in their essential details to offer a genuinely alternative image of the South. Whether their authors were indirectly expressing concern for northern society or whether they were genuinely impressed by the South, such accounts failed to make the region seem any less foreign. Indeed, they merely reinforced the growing impression that the South was a world apart and clearly out of tune with the North. This in itself was not a problem. It became so in the 1850s only because an increasing number of northerners felt that North-South differences, far from enhancing the cultural and social diversity of the nation, actually posed a threat to it. It was not only the mounting opposition to slavery that informed this shift. In the image of an aristocratic South, a growing number of northerners detected a challenge to the democratic ideology on which the nation had been founded. Increasingly, American national ideals were perceived as existing only in the northern states.

By the 1850s, the impulse to prove the superiority of the North had led to the appearance of travel accounts that were either wholly or partially fabricated. Although purported to be written by visitors to the South, it is clear from their content as well as their ideological thrust that they were compilation volumes designed to criticize both the South and its "peculiar institution." However, although these volumes did not represent actual travelers' accounts, their contents were derived from genuine reports by travelers and others. Neither their strongly abolitionist slant nor their negative image of the South was in any sense made up. What such volumes did was to bring a variety of criticisms of the South together under one cover, thereby reinforcing what was already a strongly sectional message. The fact that some northerners felt motivated to produce such works reveals a growing hostility to the South and to all it represented. And the fact that they were presented as travel accounts rather than simply as writings on the South underlines the importance of travel literature to northerners.

At a time of growing sectional tension, firsthand reports from the South offered northerners an opportunity to come to terms with a part of their nation that increasingly seemed like a foreign country. The eventual dominance of the negative image of the South over the positive, however, meant that it was an opportunity missed. In assessing why northerners were more inclined both to produce and to believe negative accounts of the South, it seems clear that the South had become, for many of them, a valuable point of comparison against which to measure the progress of the North and the nation. In their criticisms of the South, northerners like Olmsted were able to express, indirectly, their concerns for the future direction of the republican experiment. Above all, by ascribing to the South all the problems of mid-nineteenth-century life, northerners managed to off-load the burden of their guilt over slavery. In the process, they made the South seem more foreign than ever.

Ultimately, northern travelers' responses to the South in the antebellum period can best be understood within the framework of the development of a northern nationalist ideology. In the image of the benighted South, northerners found proof that their nation's success was predicated on the free institutions of the North, not on the slave society of the South. The South seemed both an affront and a threat to these institutions. In the image of the aristocratic South, northerners recognized a way of life that they responded to emotionally but were forced to reject intellectually. Antebellum travel accounts, therefore, both reflected and informed northern concerns about the nation as a whole that prevailed at the time. The image of the South as promulgated by William Cullen Bryant, Frederick Law Olmsted, and other northerners who visited the region was a response to the contradictory elements inherent in antebellum American society: freedom and slavery, democracy and despotism, a feudal past that the nation never had and a democratic future it had not yet achieved.

❦

FIVE

Representative Mann

The Republican Experiment and the South

It may be an easy thing to make a republic, but it is a very laborious thing
to make republicans.
— Horace Mann, 1848

Northern reactions to the antebellum South can be fully understood only in
the context of northern concerns for the future of the American republican
experiment, which was basically the search for an American national identity.
Central to antebellum concerns was the issue of freedom in a nation that retained slave labor. In the nineteenth century, the belief in freedom was, in
Fred Somkin's words, "the *res Americana, the matter of America.*"[1] In the decades preceding the American Civil War, however, North and South came to
hold very different ideas of what freedom meant and what it entailed. In time,
northern concerns over slavery and the society that relied on it found political
expression in what Eric Foner termed the "Republican critique of the South."
This critique was focused not on slavery alone but on the South as a whole—
its society, culture, industry, and intellectual achievements. It was simultane-
ously an attack on the South and an affirmation of northern superiority.[2] Ultimately, it was a sectional message with national ambitions. It transformed
the matter of America into the matter of the North.

It was in the run-up to the election of 1848 that Daniel Webster, the man
who had "consecrated the Union" in 1830, first invoked the concept of a
"North."[3] In April of that year, the Eighth District of Massachusetts sent
Horace Mann to Congress to take the seat left vacant by the death of John
Quincy Adams. Mann's congressional career was destined to be brief (1848–
1852), but in this short time he adopted an increasingly confrontational stand
toward slavery and the South. Indeed, Mann's political career reveals a great
deal about the background to and the lineaments of the northern ideology
that Webster had anticipated and that the Republican Party would use so effectively for its own political ends.

When Mann arrived in Washington, slavery was making itself felt as a divisive, increasingly sectional issue. As Mann himself put it, the furor over slavery was, by this time, "the salt of all political cooking."[4] Mann quickly became aware of the intensity of the debate at the political level, as his comments to Samuel Gridley Howe clearly indicate. "For two days past," he wrote, "we have had a Southern tornado,—not a meteorological affair, but a psychological one. Slavery, of course, has been the theme." However, the full effect of the debates, the "threats, insults, the invocation of mob-rule and lynch law," could barely be discerned from the published reports. Mann painted an evocative picture of southern congressmen whose manner was so threatening and violent that he was prompted to suggest that "if this represents the manner and the wrath with which they put it on to the poor slaves, with scourge in hand,—and I presume it does,—then you must conceive how the skin is dropped and the blood spilled."[5]

Initially, Mann held off from stating his position on the slavery issue, despite Charles Sumner's persistent encouragement to do so. Before Mann declared himself, he had occasion to visit the South, going to Richmond and Norfolk, Virginia. Although impressed by certain aspects of Richmond, he, like many northern visitors, was struck by how backward the place seemed compared with Boston. On his return he confided to his wife, Mary, that the "whole face of the country is stamped with the curse of slavery: its riches are turned into poverty, its fertility into barrenness; and man degrades himself as he degrades his fellows."[6] Barely a month later, Mann took the floor for his maiden speech in Congress and expanded on this theme of southern backwardness and degradation.

In the course of his speech, Mann drew on and developed several of the main ideas concerning the South that were becoming common. Considering the moral and economic aspects of slavery, Mann indicated that slavery as an institution stifled the progress of the southern states. Although deemed to be property themselves, slaves were, Mann argued, "the preventers, the wasters, the antagonists, of property." Slavery in no way increased either individual or national wealth but hampered both, destroying "worldly prosperity." The root of the problem, as Mann perceived it, was that slavery by its very nature destroyed the ambitions of the slave and thus undermined the natural human impulse toward "bettering one's condition." On the main points of the free versus slave labor argument, Mann turned for support to the writings of William Gregg, a southerner whose pamphlet *Essays on Domestic Industry* included some telling differences between the free and the slave states. In his comparison of North and South, Gregg concluded that "the true secret of our difficulties lies in the want of energy on the part of our capitalists, and ignorance and laziness on the part of those who ought to labor." The vast resources of the South—the forests, quarries, and mines—Gregg noted, lay idle, as the South contented itself with purchasing goods from the North instead of developing its own manufacturing capabilities. As his biographer noted, Gregg's perception of the differences between North and South "was essentially that between conservation and waste, economy and exploitation."[7]

This was a familiar theme, and Gregg was not the first or the last southerner to provide northerners with such damning arguments against the South. As early as 1837, W. C. Preston, like Gregg a South Carolinian, noted with shame "the prosperity, the industry, the public spirit" of the northern states compared with the "neglected and desolate" South. His comments were picked up by John Gorham Palfrey—who would later listen with great interest and approval to Mann's 1848 address—and reprinted in the *North American Review* that same year.[8] In 1843, the *Pittsburgh Daily Gazette* carried an article written by a South Carolinian that criticized southern educational failings. While the North sustained "schools at the public expense all over the country, supplied with good teachers," it was argued, the South enjoyed no such system. "Hence, in New England, you can seldom find a man who cannot read and write," whereas in South Carolina, "one fifth part of the adult whites cannot read." This, the southerner concluded, was "the necessary policy of a slave-holding aristocracy."[9] Similarly, in the composite volume of Mann's writings on slavery, which appeared in 1851, Mann's maiden speech was followed by extracts from a tract written by a Virginian that had appeared the previous year. The Virginian in question, the Reverend Henry Ruffner, president of Lexington College, held views similar to those of both Gregg and Preston, as well as to those of Mann himself. Slavery was indeed a curse, Ruffner declared, and it condemned the South to stagnation and decay, while the North exhibited "a dense and increasing population; thriving villages, towns and cities; a neat and productive agriculture, growing manufactures, and active commerce." Under slavery, the potential of the South would never be fulfilled, and the presence of slaves only served to bring white labor into disrepute. "Thus general industry gives way by degrees to indolent relaxation," Ruffner concluded, creating "false notions of dignity and refinement, and a taste for fashionable luxuries."[10]

That Mann should be critical of this lack of industry is unsurprising. His support for and belief in the role of industrial development had been evident much earlier in his career. As a member of the Massachusetts General Court, Mann found an occasion to voice "his general faith in science and technology," a faith that led him to regard industrial development as "the long-awaited touchstone for greater human happiness."[11] It was little wonder, then, that Mann concurred so strongly with the views of men like Gregg and

Ruffner.[12] Mann's arguments in 1848 represented the summation of years of thought on the subjects of education and slavery, subjects that were twinned forever in Mann's worldview. On the occasion of a Fourth of July oration in 1842, Mann had touched on similar themes. "We are a Union made up of twenty-six States, a nation composed of twenty-six nations," he observed. Yet, "[a]cross the very center of our territory a line is drawn, on one side of which all labor is voluntary; while, on the opposite side, the system of involuntary labor, or servitude prevails. This is a fearful element of repugnance,—penetrating not only through all social, commercial, and political relations, but into natural ethics and religion."[13]

The subject of slavery was clearly uppermost in Mann's thoughts at this time. He had referred to it earlier that year in a letter to Scottish phrenologist George Combe, in which he expressed the hope that "our boisterous democracy could furnish you with a peaceful retreat," but concluded that "in our political latitudes there reigns one storm, & that is endless."[14] In his final annual report to the Board of Education of Massachusetts, delivered just before he went to Washington, Mann made his position quite clear. "The slave States of this Union may buy cotton machinery made by the intelligent working mechanics of the free States, and they may train their slaves to work it with more or less skill," he argued, but they would never be able to keep abreast of progress. The South, he concluded, would always be dependent on northern ingenuity and skill; "the more educated community [would] forever keep ahead of the less educated one." It was not simply southern backwardness that concerned Mann, but its effects on the republican experiment that was America. As he put it, "the establishment of a republican government, without well-appointed and efficient means for the universal education of the people, is the most rash and fool-hardy experiment ever tried by man." "It may be an easy thing to make a republic," he continued, "but it is a very laborious thing to make republicans; and woe to the republic that rests upon no better foundations than ignorance, selfishness, and passion." This was a theme he expanded on. "We are part of a mighty nation, which has just embarked upon the grandest experiment ever yet attempted upon earth,—the experiment of the capacity of mankind for the wise and righteous government of themselves," he declared. However, in more than half the nation "no provision worthy of the name is made for replenishing the common mind with knowledge, or for training the common heart to virtue."[15]

Mann's thinking on this subject was in line with the reform impulse of the age, particularly its more aggressive side. Clearly, nineteenth-century reformers were concerned about the changes that America as a whole was undergoing, and they devoted a lot of thought to how these might be controlled. In the free-labor ideology of the North, Mann and his contemporaries believed that they had, in David Nasaw's words, "discovered a republican solution to a universal problem." The answer was a free public school education, which would ensure that the population was both more moral and less prone to social upheaval and civil disobedience. These reformers sought to inculcate the necessary republican principles from the outset, "not only through the history and geography texts but in the readers and spellers . . . that formed the core of every curriculum." This reform impulse and the impetus toward universal education was very much in a northern mold. The type of education that Mann and others hoped to impose on the nation represented a form of republicanism that "was in fact no more or less than the Whiggism preached and practiced by the reformers themselves; it was a republicanism that emphasized the need for public obedience rather than public participation." In the reformers' worldview, America represented liberty, and the "republic that had survived into mid-century was sacrosanct in form and function."[16]

Education was not, in any sense, a secondary or subsidiary issue as far as the North-South debate of the antebellum period was concerned. One of the first things the South did in response to growing sectional tension was to ban "Yankee" texts from the classrooms and substitute those that preached a more "southern" line.[17] The *New York Tribune* reported this trend and expressed dismay at its implications. "Southern men now require Southern schoolbooks for their children, and Southern teachers for themselves," the *Tribune* noted. It concluded that "the tendency, in and out of Congress, is toward sectionalism."[18] That something as seemingly innocuous as schoolbooks should become a source of sectional disagreement is less surprising than it seems. In the mid-nineteenth century, America was very much a nation in search of an identity. The revolutionary generation had laid the groundwork for the creation of the American nation, but it was the particular responsibility of nineteenth-century Americans to make explicit the ideals that were implicit in their national identity. Any people with "a growing spirit of nationalism" require an "education for patriotism," and nineteenth-century America was no different in this regard from many European states. On both sides of the Atlantic, one can trace "the growth and development of conceptions which viewed popular education as a tool of the national state." The American impulse in this direction was "just one phase of a broader movement in the Western world toward education for national, as opposed to purely religious or personal, ends."[19]

The question for Mann was whether America would "be reclaimed to humanity, to a Christian life, and a Christian history," or whether it would be "a receptacle where the avarice, the profligacy, and the licentiousness of a corrupt civilization shall cast its criminals and breed its monsters." The nation's only salvation, he averred, lay in the beneficial influence of "the mother States of this Union, those States where the institutions of learning and religion are now honored and cherished."[20] For Mann, his own state of Massachusetts had already achieved the necessary conditions for the maintenance of a virtuous republic. "The people of Massachusetts have, in some degree, appreciated the truth," he boasted, "that the unexampled prosperity of the State, its comfort, its competence, its general intelligence and virtue,—is attributable to the education, more or less perfect, which all its people have received."[21] Ten years after Mann made this observation, the *New York Daily Times* expressed similar sentiments. Education, the paper's editorial argued, was the bedrock of the American Republic, since in "proportion as the Government departs from a democratic form, and gathers within itself despotic powers, is the enlightenment of the people considered undesirable and dangerous." In an echo of Mann's position, the paper concluded that New England's common schools were "the mental architects of this age. They lay the granite foundation for the mind of the country."[22]

Education was clearly the root of all good in Mann's America, and he proudly observed that "[i]t has been justly remarked by the most intelligent foreigners that the nature of our political institutions does much to educate our people . . . that from being called upon to decide so many questions, their minds are honed [trained] to a great degree of activity."[23] Mann did not, however, include the South in his version of America. Mann was of the same mind as the reformers identified by Richard Abbott who ascribed to the North all the positive values of free labor, education, and individual advancement.[24] Given Mann's general philosophy on matters of free labor and education, it is perhaps unsurprising that he chose to present the South in the manner he did in his maiden speech. That Mann chose to paint such a negative picture of the southern states indicates quite clearly that he, too, subscribed to what was fast becoming an accepted critique of the South.

What was significant about this critique was that it focused less on the economic failure of the southern states per se and more on the comparative success of the North. Likewise, although slavery was promulgated as the root cause of so much southern distress, concern for the slave took second place to concern for white southern society. Much of this hostile imagery drew on, and influenced, abolitionist rhetoric, although its exponents were often suspicious of William Lloyd Garrison's call for the immediate and total abolition of slavery.[25] What gave this image particular efficacy, however, was that conservatives in the North also subscribed to it; it was not the preserve of any particular faction but was a fundamental part of the northern response to the South. The critique itself often represented no more than a simple inversion of the positive images of the South that Taylor, among others, has identified.[26]

Those who were concerned about the social effects of the North's increasing industrialization and diversification looked to the South for evidence of a conservative, stable society rooted in what were perceived to be traditional English values. Those who welcomed progress—and we must include Mann in this category—and who sought to create a society sustained by essentially republican values regarded the southern way of life with suspicion and tried to show how backward it was. Conservative northern statesman Edward Everett, like Mann, believed strongly in the power of the intellect. "Mind, acting through the useful arts . . . is the vital principle of modern society," he declared in 1837.[27] However, Everett believed that the South did not show much evidence of this. The abolitionists and other like-minded reformers of the period had even more cause to play up the negative side of southern life, focusing on the suffering it caused not only to the slaves but also to the non-slaveholding white majority, and it was on the plight of this latter group that politicians often focused.

Since the war against ignorance represented so much of his life's work, it is unsurprising that Mann expressed such concern over the educational backwardness of the South. However, he was far from alone in either his concerns or his criticisms. The ignorance induced by slavery had been a useful stick with which to beat the South as early as the 1830s. Slavery, one Ohio senator argued in 1832, reduced the South's "capacity for commercial enterprizes. A negro slave is unfit for a ship carpenter or a sailor," he continued, "and, in a country where there is no laboring class, except slaves, ships cannot be built, or manned to the same advantage, as in the Eastern and Middle States, where laborers are freemen, and possess intelligence and enterprise."[28] In a similar vein, a senator from Pennsylvania argued that, because of slavery, the "lights of science, and the improvements of art" could not penetrate the South. "While the intellectual industry of other parts of this country springs elastically forward," he concluded, the South remained "stationary."[29] Such views of the South were echoed increasingly by northern abolitionists. Theodore Parker, for example, argued that while "the South can grow timber, it is the North which builds the ships," and whereas the South could "rear cotton, the free intelligence of the North must weave it into cloth." The South, Parker concluded, would never match the North in either industrial or intellectual development. "Steam-engines and slaves," he asserted, "come of a different stock."[30]

By the 1850s, such arguments had become all too common. Northern newspapers and journals picked up on this and frequently drew their readers' attention to southern educational and intellectual deficiencies. Slavery, according to the *Boston Daily Courier,* served only to hinder the progress of the South "in population, in wealth, in intelligence, in cultivation . . . of the mind or the soil"—a viewpoint that many northern papers concurred with. The *New York Daily Times* was periodically up in arms about southern educational backwardness and stressed both the importance to the nation of an educated workforce and the superior intellectual capacity of northerners. Similarly, the *Albany Evening Journal* argued that southern intellect was not as "practical or diffused as at the North." For evidence, the paper cited the number of patents applied for in the nation and noted that "at least one half the Patents applied for from the South are sought by Northern mechanics who have magnanimously migrated to the Southern desert." Only a few months later, the *Journal* remarked that in Mississippi, "one third of the population do not know the letter B from an ox-yoke."[31] Of all the papers, however, the *New York Tribune* was the most vehement on this subject from the 1840s onward. The lack of education that was an inevitable corollary of the system of slavery, the *Tribune* argued, condemned the South to a position of inferiority within the Union. The South, according to the paper, "has not only comparatively little in the arts of civilization, but what she has she borrows. She has no superior industry or art. What she enjoys she does not originate. She buys the iron; she imports her engineers; she gets Fulton to invent her steamboats and Whitney her cotton-gin."[32]

Mann was clearly both cognizant of and fully in agreement with such arguments. Ignorance, he opined, was the root cause of all the problems facing the South, and this ignorance was fostered by slavery. "Create a serf caste and debar them from education," he observed, "and you necessarily debar a great portion of the privileged class from education also." By destroying common education, Mann argued, "slavery destroys the fruits of common education— the inventive mind, practical talent, the power of adapting means to ends in the business of life." As he took pains to show, it was certainly not the southern states that were producing "all those mechanical and scientific improvements and inventions which have enriched the world with so many comforts, and adorned it with so many beauties."[33]

This was an issue that Mann had worked out at some length in private over the years and was an expression of some of his most deeply held beliefs concerning human development and the responsibilities of living under a republican form of government.[34] Turning again to the writings of his previous career as secretary of the State Board of Education in Massachusetts, it becomes clear how vital education was to Mann. For him, education was "much more than an ability to read, write, and keep common accounts." Education meant "such a training of the body as shall build it up with robustness and vigor,—at once protecting it from disease, and enabling it to act, *formatively*, upon the crude substance of Nature,—to turn a wilderness into cultivated fields, forests into ships, or quarries and claypits into villages and cities." "It is a truism," he continued, "that free institutions multiply human energies. A chained body cannot do much harm; a chained mind can do as little. In a despotic government, the human faculties are benumbed and paralyzed; in a Republic, they glow with an intense life, and burst forth with uncontrollable impetuosity." It was therefore the duty of a republican government to confer, via education, the necessary "wisdom and rectitude" upon its people, that they might harness this energy for the greater good. Mann again made explicit the link between education and republican government and the necessity of the former if the latter was to have any chance of success. "If republican institutions do wake up unexampled energies in the whole mass of a people, and give them implements of unexampled power wherewith to work out their will," he argued, "then these same institutions ought also to confer upon that people unexampled wisdom and rectitude."[35]

The role of education in rendering democracy safe by creating "universal elevation of character, intellectual and moral," along with it occurs throughout Mann's writings. It is little wonder that he regarded the lack of education in the southern states with such concern. It did not simply result in intellectual backwardness, in a population that could neither read nor write (although that was bad enough in Mann's opinion); it threatened to undermine the very foundations of what Mann considered to be successful republican government.[36] In a rare example of understanding toward the South, Mann wrote to his wife: "I begin to have more charity than I ever had for the Southerners. Does not the aberration of mind they evince in regard to the eternal principles of truth & justice excite your profound compassion, & induce you to look upon their acts in a somewhat more charitable spirit than before?" he asked her. Of course, the problem of the South could be traced to its educational deficiencies. "Should we have been any better," he inquired, "if so educated? It makes me look upon Mr. Clay with much admiration."[37]

However, Mann could not be reasonable on this subject for long. As he saw it, the educational failure of the South threatened all American free institutions—with ignorance lay danger and the threat of despotism. Addressing the South across the floor of the House of Representatives in 1850, he went on the attack:

We of the North, you say, are Abolitionists; but abolitionists of what? Are we abolitionists of the inalienable, indefeasible, indestructible rights of man? Are we abolitionists of knowledge, abolitionists of virtue, of education, and of human culture? Do we seek to abolish the glorious moral and intellectual attributes which God has given to his children, and thus . . . make the facts of slavery conform to the law of slavery, by obliterating the distinction between a man and a beast? . . . Do our laws and our institutions seek to blot out and abolish the image of God in the human soul?[38]

Having warmed to his theme, Mann pursued it throughout his congressional career. In one thing, he opined, the South excelled, and that was in the training of statesmen. For evidence, he turned to a famous pamphlet written by the Reverend Horace Bushnell and published for the American Home Missionary Society the previous year, entitled *Barbarism the First Danger.*

Slavery, Bushnell argued, hampered progress in the South, yet made politicians and statesmen out of southerners. The planter class had the leisure to develop "that kind of cultivation which distinguishes men of society." This allowed the slaveholding southerner to excel in public life, "where so much depends on manners and social address." Again, this was a common theme, especially in New England. Southerners, Bushnell continued, lived isolated lives that, significantly, prevented the successful establishment and maintenance of both public schools and churches. "Education and religion thus displaced," Bushnell concluded, "the dinner table only remains, and on that hangs, in great part, the keeping of the social state." This, he warned, "cannot be regarded as any sufficient spring of character. It is neither a school nor a gospel."[39] Having cited this damning indictment of southern life and manners, Mann concluded that "[a]ll this proceeds from no superiority of natural endowment on the one side, or inferiority on the other. . . . [T]he difference," he stressed, "results from no difference in natural endowment; the mental endowments at the South are equal to those in any part of the world; but it comes because in one quarter the common atmosphere is vivified with knowledge, electric with ideas, while slavery gathers its Boeotian fogs over the other."[40]

For Mann and other like-minded northerners, America was clearly the once and future nation, although in the antebellum period, Americans expressed increasing concern for the future success of their national experiment and the ideals the nation stood for. For Mann, "sin had become the failure of self-cultivation, of which ignorance was only one facet."[41] Mann was not alone in his views. Much earlier, in New York, William H. Seward had made the link between internal improvements, social development, and education, and he stressed it repeatedly in an attempt to encourage "the American people to make their educational system match their democratic hopes."[42] In a similar vein, but over a decade later, the noted minister and reformer Henry Ward Beecher traced southern deficiencies in morals and enterprise to a basic deficiency in education. "The disease is not on the skin," Beecher declared, "but in the bones and heart; in the political and social system. The South has made slavery to be its heart." Consequently, southerners "are made to lag behind the march of civilization, and to see the whole world running past them in social elevation, popular intelligence, and industrial enterprise."[43] Beecher would have concurred with Frederick Law Olmsted that "[t]here is no life without intelligence—no intelligence without ambition."[44]

Significantly, it seemed to intellectuals like Bushnell, Beecher, Olmsted, and Mann that, to a great extent, the South was hampered not only by slavery but also by a fundamental lack of ambition for improvement. Bushnell was one of the few commentators who even came close to acknowledging that geographic factors, combined with the South's lack of cities, worked against the establishment of the kind of educational and social facilities enjoyed by the North. The *Boston Daily Courier* had touched on this in its coverage of Mann's maiden speech, but it identified slavery quite clearly as the cause and laid the blame for this state of affairs with southerners themselves. The population of any slaveholding country, the paper noted, "must be too sparse, and the land too badly cultivated, and the forces of nature, in water, wind, steam, and mechanical power, too much neglected, to enable it to reach a high point of elevation in the scale of power, intelligence, wealth, comfort and elegance."[45]

Ralph Waldo Emerson had reached a similar conclusion a few years earlier when he noted that slavery was "no scholar, no improver; it does not love the whistle of the railroad; it does not love the newspaper, the mail-bag, a college, a book or a preacher who has the absurd whim of saying what he thinks." In any slaveholding society, Emerson concluded, "everything goes to decay."[46] Emerson's hostility toward the South predated, and often precluded, his concern for the slave. Instead, Emerson's critique of the South originated in his own ambitions for the North, particularly New England. Events in the 1840s and 1850s—especially the expulsion of Samuel Hoar from South Carolina (1845) and the revised Fugitive Slave Law (1850)—prompted Emerson to declare his antipathy for the South. Such events were not, however, the decisive factor in Emerson's reaction to the South. It has been argued that for Emerson, as for others, the increasing sectional tension caused him to modify his views, to become more overtly hostile to the South.[47] Yet there is, in Emerson's case, clear evidence that his views on the South were consistently negative. The political upheavals of the 1840s and 1850s only confirmed his concerns regarding that region; in no sense did they alter them.

Like Mann's, Emerson's views on the South were shaped not only by an antipathy to slavery but also by more general concerns for the American republican experiment. Education was lacking in the South, but much more worrisome for Emerson and Mann was the fact that any obvious desire for education seemed to be missing as well. The suspicion that the South did not want to heed the lessons that the North was desperate to teach it caused both men increasing concern. Despite Emerson's friendships with southerners and his visits to the South, his general view of southern intellectual ability was, in common with Mann's, a fairly damning one. He could be almost jocular on the subject, as he was in an early letter written to John Boynton Hill. "What kind of people are the Southerners in your vicinity?" Emerson asked. "You know our idea of an accomplished Southerner—to wit—as ignorant as a bear, as irascible & nettled as any porcupine, as polite as a troubadour, & a very John Randolph in character and address."[48] Despite Emerson's lighthearted tone, there was an underlying sense of northern superiority in his query, as there was when he advised his friend to "pluck out thy lot of life from the abundance of the North."[49] There was real vitriol, however, in a journal entry Emerson wrote many years later.

In 1837, writing in his journal about southern students at Harvard, Emerson concluded that the southerner was "a spoiled child with graceful manners, excellent self-command, very good to be spoiled more, but good for nothing else." Drawing on the general image of the South as a region influenced by the lifestyle of the English landed gentry, Emerson suggested that the southerner "has conversed so much with rifles, horses and dogs that he has become himself a rifle, a horse and a dog, and in civil, educated company . . . he is dumb and unhappy." Ultimately, Emerson believed that southern students were "mere bladders of conceit. . . . Their question respecting any man is . . . how can he fight? In this country," Emerson noted, "we ask, What can he do?"[50] In referring to the North (or he might have meant only Massachusetts) as a country distinct from the South, Emerson revealed a singularly sectional perspective that viewed the South as a world away from the intellectual and cultural achievements of the North.

It is clear, therefore, that when Mann addressed these themes, he established himself as being of a mind with many other northerners. He expressed similar concerns about the future of the nation as Seward had in 1835, concerns that would be repeated by many others throughout the 1850s. For Mann, "hard work was the key to the kingdom of riches, power, and personal glory because that had been his own experience," but the South did not exhibit any such ability. Southerners were, as the critique went, lazy aristocrats, who relied on others for their survival.[51]

In the course of his denunciations of the South, Mann also focused on another common idea, that of southern despotism. He frequently alluded to it in his private correspondence, and although he was able to converse with particular slaveholders without an "uncivil word" being exchanged, his response to the slaveholder class became increasingly denunciatory as his congressional career continued.[52] In part, this image of the despotic southerner derived from the prevalent image of the aristocratic and lazy southerner, who by virtue of the "serf caste" in his section could devote time to the cultivation of manners, which, as Bushnell had noted, were so necessary to a successful statesman. Although Mann and others clearly felt that the North was further advanced than the South in many ways, their confidence in the efficacy of northern intellectual superiority was not complete. The suspicion that southerners managed very well without the educational accomplishments of the North worried some northerners. The *New York Times*, for instance, noted that the "people of our Northern States are strongly inclined to reverence Books, and to lay very great stress on Book-culture." For once, the paper did not see this as an advantage. Northerners, the *Times* suggested, devoted too much time to purely intellectual pursuits and not enough to the business of politics. Northern statesmen, the paper concluded, needed to develop more "practical power over men," particularly in their dealings with the South.[53]

Another element in this image of the despotic southerner arose from the perception that in Congress southerners acted in concert with other members of their section, effectively blocking northern votes on such issues as the tariff and, more importantly, slavery and its extension. Mann made this point in 1850 and again two years later.[54] "Nominally the South is divided into the same parties" as the North, he argued, "but, in whatever regards slavery, it is undivided and a unit—indissoluble as the Siamese twins. . . . On tariffs, river and harbor improvements, and so forth, they carry on a feeble and somnolent warfare among themselves, but whenever the tocsin of slavery is sounded, they awaken to seize their arms, and form in solid column for a quick-step march to the point in contest."[55]

Whereas hostility toward slavery was often a significant element of the northern critique of the South, the focus was not on the moral wrong of slavery but on the economic, social, and political danger arising from the power of the white, slaveholding inhabitants of the southern states—a power that was expressed by, and drew its strength from, the ownership of slaves. As Larry Gara noted, this distinction is crucial to an understanding of the increasing sectional tensions of the antebellum period.[56] The northern critique of slavery all too often evolved out of a deeply racist concern for the continued well-being of American white society; in other words, concern for the slave was not necessarily the motivating factor behind northern attacks on slavery. For Mann, too, concern for the slave was not an issue, and he admitted to harboring racist sentiments. In his defense, Mann struggled just a bit harder with this idea than most, but he was unable to overcome a deeply felt antipathy for blacks.[57]

In Mann's continuous opposition to the extension of slavery, and in his increasingly hostile denunciations of slaveholders, we can trace a growing perception that there was a real danger in the "slave power." Slavery, the cause of southern difficulties, now threatened to subvert northern institutions. Mann argued that were it not for slavery, the South "would today possess, threefold the population of the northern section—all free, all blessed with more abounding comforts and competence, and with all the means of embellishment, education, and universal culture. . . . It is slavery," he reiterated, "and slavery alone, that has struck them down from their lofty preeminence; that has dwarfed their gigantic capacities, and driven them to maintain an ascendancy—ultimately worthless, and worse than worthless—by subordinating Northern politicians, instead of exulting in the legitimate superiority of home-born and undecaying vigor."[58] This represents a change of direction for Mann. The blight of slavery was no longer contained within the South; because of its effect on northern politicians, it was extending its pernicious influence over the northern states.

As the sectional struggle in Congress became more vehement, Mann's concern for the North's position increased. The furor at the start of the 31st Congress over the choice of Speaker prompted him to criticize his own section for allowing Howell Cobb to be elected.[59] Writing to his wife, Mann expressed his increasing concern over the power that slaveholders wielded in the national arena and his fears that the North was losing ground to the South. "You are in error," he informed her, "in supposing that the exclusion of slavery from the Territories will affect the growth of cotton or rice unfavorably. Slaves are in great demand now for the cotton and the fields." Instead, he stressed that the southern determination to extend slavery into the territories arose from their "fear of losing the balance of power, as they call it." On this subject, he concluded, "they are not a reasoning people."[60] In this period, Mann stressed his concerns for the North both in his speeches and in his private correspondence.[61] Two main events prompted his most extreme outbursts: the Compromise of 1850, in particular its fugitive slave resolution, and Daniel Webster's infamous pro-Union 7 March speech. In the latter, Webster supported the proposed revised Fugitive Slave Act and argued that there was no need to legislate against slavery in the territories.

Again, Mann was not alone in his reactions to these events. Emerson's most hostile invectives against the South occurred after the Fugitive Slave Act was passed. Attempting to salvage what he perceived as an unimaginable betrayal by Webster, whom he had virtually deified in the past, Emerson turned to consider what role his native state might play in the future. It is imperative, he stated, that "we keep Massachusetts true. It is of unspeakable importance that she play her honest part." Emerson acknowledged that Massachusetts was a small state, but he believed that even little states might "furnish the mind and the heart by which the rest of the world is sustained." Massachusetts, Emerson declared, could "be the brain which turns about the behemoth."[62] Despite his belief in the importance of Massachusetts' role, Emerson's criticisms were directed as much at his home state as at the South. For Emerson, the Compromise of 1850 had sullied forever the good name of Boston:

> Boston, of whose fame for spirit and character we have all been so proud; Boston, whose citizens, intelligent people in England told me they could always distinguish by their culture among Americans; the Boston of the American Revolution, which figures so proudly in John Adams' Diary, which the whole country has been reading; Boston, spoiled by prosperity, must bow its ancient honor in the dust, and make us irretrievably ashamed.[63]

Seeking an explanation for what he clearly regarded as a betrayal by his native state, Emerson proposed the idea that there were really two nations under the Union: North and South. It was not slavery that divided these, he asserted, but "climate and temperament." The onus of responsibility rested, unsurprisingly, on the South. "The South does not like the North, slavery or no slavery, and never did," Emerson asserted. The more reasonable, intellectual North "likes the South well enough, for it knows its own advantages."[64]

What really offended Emerson about the passage of the Fugitive Slave Act was that it marred the perfection, as he saw it, of northern society and brought the problem of slavery into the northern states. Mann, too, believed that his home state, formerly "the impregnable citadel of freedom," had been irredeemably tainted by the passage of the revised Fugitive Slave Act, and the South was entirely to blame. The southern planter, Mann argued, "seems to possess some wizard art, unknown to the demonology of former times, by which he impregnates his bales of cotton with a spirit of inhumanity." Yet even on this subject, Mann never lost sight of the importance of education or missed the opportunity to make a sectional point. Although he was doubtful that the planters would ever "abandon their slothful habits, become industrious, and manufacture for themselves," he hoped that they might. Then, Mann argued, southerners "would become better customers for those ever new forms of commodities which our industry and inventive skill, while we keep our schoolhouses in operation, will always be able to supply."[65]

Mann was even more riled, however, by Daniel Webster's 7 March speech. Mann, in common with Emerson, never forgave Webster for his apostasy and his betrayal of the cause of freedom. In speeches, letters, and his private journals, Mann criticized Webster as a "fallen star" and a "hireling of slavery" who had betrayed the North.[66] Webster's speech, together with the effects of the Fugitive Slave Act, created for Mann the specter of the slave power encroaching on the rights and freedoms of the northern states. Although he confidently informed his wife that Massachusetts would never permit a slaveholder to recapture runaway slaves on its soil, he was less than convinced that this would be so.[67] He feared that "the slave-power of the South and the money power of the North have struck hands." Between them both, Mann believed that the republican form of government, on which he pinned so many hopes, would be destroyed.[68] In his final year in Congress, Mann wrote to his friend George Combe, setting out his fears that northern politicians were too keen to placate the South. If the North could only "unite for freedom as the South do for slavery, all would be well," he wrote, "but the lower and hinder half of the brain rules, and we do not."[69]

Two years after Mann had left Washington and moved to Ohio, he still maintained his stand against southern educational and social backwardness and the danger this posed to the Republic. "In all the free states of this Union there is a Government system of Public Schools, more or less perfect," he declared, but "in the Southern States there is nothing really worthy of the name of Free Schools & whatever semblance of these exists is miserably administered." The result, he noted, was widespread illiteracy throughout the South, from Virginia to Tennessee. "And were it not for the reflected light that is cast upon these people from the luminous that is the educated communities around them," he concluded, "they would all be heathens & cannibals."[70]

Mann and other northern reformers and intellectuals reaffirmed the moral, intellectual, economic, and social superiority of their own section by contrasting it with the educational, economic, and moral backwardness of the South. Many of these reformers were from New England, but certainly not all. The arguments they drew on had been expressed from the 1830s onward in Congress, in the northern press, and in books and journals published in the North. They therefore can be taken as representative of a broad range of northern opinion rather than as a specific reflection of New England imperialism. Although not abolitionists, northern intellectuals like Mann paralleled the arguments proposed by both the abolitionist and the more conservative elements in the North.

Mann's own position was not far removed from that of the rather extreme abolitionist Wendell Phillips, who argued that the "North thinks,—can appreciate argument,—[it] is the nineteenth century," whereas the South "dreams,—it is the thirteenth and fourteenth century,—baron and serf,— noble and slave." The struggle, in Phillips's view, was "between barbarism and civilization."[71] For Mann as well, the division between South and North was a division between the corporeal and the spiritual nature of man, between Caliban and Prospero, between nature and nurture. Theodore Parker similarly argued that the North alone sustained all the necessary accouterments of civilization. The nation's "learned and philosophical societies, for the study of Science, Letters, and Art," could be found only in the North. "Whence," he asked,

> come the men of superior education who occupy the Pulpits, exercise the professions of Law and Medicine, or fill the chairs of the Professors in the Colleges of the Union? Almost all from the North. . . . Whence come the distinguished authors of America? The poets—Bryant, Longfellow, Whittier; Historians—Sparks, Prescott, Bancroft; Jurists—Parsons, Wheaton, Story, Kent! Whence Irving, Channing, Emerson; whence all the scientific men, the men of thought, who represent the Nation's loftier consciousness? All from the free states; north of Mason and Dixon's line.[72]

Emerson best summed up the problem as northerners saw it. In his view, the southerner "has personality, has temperament, has manners, persuasion, address and terror," whereas "the cold Yankee has wealth, numbers, intellect, material power of all sorts, but not fire or firmness."[73] In this contrast between southern temperament and northern intellect, northern intellectuals made a clear distinction between what Lewis Simpson termed "the culture of no mind" and a "culture of mind." This distinction, Simpson noted, was hardly "the sentiment of a cohesive American nationalism."[74] Yet the belief that fundamental and irreconcilable differences separated North and South was not confined to New England. The fact that Emerson's viewpoint found an echo in northern society as a whole represented a dangerous shift in the reform outlook as far as the nationalist impulse was concerned. Again, it is a shift that can be traced through Mann.

Although Mann often reiterated his belief in freedom over slavery, and often cited the strength of that belief as his only reason for entering Congress initially and then for staying, against the encroachments of the slave power he drew on the arsenal of the antebellum critique of the South.[75] It is indisputable that Mann truly believed that there was "no evil so great as that of the extension of slavery," yet his concern was consistently focused on southern white society and its effects on the North, rather than on the question of slavery itself.[76]

Mann was certainly not insensible to the legal and moral arguments that could be used to oppose slavery; he did, after all, act as defense attorney in the famous Drayton and Sayres trial. Nevertheless, in his public rhetoric in Congress and in his private correspondence, Mann developed his image of the South from that of a blighted society into that of the slave power whose aspirations for its peculiar institution threatened to encroach on northern soil. "Our laws and institutions," he wrote, referring to the North, "are all formed so as to encourage the poor man, and, by education, to elevate his children above the condition of their parents; but their [the South's] laws and institutions all tend to aggrandize the rich, and to perpetuate power in their hands."[77] In true Enlightenment style, knowledge, for Mann, led to freedom, and the North, to him, was the epitome of a free society, with all the potential that offered for the nation as a whole.

As secretary of the Board of Education of Massachusetts, Mann had contrasted Massachusetts with Europe. European theory, according to Mann, allocated to some the right to labor, to others the right to enjoy the fruits of labor. In Massachusetts, by contrast, everyone had the right to both. In Massachusetts, Mann boasted, equality of condition prevailed, whereas in Europe, inequality was the norm.[78] Yet in the course of his congressional career, Mann increasingly came to contrast Massachusetts, and the North in general, not with Europe but with the South. The implications of this shift for national unity and stability are clear. America had, for much of its history, defined itself against the Old World. Europe was the negative reference point "which helped Americans to define their own positive qualities."[79] By the 1850s, however, Americans from both North and South were no longer looking across the Atlantic for definition but at each other. In such circumstances, a truly *national* outlook became impossible to sustain.

Horace Mann was thus not only representative of a nationalist impulse that regarded education as the sine qua non of a successful republic but also instrumental in the exclusion of the South from the American nation. In the opinion of men like Mann, Seward, Emerson, and Beecher, the increasing power of the South could only be detrimental for the future of the American nation. There was no distinction in their minds between the various components of their ideological outlook. What concerned them were the future of republican government and the success of the American experiment in this regard. Free government itself, in their view, relied on a solid educational base. These were the ingredients for a viewpoint that was never going to admit the South as it existed in the 1850s into the American republican experiment.[80]

It was in this spirit of sectional antagonism that the northern critique of the South emerged and developed. It drew on the concerns of many northerners, including Horace Mann, that the South represented a threat to the American republican experiment. It also confirmed their view that only the North contained all the necessary ingredients—intellectual, social, economic, and spiritual—that a successful republic required. Although Foner has detailed the form this critique took, particularly in the late 1850s, its origins have received less attention. Through the concerns of an individual like Horace Mann, who was neither an abolitionist nor a career politician and who left Congress before the Republican Party rose to prominence, one can better identify the origins of what became the Republican critique, as well as the ideology behind it. Mann's antisouthern views, derived from and sustained by his focus on the importance of education in a republic, were reiterated time and again by a much broader group of northerners in the later antebellum period. In this sense, Mann was very much a representative man for the antebellum North: in his denunciations of the South, one can identify the main elements of a sectional ideology distinctly at odds with the national ideals it proclaimed.

SIX

❧

When Is a Nation Not a Nation?

The Crisis of American Nationality

The North, which Daniel Webster desired to see, but died without the sight, is discovered at last.
— *New York Tribune*, 25 November 1856

Given the increasing sectional animosities in antebellum America, it is difficult to see how a specifically northern nationalism could have failed to develop. Daniel Webster's 1848 invocation of the idea of the "North" had an impact that he could hardly have anticipated or relished. In the wake of the Republican defeat in the election of 1856, one northern abolitionist exulted in the belief that although the Republicans "have not yet got a President . . . they have what is better, a North."[1] Indeed, Webster's idea of the North became a rallying cry of sorts for those northerners most disaffected by the South and increasingly concerned not just for the future of their own section but also for the future of the nation as a whole.

As historians have long recognized, the issues raised by the Kansas-Nebraska Act had much to do with northern hostility toward the South and southern behavior. The bill also prompted a resurgence of specifically northern sentiment. The North, according to one congressman, was "*at last aroused, at last united.*"[2] The *Springfield Republican,* in contrast, was far from optimistic. Although it believed that if northerners were to "sink their little prejudices and their effete party trammels" to form "an impregnable platform of opposition . . . there *would be* a North," it held out little hope that its advice would be followed. "'There is no North,' said Mr. Webster in 1848," the paper recalled, adding in a pessimistic note, "It is just as true in 1854."[3] Charles Francis Adams expressed a similar pessimism. In his opinion, the free states had "no self reliance" and were, as a result, continually humiliated by the South. Charles Upham took a more confident line and argued in Congress that the South's behavior had "united the free States, at last." The North, he declared in an article written the following year, was "at last a unit, as the South always has been, on the slavery question."[4] Israel Washburn concurred and, like the *Springfield Republican*, recalled the words of Daniel Webster. "Let this [Kansas-Nebraska] bill become a law," he declared, "and prophecy will not loiter on the way to fulfillment. There will be a North."[5]

Thurlow Weed's *Albany Evening Journal* picked up on this shift in both public and political sentiment. It echoed Washburn's words almost exactly and argued that while northern congressmen "have seemed content to be 'hewers of wood and drawers of water' for Slaveholders," if the Kansas-Nebraska bill was passed, "THERE WILL BE A NORTH."[6] Once the bill had passed, the paper argued that the South had "laid its hands on the bargain made with Freedom thirty years ago, flung it aside and pronounced it null and void. This roused the Free States from their lethargy. They united."[7] The concept of unification in the face of the enemy was a fundamental aspect of northern nationalism in this period. This is how the northern critique came to be achieved and how it was sustained. By June 1854, even the *Springfield Republican* was in a more optimistic mood, declaring that "a determination that henceforth there shall be a North" had "sprung up through the Northern states." The paper had no doubt that this North would find political expression via "a party whose foundation and watchword is freedom."[8] Ultimately, however, this party—the Republicans—would conclude that the best guarantee of freedom lay in a process of "Northernization," whereby the South would be forced to conform to northern ideals and values. A brief examination of the northern response to several key events between 1854 and 1856 reveals that the fledgling Republican Party was drawing on, and at the same time encouraging, a distinct antisouthernism. The development of the idea of the North was part of a process whose logical conclusion was that the Union would exist on northern terms, or not at all.

I t is possible to trace the development of this northern idea between 1854 and 1856. In Massachusetts, especially, the Fugitive Slave Act of 1850 had a significant impact once its full effects were felt, as they were in the notorious Anthony Burns case of 1854. Amos A. Lawrence, hardly a noted radical, commented that, following the rendition of Burns, Bostonians "went to bed one night old fashioned, conservative, Compromise Union Whigs & waked up stark mad abolitionists."[9] Thomas Wentworth Higginson, whose Civil War experiences as commander of the 1st South Carolina Volunteers were published as *Army Life in a Black Regiment* (1870), was upset enough to devote a sermon to the affair. "If we are all Slaves indeed . . . if our own military are to be made Slave-catchers . . . if Massachusetts is merely a conquered province and under martial law," Higginson declared, "*then I wish to know it*."[10] Toward the end of the year, the *Boston Courier* identified a shift in northern public opinion when it covered one of Wendell Phillips's antislavery lectures. "Sentiments the most repugnant to the feelings of every patriot, and to those of nine-tenths of the Abolitionists themselves," the paper reported, were now "absolutely applauded.... Topics of the most odious character ... such as the dissolution of the Union and the destruction of the Constitution. ... Truly," the *Courier* concluded, "there has been a great change since 1850."[11] The *Springfield Republican* concurred and suggested that there was "now the best prospect for a North, that the political history of this country has ever afforded."[12]

Ralph Waldo Emerson had been critical of the Compromise of 1850 at the time, but the impact of the Fugitive Slave Act on Boston moved him to address the subject again in 1854. "I have lived all my life without suffering any known inconveniences from American Slavery," he announced. "I never saw it; I never heard the whip; I never felt the check on my free speech and action, until ... Mr. Webster, by his personal influence, brought the Fugitive Slave Law on the country."[13] This was disingenuous. Doubtless Emerson had suffered no personal inconvenience from slavery, but he had most definitely seen slavery on his trips to the South. He may not have heard the whip, but he had witnessed a slave auction. Emerson, in common with many northerners, had not regarded the problem of slavery as a national one. He was quite content that the South be blighted by its "peculiar institution," so long as the North remained unaffected. The Fugitive Slave Act, by effectively removing the North's cordon sanitaire, made men like Emerson suddenly aware that the North was fully implicated in, and affected by, the South's crimes.

New England's most famous radical, Theodore Parker, shared Emerson's concerns and regarded the application of the Fugitive Slave Act as the disgrace of Boston. The rendition of Anthony Burns, coupled with the Kansas-Nebraska Act, prompted Parker to conclude that North and South had become "utterly diverse and antagonistic in disposition and aim." The North, he argued, "has organized Freedom, and seeks to extend it; the South, Bondage, and aims to spread that. The North is progressively Christian and democratic; while the South is progressively anti-Christian and undemocratic."[14] Josiah Quincy thought the problem went beyond the impact of the Fugitive Slave Act. He argued that "a taint of slave influence can be seen and shown in the morals, literature, and religion of the Free States." Higginson concurred: "Let us speak the truth," he declared, "under the influence of Slavery we are rapidly relapsing into that state of barbarism in which every man must rely on his own right hand for protection. ... I deny that we live under a Democracy. It is an oligarchy of Slaveholders, and I point to the history of half a century to prove it." Which, he asked, "is the most influential in Congress—South Carolina . . . or Massachusetts? . . . Name if you can," Higginson continued, "a victory for Freedom, or a defeat of the Slave Power, within twenty years, except on the right of petition, and even that was only a recovery of lost ground."[15]

Northerners' reactions to the Kansas-Nebraska Act and to the Fugitive Slave Act revealed that they felt that matters were getting out of control. Like Higginson, they turned to the past for evidence of the South's exploitation of both the Union and the goodwill of the free states. The *New York Tribune* reminded its readers that the new territories of Florida and Texas benefited the South far more than the North. "The area of slavery must be enlarged at any cost, but that of freedom must not," the *Tribune* declared. "The North dares not even recognize the existence of freedom in any community the members of which are suspected of having African blood in their veins. We can have no commercial treaty with the people of Hayti. . . . We dare not recognize the Republic of Liberia, lest it might offend the South. Look where we may, the South dictates the policy of the whole Union."[16] Similarly, the *Albany Evening Journal* criticized the "aggressions" of the South and argued that the North had always given way. "In all the conflicts between Slavery and Freedom," it argued, "from the Compromise of 1821 to that of 1850, Freedom has yielded most. Indeed Freedom has yielded all that Slavery demanded."[17] Such arguments were not without foundation. Clearly the South wished to extend the boundaries of slavery. So if slavery represented no more than the sins of their fathers, as some in the North continued to argue, southerners were certainly making the best of a bad situation.

The realization that slavery was not going to disappear of its own accord intensified northern hostility toward the South. The South was now seen to be consciously and deliberately betraying the nation's ideals. It was this betrayal, rather than the existence of slavery, that most upset northerners. As the *Tribune* put it, "while the great mass of the American people, north of Mason and Dixon's line, have remained fast and firm in the faith of Washington, Jefferson and Madison, and have carried their idea into practical effect by abolishing slavery, those south of the line have been gradually taking up a new faith, which teaches that the relation of master and slave is of divine origin, and is to be maintained now and for evermore." Now, the paper concluded, "the North and the South are steadily moving in opposite directions; the one becoming more averse to slavery, and the other more enamoured of it." The problem, as the *Tribune* saw it, was not simply that the two sections were moving apart but that they now found themselves in opposition over important national matters. Again, however, the criticism of the South was slanted to show the North in the best possible light. The North, the *Tribune* argued, was always in search of improvement and therefore required canals, railroads, lighthouses, navigable rivers, and roads, which the South opposed. Southerners, the paper asserted, "do not endeavor to render productive what they have."[18] There was nothing new in this argument. What was different was the use to which it was ultimately put.

The most notable cause of sectional disharmony in this period was the violence in Kansas. This, together with the infamous attack on Massachusetts senator Charles Sumner by southern congressman Preston Brooks, did much to convince the North that southerners were dangerous fanatics, educated by slavery to violence, and determined to dominate the free states. One New Hampshire paper argued that the attack on Sumner was only "one link in a chain of flagitious outrages upon the North by which we are debased forever; one further evidence that the South intends 'to drive us to the wall and nail us there'; new proof that the South desires to treat us as it does its bondsmen at home."[19] Even the conservative Edward Everett was moved to comment on the "all but murderous assault made on Mr. Sumner." He conceded, too, that this "outrage has produced intense excitement in the non-slaveholding States."[20] In a more radical vein, Samuel P. Chase suggested to Theodore Parker that "Sumner's grievous wrong will do more to open men's eyes to the true character of the men that Slavery makes than ten thousand speeches." John P. Hale concurred, adding that "it seems as if it required something of that kind to arouse the North."[21] The portents, however, were ominous. Robert Winthrop, like Everett, was fully aware of this fact. Writing to a friend, he recounted a recent discussion he had held with Ephriam Peabody, who had pronounced "the Republican movement to be, in his judgement, little less than an organization of Disunion." This, Winthrop declared, "is farther than I am prepared to go myself, but I fully agree with him when he spoke of Theodore Parker & Wendell Phillips & Charles Sumner & the rest as having gradually educated our people to relish nothing but the 'eloquence of abuses.'" Brooks's attack, Winthrop concluded, "has made great men of more than Sumner."[22]

In the wake of the assault on Sumner, one well-wisher advised William Pitt Fessenden that he saw "no other safety for you northern members, who dare to speak out like men, but that you go constantly armed with pistols and bowie knives."[23] To New York lawyer George Templeton Strong, the caning of Sumner offered proof positive that "civilization at the South is retrograde," and he was appalled that southern editors and congressmen talked "about the 'chivalry,' 'gallantry,' and 'manliness' of the act."[24] It would be a mistake to conclude, however, that this episode alone produced a marked antisouthernism in Strong. Distinctly antisouthern elements had been evident in Strong's thinking prior to the events of 1856. Strong generally viewed the South as "clamorous, querulous, and absurd." Southerners, he declared at one point, prevented "people from seeing their just grounds of complaint by the preposterous vaporing, bombast, and brag wherewith they make themselves and their concerns ridiculous."[25] For Strong, as for many northerners, the events of 1856 only confirmed his worst suspicions about the South. The difference after the Brooks incident was that, far from being ridiculous, southerners were viewed as positively dangerous, doubly so since the attack on Sumner was not an isolated incident. Indeed, it was only the best known of four such violent assaults in the space of six months.

The first attack took place in December 1855, when the editor of the *Evening Star* was assaulted by William Smith, the former governor and current representative of Virginia. Only a few months later, Horace Greeley, the editor of the *New York Tribune,* was attacked by Albert Rust, a representative from Arkansas, following some typical antisouthern comments in the *Tribune.* Then, in the same month as Brooks's attack on Sumner, an Irish waiter at Willard's hotel—an establishment favored by congressmen who did not maintain homes in Washington—was shot and killed by Philemon T. Herbert following a row over, of all things, breakfast. Herbert was a representative from California but a native of Alabama.

The newspapers, in particular, promptly drew what was fast becoming a common conclusion. The *Springfield Republican,* for one, argued that Herbert's "education has been such as to lead him to regard the life of a menial as a cheap article. He has been in the habit of ruling menials . . . and it is part of the policy to which he has been bred that resorts to abusive language, and defense from physical violence, are never to be allowed in a menial." The *Republican* did not believe, however, that this attitude was limited to Congress. "The whole slaveholding interest looks with contempt upon the free laborers of the country," it asserted, and worst of all, northerners had "suffered it to come into our politics, into our pulpits, and into our social circles, until we are all tainted."[26] Speaking in defense of Sumner in the Senate following Brooks's attack, Henry Wilson developed this line of argument: "There are a great many men," he observed, "who have swung the whip over the plantation who think they not only rule the plantation, but make up the judgment of the world, and hold the keys not only to political power, as they have done in this country, but to social life." On this point, he declared, "the sentiment of Massachusetts, of New England, of the North, approaches unanimity."[27]

Horace Greeley summed the matter up succinctly. Southerners, he dryly observed, "are accustomed to beating us and we to being beaten."[28] For men like Greeley, the apparently growing tendency among southerners in Washington to respond to northern criticism with violence was proof that southerners were both uncivilized and a threat to American democratic institutions. It certainly allowed Greeley the opportunity to bring "the monstrous specter of slavery into the Yankee living room and [seat] it before the fireplace."[29] Parker, likewise, expressed no surprise "at this attack on Mr. Sumner. It is no strange thing," he argued. "It is the result of a long series of acts, each the child of its predecessor, and father of what followed. . . . Look first at the obvious cause of the blows dealt. . . . It is the ferocious Disposition of the Slaveholder."[30] The southern response to these incidents only exacerbated matters. In all but one case, the southerner suffered no repercussions within his own section, and in the case of Brooks, was warmly supported by southerners—many of whom sent him new canes to replace the one he had broken over Sumner's head.[31] The South's reaction to these assaults convinced many northerners that southern society was despotic, violent, and bent on getting its own way.[32]

As Quincy saw it, southerners were educated "under circumstances which make pride and exercise of power, the chief elements of their character." Southern politicians came to Congress, he averred, "with the arrogant spirit of aristocratic despots, looking down on the Representatives of the Free States as an inferior class." Further, he argued,

> the different state of sentiment and opinion, in the different sections of the United States, brings into action, in Congress, that arrogance, which . . . is an inseparable element of a slaveholder's character. The disposition to insult, and endeavor to brow beat, whoever from the Free States dares to cross his path, is excited into constant action, not only from the belief that, toward members from the Free States, they can do it with impunity, but from the fact that such bullying is a sure path to popularity among their own constituents.[33]

The *New York Times* likewise expressed the conviction that the South intended "to drag, or drive, the North back to its level,—to break down the sentiment which at the North recognizes a man as a gentleman even if he does not fight,—and to substitute for the moral, social and religious influences which prevail here, that personal intimidation and personal violence which take their place in the Southern section."[34] William Cullen Bryant's *New York Evening Post* concurred. "Has it come to this," the paper asked, "that we must speak with bated breath in the presence of our Southern masters. . . . Are we too, slaves, slaves for life, a target for their brutal blows, when we do not comport ourselves to please them?"[35]

Although the dual symbols of "bleeding Kansas" and "bleeding Sumner" did much to encourage northern fears of the slave power, neither one had created such fears or the image of the South that supported them. Overt hostility toward the South had been building for years throughout northern society as a whole. "The South is to the North," Strong wrote, "nearly what the savage Gaelic race of the Highlands was to London *tempore* William and Mary . . . except that they've assumed to rule their civilized neighbors instead of being oppressed by them, and that the simple, barbaric virtues of their low social development have been thereby deteriorated." Strong acknowledged the existence of the "rich Southern aristocrat," with his "fine nature," his "self reliance" and his "high-tone." However, like so many others, Strong did not consider the southerner to be representative of a true, "high-bred chivalric aristocracy." Rather, the southerner belonged to "a race of lazy, ignorant, coarse, sensual, swaggering, sordid, beggarly barbarians," a world away from the "law-abiding and peace-loving" democracy of the North.[36] The *New York Times* was equally critical. Southerners, it declared "no more recognize the right of a Northern man to hold and express opinions on Slavery different from theirs than they do the right of a slave on their plantations to resist their commands. They are intolerant, domineering and insolent, not occasionally nor by accident—but habitually and on principle."[37]

Wilson, speaking on behalf of Sumner in the Senate in the aftermath of Brooks's assault, defended Sumner's charge that the South was only nominally republican and retained aristocratic features. "Well, sir," Wilson asked "is not this true? To be a member of the House of Representatives of South Carolina, the candidate must own ten men." In declaring himself opposed both to slavery and to the "aristocratic inequalities" of the South, Wilson did no more than repeat ideas about the South that had been common in the North since at least the 1830s. When he suggested that slavery had impaired South Carolina's performance during the Revolution, he was only following a long line of northerners who had uttered similar sentiments in the past. "South Carolina," Wilson noted, "makes rice and cotton, but South Carolina contributes little to make up the judgment of the Christian and civilized world. I value her rice and cotton more than I do her opinions on questions of scholarship and eloquence, of patriotism or liberty." Washburn, likewise, was hardly pointing out something new when he drew a contrast between the "intelligent, thrifty, respectable free labor" of the North and the "ragged, unhoused, untaught, white labor of the slaveholding states."[38]

In the invidious comparisons that northerners made between slave and free labor, the southerner came to be portrayed as ever more helpless, lazy, and unproductive. The moderate view recognized slavery's propensity to make manual labor unacceptable to whites, but the more hostile critics focused on this and embellished it to create an image of a society totally atrophied by its peculiar institution. One of the most vehement on the subject was Republican spokesman George Melville Weston, whose series of pamphlets published in 1856 did much to support and influence the Republican critique of the South.[39] Weston promulgated a free-labor doctrine, combined with a strong element of racism. As was the case with many northerners, his concerns were only for southern white society and the north's free-labor system. He presented an image of the South as totally ground down by slavery, agriculturally backward, with little or no manufacturing or industry worthy of the name. Throughout the South, he argued, "towns are built up only by Northern and European immigration, and without it there would be scarcely any manifestation of civilization. Mills, railroads, cotton presses, sugar boilers, and steamboats, are mainly indebted for their existence in the Southern States to intelligence and muscle trained in free communities."[40]

Hostile critics such as Weston had a wealth of published data at hand, much of it from southern sources, to support their contention that the majority of southerners existed in abject poverty, beaten down by the slaveholders to a social position well below that of the slaves. The most widely used document was the census of 1850, which was quoted liberally and at length by the northern press, by journals, by travelers such as Frederick Law Olmsted, and by politicians such as Horace Mann. Armed with the census, these northerners were able to prove how far behind the South was in terms of agricultural development, manufacturing output, education, and industry.

In their responses to the reports of violent southern congressmen, northern politicians did not have to cast around for suitably negative images of the South. Nor did they have to put much effort into working up the appropriate level of indignation. By 1856, the negative image of the South was so prevalent in the North, and manifested in so many different ways—in newspaper articles, journals, books, travel accounts, and political speeches—that all politicians had to do was repeat arguments and conjure up images that were, by then, completely familiar. Positive reactions to the South, in this context, did little to counteract the negative response, based as they were on exactly the same set of images. It was but a small step for the northern mind to transmute the image of the chivalrous, aristocratic, landed gentleman into that of the cruel, whip-wielding tyrant who, as Thomas Jefferson had pointed out many decades before, had learned despotism in childhood.

Reiterating arguments about the lazy South that the commercial and agricultural journals had been reinforcing for years, Quincy reminded northerners that it was the inordinate amount of free time available to southerners that made them so dangerous. "Having no necessity or inclination to labor," Quincy argued, southerners had "more idle time than the generality," time that they devoted "to politics; which, in their vocabulary, means how to govern their slaves and how to control the Free States." This, he concluded, "is the topic of discussion at their homes, in their court-houses, their caucuses, and in their senate-chambers."[41] Emerson invoked similarly common images in his address on "The Assault upon Mr. Sumner." As he had done many times before, Emerson represented the differences between the North and the South in terms of education, skilled labor, the arts, "sacred family ties," honor, and justice on the part of the former, and animal pleasures, frivolity, hunting, and "practicing with deadly weapons" on the part of the latter. Emerson bemoaned the fact that a southern minority dominated the federal government, although he was not surprised by that fact. It was, in his view, a direct result of the southerner's fighting skills; "the shooting complexion, like the cobra de capello and scorpion," he observed, "grows in the South." The South, for Emerson, remained to the end a land of "no wisdom, no capacity of improvement," which "looks in every landscape, only for partridges; in every society for duels."[42]

As the 1856 election drew closer, the Republican Party and its supporters increasingly used this kind of rhetoric to differentiate the free from the slaveholding states. In a speech given that year, the Speaker of the House of Representatives, Nathaniel Prentiss Banks, concurred with Parker's oft-repeated dictum that the North could manage steam and water power while the South could manage men:

> They lack no energy—they lack no intelligence—they lack no capacity—they want no ability that we possess. . . . But the power that they manifest is directed differently from the power that we exhibit. . . . We have been busy in science, in literature, in the mechanic arts, in improving agriculture, and we have given less attention to the affairs of government than we otherwise ought . . . the men of the South, abandoning agriculture for the time being, having no literature of its own, having no science of its own, having no mechanical and manufacturing industry of its own, having little or no commerce of its own, and having no inventive power—no results or products of these combinations of elements of power that distinguishes our civilization, except such as is forced upon them by our example . . . they have given their undivided attention to matters connected with government . . . they are in the army; they are in the navy; they are in the treasury; there is not any place which is distinguished by commission, or profit, or honor, where they are not. . . . They say there is something in the race—something in the origins of the people of the South—that gives them peculiar power, and efficacy, and skill in matters of politics and government.[43]

Banks's lengthy diatribe summed up the northern Whig-Republican response to and understanding of the South by 1856. This response was by no means confined to the limits of partisan debate, however. It was devoted as much to praising the North and stressing its adherence to American national virtues as to showing the South to be deficient and fundamentally un-American in its intellectual and economic backwardness. In Banks's speech, one can identify all the ingredients that had, over the years, combined to create an image of the South as not only different from the North but also actively at odds with the national ethos. Republican spokesman William Seward had no doubt about the reasons for this. He regarded the South as an aristocracy—the dominant class in the Republic—which was not only undermining the Republic but holding back the South as well. His 1855 speech to that effect was seen by some as the "key note" of the newly formed Republican Party.[44] "Think it not strange or extravagant," Seward declared, "when I say that an aristocracy has already arisen here, and that it is already undermining the republic . . . a privileged class has existed in this country from an early period. . . . Slaveholders constitute that class."[45]

This was not a new idea for Seward. Eleven years earlier, he had expressed the view that slavery "is the bane of our social condition . . . [it] is an aristocratic institution compared with our democracy."[46] Seward was far from alone in his views. In a letter sent to the *New York Courier and Enquirer* in response to the Sumner-Brooks affair, James Watson Webb had argued that slavery was an "Aristocratic and Anti-Republican Institution . . . and, like all other aristocratic institutions, it produces specimens of the highest refinement, the gentlest habits, and the greatest culture, only to render more conspicuous the general brutality and debasing recklessness which it imposes upon the great mass of people."[47] Webb clearly was of two minds about the South. He managed to combine what almost amounted to praise for the southerner with criticism of southern institutions. On the subject of aristocracy, however, he was adamant that this was incompatible with the American republican experiment. The image of the South as aristocratic, and therefore antirepublican, was perhaps the most powerful and resonant aspect of the northern critique for the Republicans to adopt. As John Murray Forbes, a Boston merchant, noted in the 1856 election year: "If there is anything in this country fixed, it is the prejudice against aught which has the appearance even of aristocracy."[48]

Throughout the antebellum period, one can trace the growth of a distinctly northern, antisouthern ideology that grew out of the North's fear that the South posed a genuine and tangible threat to the northern way of life. This ideology culminated in the portrayal of the South as an aristocratic slave power, which indicates that issues other than slave versus free labor were involved in the northern critique of the South, a point that historians have long recognized. The southern slave power, standing for aristocracy, minority rule, and despotism, appeared to be the negation of republican values. The Republican Party picked up on and exploited this point in the buildup to the 1856 election. However, the negative view of the South promoted by the Republicans was more than mere propaganda devised for political ends. It was a reflection, as well as a development, of the increasing concern felt by a growing element in the North. Although the Republicans' attempts to attach the ideology of republicanism to themselves alone may be regarded as political posturing, we should not overlook the obvious fact that the Republicans chose to focus on republicanism and got significant political mileage out of it. In light of this, it seems clear that they had identified an issue of increasing concern for the northern population. For evidence of this, one need only consider how they redirected nativist concerns in the Speakership debate at the start of 1856.

The year had opened with Congress in deadlock, as North and South blocked each other over the election of the Speaker of the House. The debate ran from December 1855 through February 1856. Nathaniel Prentiss Banks, a former Democrat who had been elected by the American, or Know-Nothing, Party, was finally elected Speaker on the 133d ballot, by which time he had expressed Free-Soil sentiments that clearly aligned him with the new Republican Party. This had considerably widened his appeal among northern congressmen. His success did little, however, for sectional harmony. Almost immediately his election was hailed as a resounding defeat of the slave power, and hundred-gun salutes were fired in his honor in Maine, Massachusetts, and Illinois.

As David Potter observed, Banks's election was a notable sectional victory in which a significant number of congressmen with both nativist and anti-Nebraska leanings finally settled on the side of the antislavery forces and, in consequence, in support of the Republicans.[49] The result of the Speakership contest indicated that, for the North in general and the Republicans in particular, the political wind was blowing in a sectional direction. Regarded by many of his contemporaries as "the first Northern victory," Banks's election had sectional overtones that swiftly became apparent.[50] One New York Republican exulted in Banks's success and harked back to Daniel Webster's 1848 speech. "For once there has been found a North," he declared.[51] He was far from alone in this sentiment. Abraham Lincoln's law partner, William Herndon, expressed his hope that Banks's election indicated that "the North will now endure no more of Southern insolence. . . . The prestige of the South is gone," he declared, "I pray God never to return. . . . The North are up."[52] The *Albany Evening Journal* regarded Banks's election as a victory "by the politics of Freedom and Equality, over the aristocratic policy of Slave-labor Economy, and Slavery-underlaid Society."[53] As the 1856 election drew closer, Republican propagandist Weston recalled how the "charm of Southern invincibility was broken forever, on the day and hour when N. P. Banks ascended to the Speaker's chair."[54] Sumner, in perhaps the most telling phrase, declared Banks's election "the first victory of the Northern idea since 1787."[55]

The intricacies of political maneuvering between the antislavery and nativist elements in each state are too detailed to pursue here. For the purposes of examining the construction of northern nationalism, the question is not how the Republicans managed, in Potter's phrase, "to eat the cake of nativist support and have too the cake of religious and ethnic tolerance," but why this was the case.[56] The answer lies in the new party's construction of the South as antirepublican and irredeemably opposed to American national values. There was, as Eric Foner reminded us, "no question that Republicanism was in part an expression of the hopes and fears of northern native-born Protestants."[57] By 1856, many of these hopes and fears were focused on the Catholic threat, a threat exacerbated by the rising numbers of immigrants to the North. It is important to bear in mind the levels of immigration after 1845 in order to understand the xenophobic tone of the period. Not only did more immigrants arrive, relative to the overall population, but many of the new arrivals were Catholic. There was, therefore, a perceived need to reassert fundamental American Protestant values, both to promote the newcomers' assimilation into northern society and to override the potentially disruptive effects of this foreign influence. As the *New York Times* put it, there "is one duty we would earnestly urge upon the calm good sense and just feeling of our adopted citizens. It is the duty of thoroughly *Americanizing* themselves. They should merge all prejudices and all feelings of race and nation into the one paramount feeling, that they have become, by their own choice, American citizens."[58] To many in the North, however, it was far from clear what, precisely, becoming American might involve. Prompted by the mass influx of immigrants, northerners, much more than southerners, were forced to reevaluate what it meant to be American.

Questions over American national identity, as Reinhold Niebuhr and Alan Heimert noted, were voiced "most hysterically when the rise of sectional prejudices cast doubt on the unity of native America itself." Nativism, they concluded, provided "a means of preserving a sense of national identity at a time when social harmony, and even the Union itself, were threatened by an apparent failure of democracy to meet the challenge of social and economic change."[59] However, based on the response to Banks's election and the gradual Republican takeover of the nativist vote, it is clear that the situation was actually the reverse of what Niebuhr and Heimert argued. Sectionalism of-fered the solution to nativism, not vice versa. Sectionalism—a distinct anti-southernism combined with overt support for all things northern—was, for many northerners, the means by which a sense of national identity was incul-cated and preserved. The *New York Tribune* was fully cognizant of what was at stake. "The national character," it argued, was "deeply involved in the ex-isting struggle, and if it ends prejudicially to Freedom, the peculiar national reputation, acquired by and grown up since the Revolution, will be almost wholly lost. . . . The struggle of the Anti-Nebraska men is thus not only a struggle against the spread of Slavery, it is a struggle to preserve the national reputation in the eye of the world and for history." The Fourth of July cele-brations in 1856 prompted the *Tribune* to repeat its message. Eighty times, it noted, "has the Anniversary of American Independence dawned upon the Republic, but never amid circumstances of such peculiar solemnity as the present . . . it is the crisis of our country's existence, the turning point in her history."[60]

Although it reflected the concerns of many northerners, nativism never had the potential to be a unifying ideology. For one thing, the new arrivals were not likely to disappear. Their influence was a cause for concern, but their presence was an unavoidable issue. More importantly, the assimilation of im-migrants was a fundamental tenet of the nation's "mission statement," and northerners never lost sight of that fact. Throughout the antebellum period, northerners repeatedly reminded themselves that "American Republicanism has been an experiment. It is destined to solve a great problem . . . it has pro-posed to exemplify a plan by which the rights of man may be happily vindi-cated."[61] Specifically, as the *Albany Evening Journal* reminded its readers in 1842, the "union of these States is a great fabric . . . it was designed as an asylum for the oppressed of other nations."[62] Nativist sentiment, therefore, was not only potentially disruptive but also clearly at odds with the national ethos. For northerners, and especially for Republicans, the sectional message could provide much more mileage than the foreign, Catholic threat.

One can draw a parallel between the buildup of antisouthern sentiment at this time and the religious revivals that Perry Miller analyzed, since both fo-cused on the future of the nation. The impetus toward revivals, Miller ar-gued, in both New England and the West, was designed to ensure "not only the conviction of innumerable individuals, but the welfare of the young coun-try."[63] Richard Carwardine's more recent study endorses this point. Evangeli-cals, Carwardine noted, were particularly concerned about the "blighting influence of the peculiar institution on southern society and economy," and the possibility that this society might spread its influence across the new territories appalled them. By the eve of the Civil War, Carwardine concluded, "Northern political postmillennialism . . . reached its apotheosis in the Republican party," whose "fusion of religion and politics drew on established modes of mobilizing revivalist enthusiasm." The Republicans may have derived their "essential moral energy from evangelical Protestantism," but in their focus on the slave power threat, this energy did much to undermine the nation they purported to revere.[64] As one Republican supporter observed, "neither the Pope nor the foreigners can ever govern the country or endanger its liberties, but the slavebreeders and slavetraders do govern it, and threaten to put an end to all government but theirs." This, he concluded, "is something tangible to go upon . . . an issue which . . . will . . . surely succeed in the long run."[65]

Opposition to the South was a far more viable cohesive force for the northern states than was opposition to a threat an ocean away. In the construction of the South as a threat both to the North and, by extrapolation, to the nation, northerners were not being totally irrational. One need only consider a map of America at that time to realize that southern—or, more accurately, slavery's—expansion, hitherto operating in an east-west direction, looked set to take a sharp right turn with the passage of the Kansas-Nebraska Act. This would have effectively boxed the free states in, and the papers often made this point visually. This, together with the intrusive effects of the Fugitive Slave Act and the violence in Kansas and in Congress, resulted in an increasing number of northerners feeling threatened, both culturally and physically, by the South. In defining the southern threat between 1854 and 1856, northerners reiterated a variety of arguments against the South that had been building in intensity since the Compromise of 1850.

The notion of the South as threat—the slave power side of the equation—was predicated on two main perceptions: first, the South's ability to produce better statesmen than the North, which derived from its labor system and the amount of leisure this afforded southerners; and second, its apparent unity, in contrast to the disunity of the northern states and northern politicians. It was this unity that gave the South strength in Congress and thereby threatened northern stability. This point had been made by Harrison Gray Otis as early as 1820 and was one that Horace Mann, among others, took up again to great effect in the 1840s and 1850s. It was made again by the *Springfield Republican* in 1854 when it argued that "while the South can unite, does unite, and presents an almost unbroken front in favor of its sectional interests and views, the North is prey to the narrow-mindedness, selfishness, ambition, prejudices and littleness of her effervescing, sputtering and struggling politicians,—and thus divided, is easily conquered."[66]

By 1856, this had become a central theme of the northern critique of the South. Southern unity, Samuel J. May argued, gave the region "an immense influence over 'the politics' of our nation." Indeed, May regarded this influence as "almost absolute." The interests of northerners, he concluded, were too diverse; consequently, the North was no match for the South in Congress.[67] Not all northerners, of course, regarded the South as a single homogeneous region defined by support for slavery and opposition to the North. Even an extreme Republican spokesman like Weston expressed doubt that there was "unanimous approbation" of slavery in the South. Weston believed, however, that "a reign of terror which has muzzled the press and silenced free speech" was what gave the South the appearance of unanimity in Congress. "It is perfectly monstrous to talk about the unanimity of the South under such circumstances," Weston averred, since it was "the unanimity of Poland, with the Russian knout brandished over it . . . the unanimity of Austrian Italy . . . the unanimity of the subjects of despotic power the world over." Weston exacerbated northern fears when he announced that, in his view, the South did not wish to "leave the Union but to rule it."[68]

In the face of the threat that a united South seemed to offer the North, there were some northerners who felt that their own section ought to respond in kind. The future secretary of the Union navy, Gideon Welles, suggested in 1854 that the only solution to southern "unanimity of feeling" was for the North to "be less national, and more devoted to state rights" itself. "The various schemes to nationalize slavery must be resisted on State-rights principles," he argued, since the "slave states are engaging in National schemes and centralizing measures to justify and extend this great interest." The states' rights position of the South, Welles averred, was no more than "*sectionalism*—a bastard principle, the offspring of *Nationalism*." In the face of this corrupted version of nationalism, Welles believed that, from a northern perspective, less national sentiment could only be a good thing.[69] In the idea of the North as it developed between 1854 and 1856, many northerners appeared to concur with Welles's general sentiment.

It is important not to exaggerate the extent of this sentiment between 1854 and 1856. The Republicans did not, after all, win the 1856 election, nor did they appeal to northern businessmen such as Amos A. Lawrence, who viewed their ideology as dangerously sectional. Defeat in the polls, however, did little to alter the party's outlook, at least in the short term. Indeed, the so-called glorious defeat of 1856 only reinforced northern nationalist sentiment. Again, Daniel Webster's 1848 prophecy was invoked. "The North," exulted the *New York Tribune*, "which Daniel Webster desired to see, but died without the sight, is discovered at last."[70] Seeking explanations for James Buchanan's victory over John Frémont in the election, the *Springfield Republican* concluded that the Republicans had been "beaten by the ignorance of the people." In a diatribe worthy of Horace Mann, the *Republican* argued:

> The excellent common schools system of the New England States and New York have given those states to Fremont. In every section of those states where a great mass of ignorance existed, the vote showed that Buchanan was in the advance. Pennsylvania, with no common school system worthy the name, New Jersey, notoriously and confessedly behind the times in all matters pertaining to popular education, Indiana with its large settlement from the South of individuals to whom common schools are entire strangers—these have gone for Buchanan; and wherever good common schools existed, or wherever the settlements were made by men who had the advantage of common schools, Fremont and freedom have been indorsed by large majorities.[71]

Certainly the Republicans' support in 1856 was strongest in New England and in those areas where New England had some influence, such as western New York, northern Pennsylvania, Ohio, Indiana, Illinois, and Iowa.[72] However, in 1856, the party's support overall was heterogeneous and reflected a wide cross section of northern opinion. What these various groups of former Democrats, Whigs, Free-Soilers, and Know-Nothings increasingly had in common was their opposition to the slave power of the South.

Integral to the Republican concept of the slave power was the image of an aristocratic, antirepublican society. The image of the South as a section separate from, and antithetical to, the North offered a convenient and plausible negative reference point for people who felt the need to reiterate, in a new and powerful way, the Yankee, Protestant values that they regarded as fundamental to the success of the North and of the nation as a whole. These values had particular resonance for—but were not exclusive to—New Englanders, many of whom viewed northeastern culture as the one to which the rest of the nation should aspire if it hoped to fulfill its Manifest Destiny. The *Springfield Republican* was not alone in its belief that Massachusetts was "doing more than any other state in the Union to shape its civilization. Her money, her schools, her religious institutions, her constantly overflowing population of intelligent and moral men and women, are felt as a vital element in the free civilization of the country. . . . Strike out what she has done for American civilization since the days of the Pilgrims, or even since she impoverished and depopulated herself in the American revolution," the *Republican* argued, "and the country would be set back a hundred years."[73] The Republican platform, however, appealed to a broader constituency than that represented by New England alone. Seward doubtless intended flattery when he advised Parker that he took his "latitude and longitude first from Massachusetts," since as Seward very well knew, in their appeal to the northern critique of the South, the Republicans had found an issue that would take them far beyond Massachusetts.[74]

The Republicans particularly appealed to those who saw southern influence in the new territories and in the nation as a whole as detrimental. As early as 1844, Stephen Douglas had argued that "North America has been set apart as a nursery for the culture of republican principles. . . . There is no room here," he declared, "for monarchy or its dependencies."[75] Ten years later, during the debates over the Kansas-Nebraska bill, it was suggested that the "present attempt to repeal the Missouri Compromise and the series of aggressive movements of the Slave Interest, give occasion to fear that the principles which led to the establishment of our independence, are losing their hold on the public mind."[76] The possible implications of this state of affairs were summed up succinctly by one of Parker's correspondents in the wake of the Republicans' defeat in 1856. "If the Slave Power succeeds in its attempts," he wrote, "farewell to the republic—farewell to liberty—and hail instead, glory, conquest, military [ideas], a military dictator, and finally a monarchy."[77]

Although it is unlikely that the majority of northerners perceived the threat of monarchy on the horizon, many were concerned about the future of republican government. Prompted by the apparently growing and potentially dominating political power of the slave South, and concerned about the effect of industrial growth and mass immigration on the northern states, northerners turned in increasing numbers toward the antisouthern, wholly sectional ideology offered by the newly formed Republican Party. In the process, they created a specifically northern nationalism, similar in origin to its southern equivalent, but ultimately more ambitious in nature. The *Albany Evening Journal* had made such ambitions clear when, in 1855, it declared that it was looking forward to the growth first of "Northern REPUBLICANISM" and then of "National REPUBLICANISM."[78] Barely two months later, the paper returned to the subject of the nation and argued:

> The vocabulary of our Politics wants reforming. 'Tis pernicious to talk of "the South" and "the North." Sectionalism comes of it. The terms "slave States" and "free States" suggest balances and compromises. . . . They introduce discord, weaken our nationality, and hinder the growth and consolidation of the Republic. . . . We are a Nation—not a Union . . . the union of the States made thirteen one—made a Nation and not a combination of nations. "The rights of the South" are rank nonsense. The North has no rights. The *Nation* has rights, and duties too. . . . Let the NATION pursue the destiny appointed to Free Politics, Free Industry, and Free Conscience.[79]

These were stirring words, but it is important to keep in mind that they appeared in a paper that regularly gave vent to sectional, distinctly antisouthern rhetoric, both prior to 1855 and afterward. This was no more than another example of the North preaching nationalism from a sectional platform. This is not to suggest that northerners were not genuine in their desire to draw North and South closer together. As the *Evening Journal* argued, the whole idea of a North and a South was at odds with the reality and the focus of the national Union. Rather, northerners almost felt too strongly about the nation, were too dedicated to the Union and too concerned that without constant vigilance it would disintegrate. What the *Evening Journal* and many Republican supporters wished to see was the nation rededicated to republicanism, recast in a northern mold, restructured around free institutions. Over time, northerners became too vociferous on this subject to permit the natural development of a nationalism encompassing both northern and southern interests. Certainly no one would argue that the North was in any sense wrong in its desire for "a new birth of freedom," but in assessing the development of what became American nationalism, one has to consider what antebellum northerners meant by the idea of freedom.

The individuals examined in this study, with few exceptions, did not mean freedom for the slave. They were not preaching abolition. What they wanted was freedom from the slave power, freedom from the effects of slavery, freedom from southern backwardness (both social and economic), freedom from southern political domination, freedom from aristocracy. They wanted "free soil, free labor, free men" in the North; the slaves of the South they were content to abandon. For them, slavery was essentially an abstract evil. Just as, during the revolutionary period, the South's "acute awareness of slavery led white southerners to a highly developed sense of liberty," during the antebellum period, the North's acute awareness of slavery in the South served the same function.[80] As the Reverend Henry Dana Ward put it, if "the South appeal to the rod of the slave for argument with the North, no way is left for the North [to escape from the southern masters] but to strike back or be slaves."[81]

Historians have recognized that a moral concern for the slave was, for the most part, confined to the more radical, abolitionist element in the North. As Horace Greeley put it, the majority of northerners cared little for the slaves of the South. "Ashamed of their subserviency to the Slave Power they may well be; convinced that slavery is an incubus and a weakness, they are quite likely to be," Greeley observed, but concerned for the slave they were not.[82] It was the existence of slavery, and the nature of the society that slavery produced, that seemed to pose the greatest threat for many of the more conservative northerners. Slavery, as Michael Holt reminds us, had other meanings aside from the system of servitude that existed in the South. Among other things, slavery "implied subordination to tyranny, the loss of liberty and equality, [and] the absence of republicanism."[83] In this sense, slavery clearly stood in opposition to what northerners understood to be American national ideals. In his analysis of Lincoln's thoughts on such matters, Peter Dobkin Hall has argued that, for Lincoln, the political upheavals of the 1850s were not concerned primarily with slavery per se. Rather, the debates over slavery's extension showed "that the promise of American life had not been realized, that the moral revolution had not taken place," and democracy itself was, consequently, under threat.[84] Lincoln had set out his objections to slavery in his 1854 speech at Peoria:

> I hate it because it deprives our republican example of its just influence in the world; enables the enemies of free institutions with plausibility to taunt us as hypocrites; causes the real friends of freedom to doubt our sincerity; and especially because it forces so many good men amongst ourselves into an open war with the very fundamental principles of civil liberty, criticizing the Declaration of Independence, and insisting that there is no right principle of action but *self-interest.*[85]

The issue for Lincoln, as for many Republicans, was the "nation's historical mission, the achievement of nationality," but this nationality was not truly national when Lincoln spoke, but wholly northern. Its essence was believed to reside entirely in the North, and its future, if it had one, lay in the free states. This ideology of republicanism had no southern reference. Indeed, the South was perceived as the very antithesis of republican values.

This is a crucial point, and in some ways an obvious one. It may be too obvious, because the moral high ground seized by the Republicans, together with the North's ultimate victory in the Civil War, obscured the process of national development in America during the antebellum period. To argue, for example, that the "cultural values that motivated Northern society and the ideas that were connected with those values were at the basis of American identity" in the antebellum period is to miss the obvious point that, prior to the Civil War, there was no American identity per se, but rather two separate identities, northern and southern, created and sustained in opposition to each other.[86] That it would come down to an internecine conflict between them was evident to Strong by 1856. Could "civil war between North and South be postponed twenty years longer?" he wondered. "I fear we, or our children," he concluded, "have got to pass through a ruinous revolutionary period of conflict between two social systems before the policy of the U.S.A. is finally settled."[87] As it turned out, the question was settled much sooner than he anticipated.

The imagined political community invoked by the Republicans in the buildup to their first national election was predicated on ideals that were perceived to be wholly antisouthern. Neither the fact that the Republicans sought to make those ideals national nor the North's eventual victory over the South in 1865 indicates that northern ideology *was* national before the Civil War. What the Republicans were doing was, in effect, denationalizing the South. By allocating to the South the role of enemy of freedom, the Republicans sought to construct a new national consensus predicated on the destruction of that enemy.[88] Northern nationalism was only one step in a process whereby the American nation was reinvented, although it was a significant one. To continue to regard the optimistic, pro-Union rhetoric of the Republican Party as indicative of a coherent, national policy embracing both North and South is to misrepresent the essence of Republican appeal in the antebellum period.

Although "Americans of both parties often invoked the national label in a cheaply partisan way to demean their political opponents by associating them with hostility to national institutions," the Republicans in the 1850s were able to do so particularly well.[89] Their success lay in the fact that their use of the national label was directed not at an opposing political party but at the South. This was a deliberate act. In developing its image of the South, the North, up until 1856, had not really concentrated on one part of that image—positive or negative—to the exclusion of the other. The North used the South in part to define its own sectional awareness, but this did not necessarily mean that the North had to regard the South as the antithesis of its own values and a threat to its future. The Republicans, however, made this connection, and although they referred to the ideological product that resulted as American nationalism, in reality, there was little that was national about it.

Contemporary opinion did not always take the Republicans' nationalist rhetoric at face value. Edward Everett, for one, believed that there was a great deal of hypocrisy in Free-Soil politics. He considered the Republican Party, in particular, to be "a body as much influenced by motives of calculation and personal interest, cloaked with pretenses of extraordinary zeal for liberty as any ever assembled in the U.S." Writing to his English friend Henry Holland about the violence in Kansas, Everett observed that the "solution really is that the leaders of the 'Republican' party are determined that no pacification should be had as that would put an end to their organization."[90] The difference between the nationalism the Republicans preached and the sectional platform from which they preached it was not lost on Boston businessman Amos Lawrence either. Indeed, he refused to join the new party because the Republicans were not only adopting a dangerously antisouthern stance but also deliberately seeking to identify the idea of republican government, the idea of America, with themselves alone. "It is a great misfortune," he bemoaned, "that so much attaches to a name." His son, Amos A. Lawrence, concurred: the Republicans, he observed, are "stealing all our American doctrines."[91]

Ultimately, Republican ideology was derived from fear of and hostility to the South. The Republican critique of the South was hardly expressive of a desire "to integrate and harmonize socially, regionally or even politically and institutionally divided sections of a people," as Peter Alter described the nation-building process.[92] Northern, like Southern, nationalism was equally destructive of the Union it purported to revere. The Union that it envisaged, and that it would go to war to save, was one in which the South was included on northern terms alone. As the *New York Times* had put it in 1854, "with the mass of the Northern mind, we can unhesitatingly say, the Union ceases to be of value when it ceases to represent a Principle."[93]

Emerson concurred with the *Times*'s sentiment. He became a Unionist only at the point at which that Union came apart. When battle between North and South commenced in earnest, Emerson exulted: "now a sentiment mightier than logic, wide as light, strong as gravity, reaches into the college, the bank, the farm-house, and the church. . . . We are wafted into a revolution which, though at first sight a calamity of the human race, finds all men in good heart, in courage, in a generosity of mutual and patriotic support . . . now we have a country again."[94] Like many other northerners, Emerson welcomed the conflict, since he saw in it "an opportunity to bring about the moral revolution in American life, that final fulfillment of the covenant that Americans had made in undertaking the political revolution of the eighteenth century."[95]

Parker's dismay at the Republicans' defeat in 1856 prompted him to reflect that "the cause of American democracy was in less terrible peril Nov. 17, 1776 than Nov. 17, 1856; for then our chief foes were abroad, the pestilent council was 3000 miles off, while now the enemy is in the midst of us and we think him a friend, and the ruinous council is chosen by the People whom it purposes to ruin."[96] The problem for Parker, as for Emerson, was that by the 1850s, the nation seemed to have lost its direction. For them, much "more was at stake than the survival of a body of ideas. Rather, as Lincoln pointed out in his speeches, the survival of the American mission and American institutions was on the line."[97]

With the emergence of the Republican Party, for the first time it seemed possible to Emerson, Parker, and many others in the North that the nation might rediscover its heritage and find a "new birth of freedom." The Republican Party, however, neither originated from nor appealed solely to a uniquely New England sentiment in this regard. Indeed, what made its version of American nationalism so potentially destructive was the fact that, in pulling together such a broad range of negative images of the South—images that originated in the concerns of abolitionists, businessmen, educators, reformers, politicians, and farmers, as well as New England intellectuals—it ensured that there were few constituencies in the North that could not find something in Republican rhetoric applicable to them. Men like Emerson and Parker were far from alone in their belief that America had departed from its revolutionary traditions and betrayed the ideals that defined the nation, and it was on this point, above all, that their worldview merged most fully and to devastating effect with the antisouthern views expressed by the Republican Party. By encouraging the development of the northern critique of the South, they laid the groundwork for the Civil War—the war that Emerson, who did not have to fight, rejoiced in, and that Parker never lived to see.

❦

From Hell to Holy

The Civil War and
the Fulfillment of American Nationality

This is the age of nationalities. Fired by our example, the oppressed of the world would have aspired to the dignity of nationalities. Shall the first to set the example, and the grandest in the procession of the nations, suffer its nationality to depart, at the bidding not of a foreign foe, but of rebel traitors of the soil?

— *Boston Post,* 16 May 1861

The process of national construction is a complex one, and nineteenth-century America was a nation with more problems than most when it came to defining a viable national identity. Not only was it a nation of many different ethnicities, with new immigrants arriving on a daily basis, but it was a nation in which sectional forces had worked against the establishment of a successful nationalism from the outset. It was also a nation that, by virtue of the manner of its founding, felt a strong impulse to live up to ideals that were fundamentally at odds with the realities of antebellum life, and not just in the South. As the "first new nation," there was also pressure to prove to a skeptical world the validity of this experiment in republican government.

In the antebellum period, the North, much more than the South, felt these pressures acutely. Partly, this was because of the forces of change that affected the northern states, and partly because the North had moved away from slavery as a labor system and could therefore position itself—albeit somewhat disingenuously—on a higher moral plane than the South. The North responded to the challenge to create an American national identity in the antebellum period in a much more positive and expansive way than did the South. Unfortunately, in the process of attempting to direct the course of American national development and create a valid national identity encompassing all the varied parts of the nation, the North succeeded in further alienating a part of that nation, the South.

National construction requires some kind of negative reference point against which to define the nation. Great Britain had, for obvious reasons, served that purpose immediately following the American Revolution. In some ways, Europe in general continued to function in this way for Americans in the antebellum period, certainly as far as the development of American culture and literature was concerned. Yet, given that America was the first attempt at modern republican government and represented a departure from the political processes of Europe, it proved difficult for Americans to use Europe in any valid way to assess the direction and success of the experiment they had undertaken. In the absence of any proximate nation against which to define themselves, the only course left to antebellum Americans was to find a suitable point of reference within their own nation. Because it retained slavery in an age when that institution was coming under attack internationally, because large areas of the region maintained a way of life very different from that in the Northeast, and because it did not experience the pressures of immigration, industrialization, and urbanization that were starting to affect the North, the South was the obvious—and perhaps the only—negative reference point for northerners to turn to.

The South was not, it must be stressed, a passive vessel for northern ideas and preconceptions. Indeed, what made the South an ideal negative reference point was the fact that it was, as historians have long recognized, involved in the process of constructing a sectional barrier against the kind of change that the North advocated. Determined to hold fast to its "peculiar institution" and to the way of life that stemmed from it, the South provided more than enough evidence, both for antebellum northerners and for historians since, to suggest that it was engaged in the construction of a sectional ideology that set it apart from the nation as a whole. Throughout the antebellum period, therefore, northern leaders, spokesmen, and intellectuals such as Daniel Webster, Frederick Law Olmsted, Ralph Waldo Emerson, and Horace Mann were not being deliberately or inaccurately provocative when they accused the South of being out of step with the national impulse, of developing an exclusive sectionalism in contrast to the inclusive nationalism of the North. Yet the inclusive nationalism of the North, because it relied so much on the South for definition, was working against itself at every step.

The Civil War offered the North the opportunity to enforce its own particular version of American nationalism, to prove by force of arms rather than by force of argument that its vision of America's future was the only viable one. Yet northern assertions of the superiority of their way of life, the value of their social, economic, and educational systems, and their forward-looking philosophy would have counted for little if their armies had not proved adequate to the task at hand. Above all, the Civil War offered north-erners the chance to establish throughout the nation the "republic of virtue" that, before 1861, they had identified as encompassing the North alone. The Civil War provided the North with an opportunity to resolve some of the troubling contradictions in the nation's life: aristocracy and democracy, lib-erty and slavery, civilization and barbarism, materialism and idealism, and, above all, nationalism and sectionalism. Here too, unfortunately, was another opportunity missed.

In the years following the Republican Party's defeat in 1856, there was little change in northern reactions to the South. The northern press con-tinued to draw comparisons between the free and slave states, to the det-riment of the latter. The image of the South as an aristocratic power at odds with American republicanism remained a central feature of northern criti-cisms. Northerners still evinced an appreciation of aristocracy, which was it-self an anachronism in the brave new republican world they claimed to in-habit, but for them, the South remained a corrupted version of this ideal. As the *Springfield Republican* put it in 1857, the "pursuits of southern planters are not those which are consonant with those of a truly aristocratic class. They are not patrons or amateurs of art, they are not cultivators of literature. They have not so much of convenience, comfort and beauty in their homes, as the working North, which they condemn. They love the race-course—they love gaming—they fight to maintain an honor which, in its weakness, is easily wounded. Their general tone of civilization is lower than that of the North."[1] In terms of both sentiment and argument, such criticisms only reinforced a sectional message that had been building in intensity up to the 1856 election and showed little sign of diminishing afterward.

As the political dust settled somewhat after the 1856 election, Amos A. Lawrence assessed the direction that events in the North were taking. He was far from impressed with the position the Republicans had adopted. Prior to the election, he had argued that the "struggle of the Northern sectional party may effect a good result. By teaching the South the danger of making en-croachments on our constitutional rights." At this point, Lawrence regarded the Republican Party as "the legitimate offspring of the repeal of the com-promise of 1820, and of the high-handed proceedings of the agents of the Southern party in Kansas and of individual members of it in Washington."[2] He was less certain that any good could come of the Republicans' overtly sectional position afterward. The recent sectional upheavals, he suggested in 1857,

should teach us to be tolerant to each other & to our countrymen. If the sins
of previous generations are visited on this, we should be willing to bear our
share of the curse, for it is light compared to that which falls on our Southern
brethren. By assuming that the honor & virtue & patriotism of the country is
concentrated in the free states, or that those qualities largely preponderate
here, we place ourselves in a position which we cannot maintain: & we cherish
that sectional exclusiveness & that love of *sectional power*, which is more dangerous to our national existence & to the true interests of liberty than anything else.

Lawrence was, as he admitted, torn: he favored the Democrats "because they
love the Union, the Republicans because they love Liberty." For Lawrence,
the Republican position "would be perfect were it drawn out by danger from
a foreign foe." As it was, however, the only foes the Republicans found were
"among their own countrymen."[3]

In an echo of Lawrence's concerns, one New York solicitor attempted to
set out a case for North-South understanding in a pamphlet published in the
wake of the 1856 election. "Are not the citizens of the South our brethren—
bone of our bone, flesh of our flesh, blood of our blood?" he inquired. "*Are
they not joint tenants and heirs with us of a common inheritance?* Were not the
institutions under which they live founded and established by our common
ancestors?" Slavery, he argued, was not the result of any voluntary act by
southerners, but an institution they were born into. He reminded northerners
that there had been a time when the whole country, not just the South, had
sustained slavery. "Do you deny, that if slavery be an evil, a wrong, and a sin,
it is a *national* evil, a *national* wrong, a *national* sin? . . . The South is now
bearing our burden as well as their own."[4] Such arguments harked back to
those of the 1830s and 1840s, but by the 1850s, they were cutting less ice. By
then, many northerners no longer considered slavery to be an institution thrust
on the South, but one that the region had willingly embraced. At the same
time, northerners had conveniently forgotten their own section's complicity in
the South's labor system, in terms of both its introduction and its retention.

More significantly, as far as northern nationalism was concerned, in their
rejection of arguments based on the North's common inheritance with the
South, northerners revealed their awareness of the unique (for the time) nature of American national identity. American nationalism could never be ethnically defined but had to be based on a civic religion. Lawrence may have
believed that southerners were "members of the same family with ourselves
& we must live on good terms with them," but his attitude was no longer
typical by the late 1850s.[5] Common descent was less important to many northerners than national ideals. This was, in many ways, understandable. A na-

tion of immigrants cannot be structured around ties of consanguinity or ethnicity—whether real or fabricated. Indeed, in the constructions of the Cavalier and the Yankee, nineteenth-century Americans of the South and North had formulated the myth of alternative ethnicities long before the mid-century's mass immigration provided an additional spur to search for an ideological base for the nation. By the 1850s, many northerners fervently hoped that southerners really were a race apart and did their utmost to portray them as such.

By 1858, Lawrence's hopes that the North might be tolerant toward the South were fast diminishing. "The numbers of us in Massachusetts who hold what are called 'national' views is so small," he admitted, although he continued to express the hope that "our people may learn to discriminate between hatred of slavery & hatred of the South."[6] By then, the number of northerners able or willing to make such a distinction was decreasing. As Lawrence noted, the Republicans' use of the northern critique of the South evinced a sectional position that undermined the Union itself. The negative image of the South, expressed, refined, and reiterated for so many years throughout the North, became dangerously concentrated once it entered the arena of partisan debate. The roots of the northern critique of the South were not, however, confined to the political arena. These had developed over many years and were drawn from a variety of images of the South that northerners had been exposed to during the antebellum period. Taken individually, none of the newspaper reports, periodical articles, sermons, travel accounts, or political diatribes against the South posed much of a threat to a Union comprising such a mix of peoples. But combined, as they were by the Republicans, at a time when the American people were forced to reassess the basis and the future of their national identity, they proved an explosive mixture indeed. Together, they produced a destructive, sectional variant of American nationalism, a northern nationalism, that worked against the construction of a truly American national identity in the years before the Civil War.

The American nation qua nation had ceased to exist long before the Civil War made the point obvious, and many Americans were fully conscious of that fact. In an echo of Ralph Waldo Emerson's exultation at the outbreak of the war, Nathaniel Hawthorne expressed his joy "that the old Union is smashed. We never were one people, and never really had a country since the Constitution was formed," he declared.[7] Frederick Douglass, the abolitionist leader, concurred. He envisioned a radical transformation for the nation. Northerners, he felt, "delude themselves with the miserable idea that the old Union can be brought to life again." The North had no business, in Douglass's opinion, fighting "for the old Union." Rather, it was fighting "for something

incomparably better than the old Union." It was fighting "for unity; unity of
object, unity of institutions, in which there shall be no North, no South, no
East, no West, no black, no white, but a solidarity of the nation."[8] Harriet
Beecher Stowe, similarly, expressed the hope that the Civil War would bring
America "forth to a higher national life."[9] For many northerners, however,
what they meant by nationalism was northern sectionalism writ large. When
they spoke of a solidarity of the nation, they envisaged it in northern terms.
For many northerners, the Civil War offered a long-awaited opportunity to
make sectional ideals national.[10] From this perspective, the Civil War was a
chance to rid the North, and the nation as a whole, of the influence of slavery
and the South. Writing to his brother during the war, Henry Adams expressed
this northern viewpoint succinctly:

> The nation has been dragged by this infernal cotton that had better have been
> burning in Hell, far away from its true course, and its worst passions and tastes
> have been developed by a forced and bloated growth. It will depend on the
> generation to which you and I belong, whether the country is to be brought
> back to its true course and the New England element is to carry the victory, or
> whether we are to be carried on from war to war and debt to debt and one
> military leader to another, till we lose all our landmarks and go ahead like
> France with a mere blind necessity to get on, without a reason or a principle.[11]

The war's outcome, of course, justified Adams's confidence in the North's
position. More significantly, as far as American nationalism is concerned, it
validated the northern interpretation of what kind of war it was, what issues
were at stake, and what kind of nation emerged from the conflict. Yet the
problems of American national construction were not likely to be easily resolved. Northern nationalism had been predicated, to a great extent, on opposition to the South, on an enemy within. Starting from that premise, there was
no obvious route back to viable nationhood. The problem the North faced
between 1861 and 1865, therefore, was twofold: the defense of the political
Union went hand in hand with the defense of the ideological nationalism that
supported that Union. Forcing the South back into the Federal fold required
military success; justifying the attempt to do so required a different approach
entirely.

In the face of the South's desire to wreck the republican experiment, to
dissolve the Union handed down to Americans by the revolutionary generation, those who supported the Union felt rightly indignant. Barely a month
after the fall of Fort Sumter, a *Boston Post* editorial argued that it was "the age
of nationalities. Fired by our example, the oppressed of the world would have
aspired to the dignity of nationalities. Shall the first to set the example, and

the grandest in the procession of the nations," the paper asked, "suffer its nationality to depart, at the bidding not of a foreign foe, but of rebel traitors of the soil?"[12] There was no easy or immediate answer to this question. As events were to show, the Federal forces were able to save the Union on the battlefield, but military victory was only one part—admittedly the major part—of the process of American national construction.

I t is generally accepted that the American Civil War of 1861–1865 and its immediate aftermath—the Reconstruction period of 1865–1877—represent a watershed in American national development. In practical terms, the war that Henry James referred to as the "great convulsion" was a definitive turning point in the timeline of American history.[13] More fundamentally, the Civil War is regarded as the event that transformed a union into a nation. The Civil War certainly succeeded in holding America together as a nation when it might otherwise have come apart. It resolved the question of whether the Union was a voluntary organization from which the states had the right to secede—as the South had argued—or whether it was, as Lincoln described it in 1861, perpetual. The Union's perpetuity, according to Lincoln, was assured not only by the Constitution and the law (although he interpreted both in such a way as to deny absolutely the South's right of secession) but also by geography. "Physically speaking, we cannot separate," he pointed out. "A husband and wife may be divorced, and go out of the presence, and beyond the reach of each other; but the different parts of our country cannot do this."[14]

However, the transition from union to nation involved much more than the establishment by force of Federal authority over the physical territory of the United States. The military and moral defeat suffered by the Confederacy changed the South dramatically and forever. For the North, the change was no less dramatic. The very process of taking up arms against the southern challenge prompted a transformation in the northern response both to the idea of union and to the imperatives of national construction. The specifics of this transformation have yet to be fully explored by either historians of America or nationalism scholars, although the words of Abraham Lincoln provide a tantalizing starting point for those interested in the process. In his First Inaugural Address in 1861, Lincoln frequently invoked the "Union," using the word some twenty times. He did not, however, refer directly to America as a "nation," relying instead on a vague phraseology concerning America's "national fabric."[15] By 1863, however, on the occasion of his famous Gettysburg Address, Lincoln's emphasis had changed. In this short but significant speech, he did not mention the Union once, but he referred five times to America as a "nation."[16] The question this epilogue addresses is how and to what extent the American Civil War brought about a perceptible shift in northern nationalist ideology.

As far as national construction was concerned, initially, it seemed as if the Confederacy had been successful. In the second year of the Civil War, the British chancellor of the Exchequer, William E. Gladstone, expressed the view that of the two sides involved in the war, it was the South that deserved the appellation "nation." The North, he argued, ought to accept the dissolution of the Union, since "Jefferson Davis and other leaders of the South have made an army; they are making, it appears, a navy; and they have made what is more than either, they have made a nation."[17] Whether the Confederacy constituted a separate nation has been debated among historians for many years. Part of the confusion stems from a lack of consensus on what is meant by nationalism: is it the construction of a strong central state; does it refer to Benedict Anderson's "imagined community"; or is it a combination of the two? Another part of the debate derives from the perceived differences between nationalist sentiment in the antebellum South and that which developed during the Civil War. Scholars acknowledge the growth, in the antebellum period, of a distinct sense of "the South," and many go so far as to argue that this constituted a fledgling southern nationalism. The Confederacy's failure in the Civil War, however, is offered up as evidence that southern nationalism as an ideology was insufficient to sustain southerners in their attempt at national construction and that it was, therefore, not a true nationalist ideology at all. Although it is recognized that "Confederate nationalists surely existed," Confederate nationalism is dismissed as "more a dream than anything else."[18]

The argument that military defeat revealed a fatal flaw in Confederate nationalist sentiment relies, however, on hindsight. The Civil War's outcome validated northern nationalist claims and placed the Confederacy firmly and forever in the "lost cause" camp. Because the nationalism of the Union triumphed, historians frequently reason that the northern variant of American nationalism had always been the stronger and more valid. At the time, however, the outcome of the Civil War was by no means certain, and in any case, the South's failure to break away from the Union does not prove that Confederate nationalism was fundamentally weak—only that it was, ultimately, unsuccessful. Nor does it prove that American nationalism as promulgated by the North was, by comparison, strong. More recent research has shown that Confederate nationalism was more than a pipe dream and that the ideology that sustained the South's attempt at secession had both form and substance.

Yet, crucially, these studies continue to examine the Confederacy almost in isolation. Lacking the wider context of the Union's search for national meaning, they continue to present the Confederacy as a world and a nation apart.[19] Certainly this is what the Confederacy had hoped to be, but despite its best efforts, the battle for Confederate nationalism was conducted both in the context of and in ironic parallel with a similar process in the North.

The Confederate struggle toward national definition was tightly bound up with the Union's defense of the Civil War and its reformulation of American nationalism during the war years. Each relied, in fundamental ways, on the other. Conflict—ideological as well as military—between the Union and the Confederacy helped each side construct and then defend its relative position. The Union victory ensured that its particular interpretation of American nationalism would dominate, but this new nationalism was both forged and, to a degree, tainted by the challenge offered to the Union by the South. In short, the experience of the Civil War operated on the construction and refinement of both Union-American and Confederate nationalism in much the same way.

Troops in both the Federal and the Confederate armies, as well as the civilians on the home front, found that military service encouraged the development of a broader, more national outlook than had prevailed before the war. Gary Gallagher argued that this was particularly the case for southern civilians, whose links with loved ones fighting far from home "broadened their horizon and led them to think nationally as well as locally."[20] However, the same was true for northerners, many of whose relatives were fighting on battlefields even farther from home. For the troops themselves, as the war progressed and casualties mounted, they often found themselves fighting alongside men from different units and other states. This experience intensified and made solid a nationalist perspective that many of them had in theory but, until the war, few had experienced in practice. Indeed, as Peter Parish argued, the Union army "was one of the most potent agencies of American nationalism." It introduced its troops to "places and people hitherto remote, but now fixed in their minds as part of the same American nation to which they belonged." And the involvement of noncombatants in supporting and maintaining the army inculcated a far stronger sense of "commitment and loyalty" to the nation than had ever existed prior to 1861.[21]

In a real sense, both North and South drew on exactly the same ideas and symbols of nationhood in their defense of the Union and the Confederacy, respectively. Both sides were completely immersed in the ideology and symbolism of the Revolution, which was held up as defense and justification for both the act of secession and the military response against it. As Reid Mitchell noted, the Civil War "proved curiously filled with echoes of the American

Revolution."[22] Keeping the example of the Revolution continuously before them, troops, noncombatant spokesmen, and politicians on both sides saw themselves as defenders of the nation's glorious past and frequently compared themselves with the revolutionaries of the previous century, albeit in different ways. A captain in the 5th Alabama Infantry, for example, felt prompted to consider how "trifling were the wrongs complained of by our Revolutionary forefathers, in comparison with ours." An officer in the 101st Ohio put a different emphasis on the nation's past when he recalled how "our fathers in coldest winter, half clad marked the road they trod with crimson streams from their bleeding feet that we might enjoy the blessings of free government."[23]

Both sides argued that they were upholding the ambitions of the revolutionary generation and sticking to the letter and the sentiment of both the Constitution and the Declaration of Independence. The point is often made that, in constructing a separate Confederate Constitution, southerners did little more than imitate the Constitution of 1787, and in their declarations of the causes of secession, the various states similarly drew on the Declaration of Independence. There were, of course, telling differences between the original documents and the Confederate versions. Most obviously, the idealistic desire "to form a more perfect union" contained in the Preamble to the Constitution became, in the Confederate version, a rather prosaic intention "to form a permanent federal government." Nevertheless, this reliance on America's founding documents by a nation that was attempting to secede from the Union not only revealed that the South was, and remained, of two minds about its actions but also demonstrated that southerners regarded themselves as "the authentic heirs of the Founding Fathers, the true defenders of the ark of the covenant."[24]

In many ways, it was easier for southerners to find historical precedents for their attempt at separate nationhood than it was for northerners to defend their opposition to secession. Southerners could far more easily align themselves with the revolutionary generation than northerners could. The South's invocation of George Washington was a particularly powerful symbol. As a southerner himself, and as the father of his country, Washington was the most impressive national figure the Confederacy could appropriate for its cause. If southerners perceived any irony in their trying to destroy the Union by using the man who had warned his countrymen to beware of sectional rivalries and to "properly estimate the immense value of your national Union to your collective and individual happiness," they did not show it.[25] As Jefferson Davis patiently explained, in "order to guard against any misconstruction of their compact, the several States made explicit declaration in a distinct article—that '*each* State *retains its* sovereignty, freedom, and independence, and every power, jurisdiction, and right which is not by this Confederation *expressly delegated* to the United States in Congress assembled.' "[26] Faced with this deadly combination of emotive and legalistic argument in favor of secession, northerners struggled to offer not just an alternative but an overwhelmingly persuasive argument in support of their assertion that America was constructed as one nation and ought to remain so.

Initially, those who supported the Union set out a variety of relatively straightforward arguments in its favor. In an article written for the *London Times* and published about a month after the start of the war, John Lothrop Motley praised the northern response to Lincoln's initial call for troops, noting that "the loyalty of the Free States has proved more intense and passionate than it had ever been supposed to be before. It is recognized throughout their whole people that the Constitution of 1787 had made us a *nation*." Motley set out the case for union succinctly, arguing that the "Union alone is clothed with imperial attributes; the Union alone is known and recognized in the family of nations; the Union alone holds the purse and the sword, regulates foreign intercourse, imposes taxes on foreign commerce, makes war and concludes peace." The Revolution, he reminded his readers, had made America "a nation, with a flag respected abroad and almost idolized at home as the symbol of union and coming greatness." Yet in recalling the Revolution, Motley had hit on an important and troubling point, although it is doubtful that he recognized it. Secession, he argued, was nothing more than a case of "rebellion." However, if it proved successful, then it became "revolution."[27]

Motley's point was much more than a distinction without a difference. The difference between rebellion and revolution, in an American context, was vast. The American nation, as well as the Union that the North was fighting to save, was the product of a revolution, a fact that the South had used in defense of its actions in 1861. Although equally keen to align themselves with the ideals of the revolutionary generation, northerners found it difficult to break through this particular part of the South's defenses. As it was understood at the start of the war, the Revolution seemed better suited as justification for the Confederacy than as prop for the Union. To acknowledge that the South was engaged in an act of revolution was, in a very real sense, to validate secession and to recognize that the South had the right to attempt to establish a Confederate nation.

One possible response, and the one favored by Lincoln, was to argue that the act of secession was less an attempt to construct a separate nation than an attack on an established union that had to be met with force. Lincoln regarded secession as rebellion, pure and simple. Further, he saw it as rebellion not of the South but in the South. This was a theme he developed throughout the first year of the war. Some months before the fall of Fort Sumter, he had questioned "what principle of original right is it that one-fiftieth or one-ninetieth of a great nation, by calling themselves a state, have the right to break up and ruin that nation as a matter of original principle?" Once war had broken out, he encouraged support for the Union by reflecting that "this issue embraces more than the fate of these United States. It presents to the whole family of man the question, whether a constitutional republic, or a democracy—a government of the people, by the same people—can, or cannot, maintain its territorial integrity against its own domestic foes." By the end of the year, he was still reiterating his firm belief that secession constituted nothing more or less than "a war upon the first principle of popular government—the rights of the people."[28] Lincoln would continue to develop and refine his arguments in defense of the Union throughout the war—putting them most succinctly and powerfully in his Gettysburg Address of 1863—but his position, however persuasive it seems with hindsight, was by no means impregnable. Throughout the conflict, Lincoln and those who concurred with his viewpoint had to work hard to defend themselves against attack not just from the South but also from opposition forces within the Union.

As the war progressed, the initial enthusiasm that Motley had described began to wane. The dreary and dangerous reality of fighting, combined with military setbacks for the Federal forces in 1861 and 1862, resulted in an overall decline in morale on both the military and the home fronts. The Emancipation Proclamation of 1863 was not especially well received at first, and this, too, led to a crumbling of support for the Union cause. Increasingly, Lincoln and his government came under attack from Democratic opponents of the war such as Clement Laird Vallandigham, who was critical of the war's impact on civil liberties. Under Lincoln, he declared, "[c]onstitutional limitation was broken down; *habeas corpus* fell; liberty of the press, of speech, of the person, of mails, of travel, of one's own house, and of religion; the right to bear arms, due process of law, judicial trial, trial by jury, trial at all; every badge and muniment of freedom in republican government or kingly government—all went down at a blow."[29]

Peace Democrats like Vallandigham walked—and frequently overstepped—a very fine line between loyal opposition to the Republican government and actual disloyalty to the Union, a fact that earned them the epithet "Copperhead" (a venomous pit viper). Nevertheless, the accusations they made had to be countered if support for the Union was not to suffer further. Lincoln defended the particular point about habeas corpus in a famous letter to his Democratic critics in 1863. There, he repeated his belief that secession was nothing more than "a clear, flagrant, and gigantic case of rebellion; and the provision of the Constitution that 'The privilege of the writ of habeas corpus shall not be suspended, unless when in cases of rebellion or invasion, the public safety may require it' is *the* provision which specifically applies to our present case."[30] But no matter how accurate it was, a constitutional defense of the Federal government's actions would not be enough to silence all criticism or persuade the northern public to continue to support a war that, by 1863, showed little sign of ending.

Increasingly, the Federal government found itself under attack on issues far beyond the constitutional. John O'Sullivan, editor of the *Democratic Review* and the man credited with coining the phrase "Manifest Destiny," argued that the North's attempt to force the South back into the Union served "to stultify our revolution; to blaspheme our very Declaration of Independence; to repudiate all our history."[31] This was a serious allegation that had to be answered. The northern response could not help but be informed by the South's swift appropriation of America's national symbols and its use of the Revolution that had created the Union for its own secessionist ends. Northerners, in a sense, had to return to first principles, not so much to reconstruct but rather to reinterpret the ideology of the Revolution and the Founding Fathers, in order to defend themselves against the criticism that by seeking to suppress secession they were acting against the basic tenets of "Americanism." Northerners were "led into far-reaching speculations on the deeper meaning of such current bywords as loyalty, patriotism, and nationality."[32] Although one of the most widely published propagandist pamphlets of the Civil War argued that "the true solution of our whole difficulty, the only force which can give vitality or permanence to any theory of settlement," was military success, the problem that the Union faced stretched far beyond the battlefield.[33]

The ideological issues accompanying the war forced the North to move toward a redefinition of nationalism that both justified its actions in challenging the Confederacy and offered a basis for postwar reconstruction of the American nation. The centrality of the Revolution, to American as well as to Confederate and Union nationalism, meant that the Union had to show that the original Revolution had been the result of "a legitimate nationalistic impulse" that bore no relation to the act of secession that had prompted the Civil War. In short, northerners had to show that "the American Revolution was over and that revolutionary ideology had no further application to American society."[34]

In the process of addressing this problem, intellectuals such as German political exile Francis Lieber and New England minister Horace Bushnell gradually shifted the ground on which American nationalism was constructed. In arguing against the South's right of secession and in favor of loyalty to the Union, these conservative intellectuals sought to bring American nationality down to earth, as it were. The Union, they asserted, merited support not because it represented the hope of liberty for the world but because it provided the more tangible and traditional basis of American national power. Further, since their arguments in support of loyalty to the Union were directly linked to support of the Federal war effort, the logical conclusion of their deliberations was to show that "the ultimate America to which allegiance was due was not some vague and improbable democratic utopia but the organized and disciplined North that was going to war before their eyes."[35] This was little more than an extension of the kind of antisouthern sentiment that Bushnell, among others, had been propounding during the antebellum years. Although the Civil War lent both weight and impetus to such arguments, the notion that the North was the preserver and protector of all that was good in American national ideology was hardly a new one.

The intellectual debate over American nationalism, although undoubtedly persuasive in terms of both defining and defending the North's position, offered little that would help North and South come together once the fighting was over. Although informed by the experience of war, the debates of intellectuals took place in a world far removed from the harsh reality of the battlefield. Northern thinkers and writers such as James Russell Lowell might have believed that the Civil War had "increased the power and confidence of the nation and certified 'to earth a new imperial race,'" but their view of the war was, as Richard Marius concluded, "humidly sentimental . . . like war imagined in a greenhouse."[36] Equally sentimental is the description of the Civil War as a "brothers' war." This glib phrase, so redolent of childhood arguments, disguises the brutal reality of a conflict in which Americans killed Americans in appallingly large numbers and in fairly gruesome ways. There was little brotherly sentiment in the reaction of one southern officer who, after the battle of Fredericksburg, described how he "enjoyed the sight of hundreds of dead Yankees. Saw much of the work I had done in the way of severed limbs, decapitated bodies, and mutilated remains of all kinds. Doing my soul good. Would that the whole Northern Army were as such & I had my hand in it."[37] Finding some basis for national reconciliation in the light of such deep-rooted hatred would hardly be a straightforward matter.

Sentimentality too frequently acts as a hindrance to an understanding of the American Civil War—both the issues involved and the outcome. The relative positions of the North and South during the war are often oversimplified. In particular, the cause for which the South was fighting is too readily romanticized. The hubris that afflicted the South is too often seen to reside in its aspirations for separate nationhood, not in its essential racism, so the romance of the "lost cause" prevails. The North, by contrast, represents the pragmatic element in the uneasy equation that was the antebellum American Union. More firmly wedded to the practicalities of union, less overtly racist though hardly enlightened in that regard, the North is seen as being more in tune with and ahead of the sweeping changes that were transforming nineteenth-century America. If Confederate nationalism was a dream, northern nationalism was the reality. There was no romance in the northern soul, scholars conclude, so during the Civil War, the "issue for the Northern states, clearly, was one of the territorial and political extent of the American nation, rather than its ideals."[38] Certainly this was the logical conclusion of much of the northern intellectual debate that took place during the Civil War. Similarly, Lincoln's famous declaration to Horace Greeley, editor of the *New York Tribune,* that his "paramount object in this struggle *is* to save the Union, and is *not* either to save or to destroy slavery," can be taken at face value to support this interpretation of northern war aims.[39]

However, if the Confederacy was, in reality, less romantic than history has chosen to portray it, then the North was certainly more idealistic than it sometimes appeared. His deceptively straightforward answer to Greeley notwithstanding, Lincoln knew very well that there was much more at stake in the Federal war effort than the maintenance of the Union. American national ideals represented the heart of the Union's position. The North continued to hanker after that "more perfect Union" of the nation's Founding Fathers and saw the Civil War as the means to achieve it. This was the essence of Lincoln's Gettysburg Address and the reason that he chose that occasion to emphasize the nation over the Union. In the Gettysburg Address, it was the nation's ideals that concerned him, and he reminded his audience not only that the Founding Fathers had brought forth "a new nation, conceived in Liberty, and dedicated to the proposition that all men are created equal," but also that men had given their lives to consecrate that nation and that proposition.

Obviously, when Lincoln spoke on the battlefield at Gettysburg, he was not addressing a truly national audience, but he was certainly reaching out to one with his carefully chosen words. It was not the first or the last time that he did so. "We are not enemies, but friends. We must not be enemies," Lincoln had urged in the emotive conclusion to his First Inaugural; as at Gettysburg, he invoked the revolutionary generation and the "mystic chords of memory, stretching from every battle-field, and patriot grave" that bound the American nation together.[40] In these statements, and in others made throughout the war, Lincoln set out his belief in the inspirational side of the American Union, his reverence for the nation's ideals, and the importance of the struggle to live up to them.

Lincoln was not alone in seeing the Civil War as an opportunity not just to save the Union but also to improve on it. African American writer and activist Frances Harper argued for a radical transformation of the American nation:

> This grand and glorious revolution which has commenced, will fail to reach its climax of success, until throughout the length and breadth of the American Republic, the nation shall be so color-blind, as to know no man by the color of his skin or the curl of his hair. It will then have no privileged class, trampling upon and outraging the unprivileged classes, but will be then one great privileged nation, whose privilege will be to produce the loftiest manhood and womanhood that humanity can attain.[41]

The North's victory in the Civil War gave impetus to such aims and hope for the future. The war was seen to have settled, once and for all, the lingering questions over slavery and states' rights that had undermined the Union. Massachusetts senator Charles Sumner certainly saw the outcome of the war as an unqualified victory for the nation, asserting that if "among us in the earlier day there was no occasion for the word Nation, there is now. A Nation is born."[42] As a result of the Civil War, the antebellum Union was replaced by an integrated state with both territorial and political sovereignty. Yet the enmity between North and South, both a cause and a consequence of the Civil War, was not so easily dispelled. American nationalism was, therefore, left in an extremely fragile position in the years immediately following Appomattox.

Ultimately, North and South used the war that had driven them apart as one means of bringing them back together. For the troops who had fought, battlefield commemoration ceremonies provided some ground—both literally and figuratively—on which the opposing sides could meet. For Confederate veterans, particularly, such ceremonies offered a way back into the American nation. This was not a quick process, but one that took several decades and involved a certain amount of compromise, to the detriment of those ideals that Lincoln considered so important to the American nation. It would be going too far to say that the Civil War was a Pyrrhic victory for the North, but it was certainly not all that Lincoln had hoped for.

As Anthony Smith stressed, the process of national construction is never "a once-for-all affair." Nevertheless, he argued, the building of nations does take place "within a definite tradition; it is not made over entirely anew by each generation, but inherits the mythologies and symbolisms of previous generations." Specifically, each generation continues to operate "within definite emotional and intellectual confines" related to the "nation's core heritage." The proven ability of past traditions "to create bonds and generate a 'society' in the past" gives them a continuing applicability in the construction of any national identity.[43] Smith was describing the nation-building process in the ethnic nation, but the argument is applicable in many ways to the American case. Lincoln's stress on the "fathers" of the nation and on the "mystic chords of memory" that bound Americans to each other was a powerful—if mythical—invocation of the core tradition at the heart of American national identity. Devotion to the civic religion of the nation, as defined by the ideals set out in the Declaration of Independence and consecrated by the blood of the revolutionary generation, re-created the sentiment of kin networks in a nation in which national construction could never be ethnically defined.

The Civil War generation, and those who came after, followed the pattern of their predecessors in the way that Smith described. The Civil War in many ways replaced the Revolution as the definitive event in American national construction. The process was far from instantaneous. The Civil War did not begin to take its place in the civic religion of the American nation until the 1880s and 1890s. In these decades, interest in the war escalated, with an outpouring of books and articles testifying to the fact. *Century Magazine*'s circulation between 1884 and 1887 almost doubled when it ran its "Battles and Leaders of the Civil War" series, and membership in the Union veterans' society, the Grand Army of the Republic (GAR), rose dramatically from around 30,000 in 1878 to 428,000 by 1890.[44] Significantly, the GAR was instrumental in the creation of an aggressive and active patriotism that glorified the Civil War and made heroes of those who had fought it, on the Union side at least.

As interest in the war grew, however, so did disagreements over the war's meaning and its part in American national construction. The road to reunion was frequently blocked by controversy, compromise, and an increasingly selective interpretation of what, exactly, North and South had been fighting for. In assessing the reasons for this, historians point to the dramatic changes that late-nineteenth-century America was undergoing and highlight the rise of industrialism and the new immigration from eastern Europe.[45] As in the antebellum period, the influx of immigrants in the 1880s and after exacerbated the need to define and construct "100 percent Americanism" to facilitate the newcomers' integration into the American national creed. The fact that the nation had only recently been divided by a civil war made this task more difficult. The response of the GAR and others was to make the war itself the focus of the new nationalism.

By elevating the Civil War to what amounted to mystical status, and by controlling the memory of what the war had been about, societies like the GAR succeeded in creating a forceful brand of American nationalism to which, Stuart McConnell argued, "all future versions of the 'nation' would feel obliged to respond."[46] Their patriotism, like antebellum northern nationalism, was sectional in origin but national in ambition. Yet, in their desire both to justify their own role in the Civil War and to create new and lasting symbols for a nation so recently and comprehensively divided, the GAR returned to the millennial rhetoric of the antebellum period. It stressed preservation of past ideals rather than future possibilities of actually living up to these ideals, and it deliberately avoided troubling questions raised by the war concerning American nationality and the African American or even the white southern role in it.

The southern response to the war, unsurprisingly, remained a divided one. In many ways, the Civil War and its outcome strengthened the myth of the South and encouraged the belief in southern distinctiveness. In the long term, the South could be included in the national interpretation of the war only if the North acknowledged that the Confederacy had fought bravely, if not wisely, and was in this sense on an equal footing with the Union forces. By emphasizing the experience of battle rather than the actual issues that had divided North and South, publications like the "Battles and Leaders" series managed to do this. Its juxtaposing of articles by Union and Confederate soldiers "signaled to the South that the North recognized its achievements even if it did not applaud its motives," making it a powerful force in the reconciliation process.[47] Over the years, in speeches and in the oratory of commemoration ceremonies held on battlefields across the nation, North and South worked toward a new modus vivendi by portraying the Civil War as a heroic "struggle between brothers whose blood had strengthened and purified the nation."[48]

Northerners, especially, were encouraged in this line of thinking by the fact that the day of Lincoln's death was significant for the postwar fabled story of the nation. The obviously religious overtones attendant upon his death on Good Friday 1865 hastened the apotheosis of the savior of the Union and lent further support to the mystical image of the Civil War. The president had been sacrificed, it seemed to many, so that the nation might endure. Lincoln consequently became a symbol of American nationality "reborn and reinvigorated."[49] In light of the tragedy of the Civil War, combined with the shock of Lincoln's assassination, northerners were already predisposed to look for evidence that their sacrifice and his death had not been in vain. The portrayal of the Civil War as a holy crusade met that need.

The assessment of the conflict by one of the North's most famous generals, William Tecumseh Sherman, perhaps best expresses the shift in outlook regarding the Civil War. In 1880, Sherman addressed a group of GAR veterans and advised them that, in his opinion, far from being glorious, war was "all hell." A decade later, addressing veterans of the Army of the Tennessee, Sherman compared the Civil War soldier to a knight of old and declared, "Now the truth is we fought the holiest fight ever fought on God's earth."[50] From hell to holy—the images Sherman portrayed summed up the nineteenth-century response to the Civil War. It was a cruel fight that became a sacred war, a holy crusade, the American nation's salvation drama. The Civil War generation succeeded in transforming a national tragedy into a triumph, thereby achieving a powerful form of national consensus.[51] Yet this transformation was achieved at a price.

The revolutionary generation had bequeathed a divided legacy to the nation, and the Civil War generation did the same. As the Civil War replaced the Revolution as the central component in the civic religion of the American nation, it came to be seen less as a brutal and bloody conflict and more as a process of redemption; the war had preserved the nation and made it both better and stronger than it had been before. Certainly the nation that emerged from the conflict was very different from the Union that had entered it. The emancipation of the slaves had been accomplished and consolidated in important amendments to the Constitution. The validity of the American experiment in democratic government had been established. As Lincoln had hoped, the federal government had proved to the world "that those who can fairly carry an election, can also suppress a rebellion—that ballots are the rightful, and peaceful, successors of bullets; and that when ballots have fairly, and constitutionally, decided, there can be no successful appeal back to bullets."[52] The antebellum Union had been open to interpretation, but after the Civil War, the nation was built on firmer ground.

Yet by resorting to warfare to compel a national identity that was clearly not going to be established by voluntary means, the North found itself in the paradoxical position of breaking the original contract of the Declaration of Independence in the process of defending it. Ultimately, the emancipation of the slaves and the passage of the Thirteenth and Fourteenth Amendments were not accompanied by any obvious lessening of racism. It was not too many years before the South managed to establish the antebellum status quo as far as its racial policies were concerned, only now it had the tacit acceptance of the North, which sought stability in the face of the social upheavals of the late nineteenth century. The focus on military glory as the basis for postwar reconciliation worked directly against some of the ideals the Union had supposedly fought for. Gradually, Frederick Douglass's revolutionary vision of a new solidarity of the nation encompassing both black and white was replaced by a conservative, preservationist impulse that defined American nationalism in an exclusionary and curiously retroactive way. From this perspective, the Civil War was still regarded as America's salvation drama, but it had saved the nation not from slavery and southern influence but from disintegration.

Union victory in the Civil War enabled northerners to overcome the challenge to the American nation offered by southern separatism. But they soon found themselves confronted with an entirely different set of challenges to the national ideal. The mass immigration of the late nineteenth century, combined with the fast development of a modern urban-industrial society, created a whole new set of problems for the nation, and northerners soon discovered that the debate over American national identity had not ended at Appomattox but simply moved to a different level.

The South had been a valuable and effective reference point against which northerners could define, and then defend, their own version of American nationalism. Yet the South could function in this way only as long as it could continue to be seen as a world apart. Bringing the South fully into the post–Civil War version of the nation meant bringing southern ideals along too. Antebellum northerners had long feared the influence of the South on the nation, and to a degree, their fears were not without foundation. Accommodation with the South meant compromising with, rather than resolving, those contradictions that had always existed at the heart of American nationalism. The "northern nation" writ large, which northerners of the antebellum period had been so devoted to defining, was never achieved. Northerners did succeed, however, in holding together the American nation, in achieving, albeit by force, the inclusive nationalism that many of them had believed in all along. If northerners discovered that, after the Civil War, the arguments over American national identity continued unabated, they could at least take some comfort from, and much of the credit for, the fact that Americans still had a single nation to argue over.

Appendix

Newspapers and Periodicals:
Selection and Assessment Methodology

Although a necessary source for the study of northern attitudes toward the South and for an understanding of the development of northern nationalism during the antebellum period, newspapers are a difficult source to examine thoroughly. For this reason, I devised a sampling method to make the study of these papers manageable. I looked at full years for the periods covering the Nullification Crisis, the Mexican War, the Compromise of 1850, the Kansas-Nebraska Act, the Speakership debate of 1856, the election of 1856, and the election of 1860. The following periods were, therefore, covered in their entirety: 1831–1833, April 1846–February 1848, July 1849–October 1850, 1854–1856, and 1860. For the other years, I examined four months; drawing on John McCardell's approach to periodicals as described in *The Idea of a Southern Nation*, I rotated the months I examined. I began with January, April, July, and October in one year; then moved on to February, May, August, and November in the next; then to March, June, September, and December, and so on. This method was essential if I was to cover the number of papers I wanted to, and it enabled me to examine, in significant depth, as much of the period as possible. For most of the papers I examined up to 1860. I wanted to see whether any significant changes occurred in the media's treatment of and reaction to the South after the election of 1856, which enabled me to clarify the development of what I call "northern nationalism" in the period preceding that date.

Newspaper Selection

The newspapers of the antebellum period were generally extremely partisan and adhered closely to their chosen party line. In the 1850 census, for example, only 5 percent of the newspapers listed were classified as independent. Nevertheless, newspapers reflect the sentiments of their readership, confirming rather than creating their prejudices and opinions. Because this study concentrated on northeastern conservative opinions—mainly, though not exclusively, on the Whig-Republican viewpoint—the newspapers I concentrated on were, with one exception, published in Massachusetts or New York and were the main Whig-Republican publications of the time. For comparative purposes, I also examined a selection of newspapers published in Pennsylvania, choosing one from Pittsburgh and one from Philadelphia, as well as a few others. In addition, the Democratic *Boston Post* and the *New Hampshire (Daily) Patriot* were examined as controls, which, when assessed with the Pennsylvania papers, enabled me to identify the predominant northeastern Whig-Republican viewpoint.

Outline of Main Papers Consulted

For Massachusetts, the *Springfield (Daily) Republican*, edited by Samuel Bowles, was most useful, although it was generally not concerned with political matters in the 1840s. Founded in 1824, it moved from weekly to daily publication in 1844 and turned its attention toward the South only in the 1850s. Samuel Bowles II actually founded the paper in 1824, but it was his son, Samuel Bowles III, who organized its transformation into a daily and was the real force behind the paper in the period under consideration. This is important, because father and son clearly held different opinions regarding the South and slavery. In 1837, for example, the *Republican* concluded that it would be unwise, indeed counterproductive, to discuss the slavery question, which was not its attitude later on. It had more to say about the South than did many other papers, and it considered the implications of southern society and attitudes for the nation as a whole to a greater degree than did the New York or Pennsylvania press.

The *Boston Daily Advertiser,* under the editorship of Nathan Hale, likewise had little to say until the 1850s, although it was more forthcoming as the political temperature rose in that decade. The *Boston Evening Transcript,* which had a variety of editors during the period covered, was unusual; it was an almost wholly apolitical paper, designed as a literary publication aimed at the Boston elite. It thus had a relatively low circulation and retained a moderate platform for most of the period 1830–1856. However, a careful examination of its pages reveals attitudes toward the South that were both hostile and derogatory, even in the early to mid-1830s. Its strongest claim to fame, as far as this study is concerned, is that it recognized as early as 1835 that the South was actively seeking to be a nation apart.

The *New York Tribune,* edited by Horace Greeley, was the leading Whig-Republican newspaper of the time, so I examined the entire run from its initial appearance in April 1841 through the election of 1860. Although I concentrated on the daily edition, I also consulted the weekly edition, which appeared on Saturdays, was nationally circulated, and reproduced articles that had already appeared in the daily edition, although often under new banner headlines. Studying which articles Greeley chose to rerun in the weekly edition and how he chose to headline them offered a clear indication of the most pertinent issues of the day. As a deliberately conceived campaign paper from the outset, the weekly edition became a strong supporter of the Republican Party in the 1850s. From the perspective of this study, the views it expressed can be regarded as a "concentrated" form of the paper's ideological stance. In my attempt to gauge the sentiments and attitudes of a proportion of the population in the North, the paper's national distribution was a strong factor in its favor, as was its circulation—some

100,000, compared with 35,000 to 40,000 for the daily. The weekly's highest circulation was in New England and among those midwesterners originally from New England, making it an extremely useful source.

The *New York Times,* under the editorship of Henry J. Raymond, is generally considered to have been more conservative than the *Tribune,* but since it did not begin publication until 18 September 1851, it is most useful for understanding the increasingly hostile attitude the Northeast displayed toward the South in the wake of the Compromise of 1850. Although the *Times* may have been more conservative than the *Tribune* politically, in the case of the South, it often had more to say. It was Raymond, for example, who commissioned and published Frederick Law Olmsted's letters, which often voiced a far more expressive critique of the society and culture below the Mason-Dixon line than even the most scathing of the *Tribune*'s editorials could manage.

Thurlow Weed's *Albany Evening Journal* was almost exclusively political. Being a smaller paper, and concentrating on political infighting, it did not publish articles, travel accounts, or letters from the South to the same extent as the larger *Tribune* and *Times* did. However, a careful reading of its editorial line, especially in the periods 1845–1848 and 1854–1860, is essential to an understanding of the rise of the Republican Party. A wider survey of its pages offers clues as to how and why that party chose to promulgate such a sectional, antisouthern ideology. Another useful paper for my purposes was the Democratic-Republican *New York Evening Post,* edited by William Cullen Bryant.

Periodical Selection

Out of the large number of periodicals published, I selected a representative sample of the more conservative publications, again mostly from Massachusetts, New York, and Pennsylvania. But since periodicals had a more national outlook than daily newspapers, place of publication was not especially relevant. My methodology for periodicals was different from my approach to newspapers. Only *Hunt's Merchants Magazine* was approached in the same way—that is, selecting four months in each year. For the others, I looked at each one in its entirety for the years covered. In the case of the *Massachusetts Quarterly Review,* which was in print less than two years, it was feasible to look at each issue; the *New Englander* I also covered for two years only. I examined the *North American Review* in its entirety but used its index to select pertinent articles and reviews, although I did not restrict myself to those. Similarly, for the *American Review, American Quarterly Review,* and *Godey's Lady's Book* I used the indexes but essentially looked at each issue for all the years covered.

My decision to approach the periodicals differently arose from the nature of the material itself. It proved feasible to read through, fairly quickly, a year's worth of issues, which would not have been possible with the newspapers. In part, this was because many of the newspapers were available only on microfilm and hence quite slow to read, whereas the periodicals were all available in the original bound volumes. With the exception of the *New Englander,* which was a religious publication that promulgated the New Haven theology of Nathaniel Taylor, I decided not to look at specifically religious periodicals, concentrating instead on pamphlets and sermons that appeared in the newspapers or were published as pamphlets.

Outline of Periodicals

The *American Quarterly Review* was essentially a resuscitated version of the former *American Review.* It did not get especially good press and has been described as "dull." Given that it ceased publication in 1837, it was of less use than the other periodicals, but dull or not, some prominent writers contributed to it for the ten years of its existence, including George Bancroft, James Kirke Paulding, and Caleb Cushing.

The *North American Review* was not much livelier and was so conservative that if one were not already aware of the sectional antagonism of the 1850s, one would not have guessed that anything was amiss from its pages. This is, paradoxically, what makes it a valid and useful source, because even here it is possible to find, if not outright criticism of the South, then certainly the sense that the South was a different country. Begun by scholars from Boston and Harvard, many of whom had been members of the Anthology Club, it had a variety of editors, including Jared Sparks, both Alexander H. and Edward Everett, and John Gorham Palfrey. The *Review*'s high point was in the first half of the 1830s, when Alexander H. Everett was at the helm; once Palfrey took over in 1836, the *Review* apparently concentrated too much on history and lost touch with its audience. Contributors to the *North American Review* included Nathan Hale, Richard Henry Dana, Jared Sparks, Caleb Cushing, and Daniel Webster. It was, however, in no sense a narrow publication aimed only at New England elites.

The same cannot be said of the short-lived *Massachusetts Quarterly Review.* Edited by Ralph Waldo Emerson, Theodore Parker, and J. E. Cabot, its articles focused on the destiny of America—political, economic, moral, and social—but it also had quite a bit to say on the subjects of Free Soil, slavery, and the South.

Hunt's Merchants Magazine was a commercial publication and concentrated on business and commercial matters. As such, it covered such topics as the agricultural and commercial position of the South, the tariff, railroads, and other matters over which North and South had cause to disagree between 1830 and 1856.

Godey's Lady's Book was of interest for several reasons. First, it is the only publication specifically aimed at women that I used; second, it was published in Philadelphia; and most importantly, it was edited by Sarah Josepha Hale, the sole woman I could find—other than Harriet Beecher Stowe—whose views on the South could be traced with any clarity through her publications. Founded in 1828 by the Reverend

John Lauris Blake, it strove to be as noncontroversial as possible and succeeded very well in this aim. Its value lies mostly in the short stories it published, as a publication of this type was not likely to carry articles addressing political or social concerns to any great extent. However, the stories proved very revealing as far as the northern picture of the South was concerned.

Notes

Introduction

1. Hugh Seton-Watson, *Nations and States: An Inquiry into the Origins of Nations and the Politics of Nationalism* (London: Methuen, 1977), p. 214.

2. Hans Kohn, *American Nationalism: An Interpretative Essay* (New York: Macmillan, 1957), pp. 94–107.

3. Patrick Gerster and Nicholas Cords, "The Northern Origins of the Southern Myth," in Patrick Gerster and Nicholas Cords, eds., *Myth and Southern History*, 2d ed., vol. 2, *The New South* (Urbana and Chicago: University of Illinois Press, 1989), pp. 43, 45. Gerster and Cords's article first appeared in *Journal of Southern History* 43 (November 1977): 567–82.

4. Gunnar Myrdal, *An American Dilemma: The Negro Problem and Modern Democracy*, 2 vols. (New York: Harper and Row, 1944), quoted in Gerster and Cords, "Northern Origins," p. 45 n. 4.

5. C. Vann Woodward, *American Counterpoint: Slavery and Racism in the North/South Dialogue* (Boston: Little, Brown, 1971), pp. 6–7.

6. Gerster and Cords, "Northern Origins," p. 51. They do acknowledge Taylor's work in their article. William R. Taylor, *Cavalier and Yankee: The Old South and American National Character* (1957; reprint, Cambridge, Mass., and London: Harvard University Press, 1979), pp. 96–97. On this point, see also Howard R. Floan, *The South in Northern Eyes, 1830–1860* (Austin: University of Texas Press, 1958), pp. 88–104, and Woodward, *American Counterpoint*, p. 62.

7. Eric Foner, *Free Soil, Free Labor, Free Men: The Ideology of the Republican Party before the Civil War* (New York: Oxford University Press, 1970), p. 9. On this point, see also Woodward, *American Counterpoint*, pp. 6–7.

8. Foner, *Free Soil, Free Labor, Free Men*, pp. 67–68.

9. Ibid., p. 51; Taylor, *Cavalier and Yankee*, p. 146.

10. Floan, *The South in Northern Eyes*, pp. 185–86.

11. Foner, *Free Soil, Free Labor, Free Men*, p. 9. On this point, see also Woodward, *American Counterpoint*, pp. 6–7.

12. Larry Gara, "Slavery and the Slave Power: A Crucial Distinction," *Civil War History* 15 (1969): 16–17; Reinhold Niebuhr and Alan Heimert, *A Nation so Conceived: Reflections on the History of America from Its Early Visions to Its Present Power* (London: Faber and Faber, 1963), p. 37.

13. Foner, *Free Soil, Free Labor, Free Men*, p. 9; Michael F. Holt, *The Political Crisis*

of the 1850s (New York: John Wiley and Sons, 1978); William E. Gienapp, *The Origins of the Republican Party, 1852–1856* (New York: Oxford University Press, 1987).

14. Bruce Collins, "The Ideology of the Ante-bellum Northern Democrats," *Journal of American Studies* 11 (1977): 103. Gienapp makes a similar point in *Origins of the Republican Party*, p. 356.

15. Foner, *Free Soil, Free Labor, Free Men*, p. 37.

16. David Brion Davis, *The Slave Power Conspiracy and the Paranoid Style* (Baton Rouge: Louisiana State University Press, 1969), p. 31.

17. On this point, see ibid., pp. 30–31, 76–86, and Holt, *Political Crisis of the 1850s*, pp. 152–91.

18. David M. Potter, *The Impending Crisis, 1848–1861*, comp. and ed. Don E. Fehrenbacher (New York and London: Harper and Row, 1976), p. 265.

19. Robert Cook, *Baptism of Fire: The Republican Party in Iowa, 1836–1878* (Ames: Iowa State University Press, 1994), pp. 116–22.

20. David Brion Davis, *Slavery and Human Progress* (New York: Oxford University Press, 1984), p. 262.

21. Potter, *The Impending Crisis*, p. 62 ff.

22. Paul Nagel, *One Nation Indivisible: The Union in American Thought, 1776–1861* (New York and Oxford: Oxford University Press, 1964), and *This Sacred Trust: American Nationality, 1798–1898* (New York and Oxford: Oxford University Press, 1971); Fred Somkin, *Unquiet Eagle: Memory and Desire in the Idea of American Freedom, 1815–1860* (Ithaca, N.Y.: Cornell University Press, 1967); Rush Welter, *The Mind of America, 1820–1860* (New York and London: Columbia University Press, 1975); and Major Wilson, *Space, Time and Freedom: The Quest for Nationality and the Irrepressible Conflict, 1815–1861* (Westport, Conn.: Greenwood Press, 1974).

23. Peter J. Parish, "An Exception to Most of the Rules: What Made American Nationalism Different in the Mid-Nineteenth Century?" *Prologue: Quarterly of the National Archives* 27, no. 3 (fall 1995): 219–29.

24. Some of the major recent studies of nationalism, none of which pursues the American case in any depth, include Ernst Gellner, *Nations and Nationalism* (1983; reprint, London: Blackwell, 1990); Eric J. Hobsbawm, *Nations and Nationalism since 1780: Programme, Myth, Reality* (London: Canto, 1990); and Benedict Anderson, *Imagined Communities: Reflections on the Origin and Spread of Nationalism*, rev. ed. (London and New York: Verso, 1991).

25. Hans Kohn, *The Idea of Nationalism: A Study in Its Origins and Background* (New York: Macmillan, 1945), and *American Nationalism;* Liah Greenfeld, *Nationalism: Five Roads to Modernity* (Cambridge, Mass., and London: Harvard University Press, 1992); and Anthony D. Smith, "Origin of Nation," *Times Higher Education Supplement* 8 (January 1993): 15–16.

26. Walker Connor, "A Nation Is a Nation, Is a State, Is an Ethnic Group," *Ethnic and Racial Studies* 1, no. 4 (1978): 377–400; Peter Alter, *Nationalism*, 2d ed. (London: Edward Arnold, 1994), p. 1.

27. One of the earliest studies of American nationalism is Kohn, *The Idea of Na-*

tionalism, followed by his *American Nationalism.* More recent studies that assess the colonial and revolutionary eras include Greenfeld, *Nationalism,* and Smith, "Origin of Nation." For additional commentary, see Susan-Mary Grant, "When Is a Nation Not a Nation? The Crisis of American Nationality in the Mid-Nineteenth Century," *Nations and Nationalism* 2, no. 1 (1996): 105–29.

28. Simon P. Newman, *Parades and the Politics of the Street: Festive Culture in the Early American Republic* (Philadelphia: University of Pennsylvania Press, 1997), p. 6. See also David Waldstreicher, *In the Midst of Perpetual Fetes: The Making of American Nationalism, 1776–1820* (Chapel Hill: University of North Carolina Press, 1997).

29. Waldstreicher, *In the Midst of Perpetual Fetes,* pp. 6, 9. See also Newman, *Parades and the Politics of the Street,* pp. 112–13, and Grant, "When Is a Nation Not a Nation?" p. 113.

30. Kohn, *American Nationalism,* p. 107.

31. Greenfeld, *Nationalism,* pp. 403, 449, 480.

32. Wolfgang Mommsen, "Power, Politics, Imperialism, and National Emancipation, 1870–1914," in G. W. Moody, ed., *Nationality and the Pursuit of National Independence* (Belfast: Appletree Press for the Irish Committee of Historical Sciences, 1978), p. 128.

33. Somkin, *Unquiet Eagle,* p. 9; Carl Bode, *Antebellum Culture* (Carbondale and Edwardsville: Southern Illinois University Press, 1970), p. x.

34. Nina Silber and Mary Beth Sievens, eds., *Yankee Correspondence: Civil War Letters between New England Soldiers and the Home Front* (Charlottesville and London: University Press of Virginia, 1996), p. 4.

35. Phillip S. Paludan, *A Covenant with Death: The Constitution, Law, and Equality in the Civil War Era* (Urbana and Chicago: University of Illinois Press, 1975), p. x.

36. John Hope Franklin, *A Southern Odyssey: Travelers in the Antebellum North* (Baton Rouge: Louisiana State University Press, 1975), p. xii.

37. Michael C. C. Adams, *Our Masters the Rebels: A Speculation on Union Military Failure in the East, 1861–1865* (Cambridge, Mass., and London: Harvard University Press, 1978), pp. 11–13.

38. Olmsted's first fifty letters for the *New York (Daily) Times* appeared under the heading "The South" between 16 February 1853 and 13 February 1854, over the byline "Yeoman." Many of these went into the subsequent volume *A Journey in the Seaboard Slave States.* Olmsted's second trip south produced fifteen letters, which appeared in the *Times* under the heading "A Tour of the Southwest" between 6 March and 7 June 1854. Much of this material went into *A Journey through Texas.* His final series of ten letters, under the heading "The Southerners at Home," appeared in the *New York (Daily) Tribune* between 3 June and 24 August 1857. These went into *A Journey in the Back Country.* Because the *Times* letters are so well known, Olmsted's letters for the *Tribune* are sometimes incorrectly attributed.

39. See Charles E. Beveridge's introduction to Volume 2, *Slavery and the South,* of Charles Capen McLaughlin et al., eds., *The Papers of Frederick Law Olmsted,* 6 vols. (Baltimore and London: Johns Hopkins University Press, 1981).

40. Olmsted edited *Putnam's Monthly Magazine* in 1855–1856.

41. Melvin Kalfus, *Frederick Law Olmsted: The Passion of a Public Artist* (New York and London: New York University Press, 1990), p. 19.

42. See Gabriel Compayre, *Horace Mann and the Public Schools in the United States* (New York: Thomas Y. Crowell, 1907); Raymond B. Culver, *Horace Mann and Religion in the Massachusetts Public Schools* (New Haven, Conn.: Yale University Press, 1929); Robert B. Downs, *Horace Mann: Champion of Public Schools* (New York: Twayne Publishers, 1974); and Edward I. F. Williams, *Horace Mann: Educational Statesman* (New York: Macmillan, 1937).

43. Jonathan Messerli, *Horace Mann: A Biography* (New York: Alfred A. Knopf, 1972), p. xi.

44. Mann had been elected as a Whig senator in Massachusetts in 1834 and later served as president of the state senate between 1836 and 1837. His career prior to that point had been devoted to law, and afterward to education. He was elected secretary of the Board of Education of Massachusetts in June 1837.

45. David Nasaw, *Schooled to Order: A Social History of Public Schooling in the United States* (New York: Oxford University Press, 1979), pp. 30–31.

46. The *Massachusetts Quarterly Review* lasted less than three years, running from December 1847 until September 1850. In 1847 and 1848 it was edited by Emerson, Parker, and John Elliot Cabot. From then until its demise it was edited almost solely by Parker.

47. Estimates of the spread of Parker's influence are taken from Michael Fellman, "Theodore Parker and the Abolitionist Role in the 1850s," *Journal of American History* 61 (1974): 667–84, and Henry Steele Commager, *Theodore Parker: Yankee Crusader* (1936; reprint, Boston: Beacon Press, 1947), pp. 144–45.

48. Theodore Parker, speech at New England Anti-Slavery Convention, Boston, 29 May 1850. Garry Wills has examined the relationship between Lincoln's and Parker's ideas in *Lincoln at Gettysburg: The Words that Remade America* (New York: Simon and Schuster, 1992), pp. 106–21.

49. See, for example, Kohn, *The Idea of Nationalism* and *American Nationalism;* John McCardell, *The Idea of a Southern Nation: Southern Nationalists and Southern Nationalism, 1830–1860* (New York and London: W. W. Norton, 1979); and Drew Gilpin Faust, *The Creation of Confederate Nationalism: Ideology and Identity in the Civil War South* (Baton Rouge and London: Louisiana State University Press, 1988).

50. A similar point is made in Adams, *Our Masters the Rebels,* p. ix; see also Dewey W. Grantham, Jr., ed., *The South and the Sectional Image: The Sectional Theme since Reconstruction* (New York and London: Harper and Row, 1967), p. 2.

51. C. Vann Woodward, "From the First Reconstruction to the Second," *Harper's Magazine* 230 (April 1965): 133, quoted in Gerster and Cords, "Northern Origins," p. 51.

52. C. Vann Woodward, "The Antislavery Myth," *American Scholar* 31, no. 2 (spring 1962): 316.

1. Myths and Memories

1. Henry James, "Americans Abroad," *The Nation*, 3 October 1878.

2. Walker Connor, "A Nation Is a Nation, Is a State, Is an Ethnic Group," *Ethnic and Racial Studies* 1, no. 4 (1978): 381.

3. Ernst Gellner, *Nations and Nationalism* (1983; reprint, London: Blackwell, 1990), p. 1; Benedict Anderson, *Imagined Communities: Reflections on the Origin and Spread of Nationalism*, rev. ed. (London and New York: Verso, 1991).

4. Anthony D. Smith, "Origin of Nation," *Times Higher Education Supplement* 8 (January 1993): 15–16, and "The Origins of Nations," *Ethnic and Racial Studies* 12, no. 3 (1989): 342.

5. Anthony D. Smith, *The Ethnic Origins of Nations* (1983; reprint, London: Blackwell, 1993), pp. 206–7, 2.

6. Peter Alter, *Nationalism*, 2d ed. (London: Edward Arnold, 1994), p. 1.

7. Ernst Gellner, *Thought and Change* (London: Weidenfeld and Nicolson, 1964), p. 168.

8. Anthony D. Smith, *National Identity* (London: Penguin Books, 1991), p. 66.

9. Josep R. Llobera, *The God of Modernity: The Development of Nationalism in Western Europe* (Oxford: Berge, 1994), pp. 172–73.

10. Theodore Parker quoted in Garry Wills, *Lincoln at Gettysburg: The Words that Remade America* (New York: Simon and Schuster, 1992), p. 77.

11. Michael Kammen, *Mystic Chords of Memory: The Transformation of Tradition in American Culture* (New York: Alfred A. Knopf, 1991), pp. 62–66; Virginia de John Anderson, *New England's Generation: The Great Migration and the Formation of Society and Culture in the Seventeenth Century* (New York and Cambridge: Cambridge University Press, 1991).

12. Reinhold Niebuhr and Alan Heimert, *A Nation so Conceived: Reflections on the History of America from Its Early Visions to Its Present Power* (London: Faber and Faber, 1963), pp. 13–42; Russell Blaine Nye, *Society and Culture in America, 1830–1860* (New York and London: Harper and Row, 1974), pp. 10–31; Rush Welter, *The Mind of America, 1820–1860* (New York and London: Columbia University Press, 1975), pp. 3–23.

13. Eden B. Foster, *A Sermon on the Crime against Freedom* (Concord, 1856), pp. 4–9.

14. David Brion Davis, ed., *Antebellum American Culture: An Interpretative Anthology* (Lexington, Mass.: D. C. Heath, 1979), p. 454.

15. John Shy, *A People Numerous and Armed: Reflections on the Military Struggle for American Independence*, rev. ed. (Ann Arbor: University of Michigan Press, 1990), p. 26.

16. This point is explored further in Susan-Mary Grant, "Making History: Myth and the Construction of American Nationhood," in Geoffrey Hosking and George Schöpflin, eds., *Myths and Nationhood* (London: Hurst, 1997), pp. 88–106; see also Shy, *A People Numerous and Armed*, pp. 25–26.

17. Daniel J. Boorstin, *The Americans: The National Experience* (1965; reprint, London: Sphere Books, 1988), p. 368. On the role of the Revolution in American historical development, see Michael Kammen, *A Season of Youth: The American Revolution and the Historical Imagination* (New York: Alfred A. Knopf, 1978). On the impact of the great migration on national myth, see Anderson, *New England's Generation.* For a fuller assessment of this process, see Susan-Mary Grant, "'The Charter of Its Birthright': The Civil War and American Nationalism," *Nations and Nationalism* 4, no. 2 (1998): 163–85.

18. Reid Mitchell, *Civil War Soldiers: Their Expectations and Their Experiences* (1988; reprint, New York: Simon and Schuster, 1989), pp. 1–2.

19. Linda Kerber, *Federalists in Dissent: Imagery and Ideology in Jeffersonian America* (1970; reprint, Ithaca, N.Y., and London: Cornell University Press, 1983), p. 34. On the Federalists and the South, see also David Waldstreicher, *In the Midst of Perpetual Fetes: The Making of American Nationalism, 1776–1820* (Chapel Hill and London: University of North Carolina Press, 1997), pp. 251–62.

20. Boorstin, *The Americans,* p. 418.

21. Albert Gallatin to Matthew Lyon, 7 May 1816, quoted in George Dangerfield, *The Awakening of American Nationalism, 1815–1828* (New York: Harper and Row, 1965), pp. 3–4.

22. Hans Kohn, *The Idea of Nationalism: A Study in Its Origins and Background* (New York: Macmillan, 1945), pp. 291, 307.

23. Welter, *The Mind of America,* p. 23.

24. Cushing quoted in Albert K. Weinberg, *Manifest Destiny: A Study of Nationalist Expansion in American History* (1935; reprint, Gloucester, Mass.: Peter Smith, 1958), p. 203.

25. Diary entry for 8 November 1854, in Allan Nevins and Milton Halsey Thomas, eds., *The Diary of George Templeton Strong,* vol. 3, *The Turbulent Fifties, 1850–1859* (New York: Macmillan, 1952), p. 197.

26. William R. Brock, *Parties and Political Conscience: American Dilemmas, 1840–1850* (New York: Kto Press, 1979), p. 140.

27. Anthony D. Smith, *Nationalism in the Twentieth Century* (Oxford: Martin Roberston, 1979), p. 18; John Plamenatz, "Two Types of Nationalism," in Eugene Kamenka, ed., *Nationalism: The Nature and Evolution of an Idea* (London: Edward Arnold, 1976), pp. 22–36. See also David M. Potter, *The Impending Crisis, 1848–1860* (New York and London: Harper and Row, 1976), p. 450; Kohn, *The Idea of Nationalism,* pp. 10–11; and John Armstrong, *Nations before Nationalism* (Chapel Hill: University of North Carolina Press, 1982), p. 5.

28. Seymour Martin Lipset, *The First New Nation: The United States in Historical and Comparative Perspective* (1963; reprint, London: W. W. Norton, 1979), p. 16.

29. Margaret Fuller, "Things and Thoughts in Europe," *New York (Daily) Tribune,* 1 January 1848.

30. Sydney Smith quoted in Alan Bell, *Sydney Smith: A Biography* (New York: Oxford University Press, 1982), p. 210.

31. John Clive and Bernard Bailyn, "England's Cultural Provinces: Scotland and America," *William and Mary Quarterly* 11 (October 1954): 207–9.

32. Ralph Waldo Emerson, "The American Scholar," in *The Norton Anthology of American Literature*, vol. 1 (London: W. W. Norton, 1979), pp. 693, 708.

33. Noah Webster in *American Magazine* (1788), quoted in Hans Kohn, *American Nationalism: An Interpretative Essay* (1957; reprint, New York: Collier Books, 1961), p. 59.

34. *New-York (Daily) Times*, 14 July 1855.

35. Plamenatz, "Two Types of Nationalism," p. 24.

36. Kammen, *Mystic Chords of Memory*, pp. 64–66.

37. Ibid., p. 66.

38. Daniel Webster, speech in the Senate, 26 and 27 January 1830, in *Webster and Haynes's Speeches in the United States Senate* (New York: Books for Libraries Press, 1971), p. 67.

39. *New York (Daily) Tribune*, 9 October 1856.

40. Wilbur Zelinsky, *Nation into State: The Shifting Symbolic Foundations of American Nationalism* (Chapel Hill and London: University of North Carolina Press, 1988), p. 127.

41. Theodore Parker quoted in Michael Fellmam, "Theodore Parker and the Abolitionist Role in the 1850s," *Journal of American History* 61 (1974): 673. See also *Massachusetts Quarterly Review* 3 (December 1848): 21–30, 105–126, for similar arguments.

42. John Hope Franklin, "The North, the South, and the American Revolution," *Journal of American History* 62 (1975): 8, 17.

43. Smith, "Origin of Nation," p. 16.

44. Abraham Lincoln, "Speech at Chicago, Illinois," 10 July 1858, in Roy F. Basler, ed., *The Collected Works of Abraham Lincoln* (1953; reprint, New Brunswick, N.J.: Rutgers University Press, 1988), vol. 2, pp. 499–500.

45. Joseph R. Fornieri, "Abraham Lincoln and the Declaration of Independence; the Meaning of Equality," in Frank J. Williams et al., eds., *Abraham Lincoln: Sources and Style of Leadership* (Westport, Conn.: Greenwood Press, 1994), p. 46.

46. Reid Mitchell, *The Vacant Chair: The Northern Soldier Leaves Home* (1993; reprint, New York and Oxford: Oxford University Press, 1995), p. 144.

47. David Miller, *On Nationality* (Oxford: Clarendon Press, 1995), p. 23.

48. Abraham Lincoln, "Speech at Peoria," 16 October 1854, in Basler, *Collected Works of Abraham Lincoln*, vol. 2, p. 276.

49. Abraham Lincoln, "Speech in Independence Hall, Philadelphia," 22 February 1861, in Basler, *Collected Works of Abraham Lincoln*, vol. 4, p. 240.

50. Wills, *Lincoln at Gettysburg*, p. 107.

51. Theodore Parker, "The Nebraska Question," in Theodore Parker, *Additional Speeches, Addresses, and Occasional Sermons*, vol. 1 (Boston, 1855), pp. 379–80.

52. On this point, see Weinberg, *Manifest Destiny*, p. 38 ff.

53. Welter, *The Mind of America*, pp. 23, 3–5.

54. Kerber, *Federalists in Dissent*, pp. 1–2. On this point, see also Jean H. Baker,

"The Ceremonies of Politics: Nineteenth-Century Rituals of National Affirmation," in William J. Cooper et al., eds., *A Master's Due: Essays in Honor of David Herbert Donald* (Baton Rouge: Louisiana State University Press, 1985), pp. 161–78.

55. Charles Francis Adams, *What Makes Slavery a Question of National Concern?* (Boston, 1855), pp. 20–22.

56. Edward Pessen, "How Different from Each Other Were the Antebellum North and South?" *American Historical Review* 65 (1980): 1119.

57. William R. Taylor, *Cavalier and Yankee: The Old South and American National Character* (1957; reprint, Cambridge, Mass.: Harvard University Press, 1979), p. 15.

58. Fred Somkin, *Unquiet Eagle: Memory and Desire in the Idea of American Freedom, 1815–1860* (Ithaca, N.Y.: Cornell University Press, 1967), p. 28.

59. Bruce Collins, "The Ideology of the Ante-bellum Northern Democrats," *Journal of American Studies* 11 (1977): 119. See also Jean H. Baker, *Affairs of Party: The Political Culture of Northern Democrats in the Mid-Nineteenth Century* (Ithaca, N.Y.: Cornell University Press, 1983).

60. Hannibal Hamlin quoted in Baker, *Affairs of Party,* p. 57.

61. On this point, see Michael F. Holt, *The Political Crisis of the 1850s* (New York: John Wiley and Sons, 1978), pp. 9–15.

62. C. Vann Woodward, *American Counterpoint: Slavery and Racism in the North/ South Dialogue* (1964; reprint, Boston: Little, Brown, 1971), pp. 13–14.

63. Ibid., pp. 6–7.

64. Dewey W. Grantham, Jr., ed., *The South and the Sectional Image: The Sectional Theme since Reconstruction* (New York and London: Harper and Row, 1967), p. 2.

65. Carl Degler, "Thesis, Antithesis, Synthesis: The South, the North, and the Nation," *Journal of Southern History* 53, no. 1 (February 1987): 5.

2. A World Apart

1. Francis Pendleton Gaines, *The Southern Plantation: A Study in the Development and the Accuracy of a Tradition* (New York: Columbia University Press, 1925), p. 3.

2. J. G. Cogswell, "Warden on America," *North American Review* 13, no. 32 (July 1821): 60.

3. Leo Marx, *The Machine in the Garden: Technology and the Pastoral Ideal in America* (New York: Oxford University Press, 1964), p. 138.

4. William Howard Gardiner, Review of James Fenimore Cooper's *The Spy, North American Review* 14, no. 36 (July 1822): 252.

5. Edward Everett in *North American Review* 22, no. 51 (April 1826): 380.

6. Lorman Ratner, "Northern Concern for Social Order as Cause for Rejecting Anti-Slavery, 1831–1840," *Historian* 28, no. 1 (November 1965): 8.

7. William R. Taylor, *Cavalier and Yankee: The Old South and American National Character* (1957; reprint, Cambridge, Mass., and London: Harvard University Press, 1979), pp. 97–98.

8. Henry De Forest to Andrew De Forest, 19 January 1839, quoted in James A. Hijiya, *J. W. De Forest and the Rise of American Gentility* (Hanover, N.H.: University Press of New England for Brown University Press, 1988), p. 9.

9. David Bertelson, *The Lazy South* (New York: Oxford University Press, 1967), pp. 179–83; Taylor, *Cavalier and Yankee*, p. 96.

10. Taylor, *Cavalier and Yankee*, p. 165.

11. Pauline Forsyth, "Sketches of Southern Life," *Godey's Lady's Book* 44 (March 1852): 368–69.

12. Pauline Forsyth, "Sketches of Southern Life," *Godey's Lady's Book* 48 (January 1854): 111.

13. Alice B. Neal, "Marrying a Planter: A New Chapter of Romance and Reality," *Godey's Lady's Book* 52 (January–June 1856): 327–28.

14. Henry F. Harrington, "The Southerner's Daughter," *Godey's Lady's Book* 24 (January–June 1842): 30–36.

15. *Philadelphia North American and United States Gazette*, 12 December 1848.

16. Review of Robert T. Howison's *A History of Virginia, from Its Discovery and Settlement by Europeans to the Present Time*, 2 vols. (1848), in *Hunts' Merchants Magazine* 21, no. 2 (August 1849): 182.

17. John P. Hale to Lucy Hale, 2 October 1850, Hale Papers, New Hampshire Historical Society.

18. Frank Bergon and C. Zeesepapanikolas, eds., *Looking Far West: The Search for the American West in History, Myth and Literature* (New York: Mentor Books, 1978), pp. 2–18.

19. *Boston Daily Advertiser*, 22 June 821. See also 16 March 1821.

20. *Albany Evening Journal*, 15 January 1833. See also 16 and 17 January 1833.

21. Mr. Ewing (Ohio), Senate, 17 February 1832, *Register of Debates*, 22d Cong., 1st sess., vol. 8, pp. 435–37.

22. George M. Dallas (Pennsylvania), Senate, 27 February 1832, *Register of Debates*, 22d Cong., 1st sess., vol. 8, p. 468.

23. Nathan Appleton (Massachusettes), House, 30 May 1832, *Register of Debates*, 22d Cong., sess. 1, vol. 3, p. 3205.

24. Mr. Stewart (Pennsylvania), House, 5 June 1832, *Register of Debates*, 22d Cong., 1st sess., vol. 3, pp. 3274–84.

25. "The Rise and Progress of Commerce," *Hunts' Merchants Magazine* 1, no. 3 (September 1839): 193.

26. "The Advantages and Benefits of Commerce," *Hunts' Merchants Magazine* 1, no. 3 (September 1839): 200.

27. "Railroads of the United States," *Hunts' Merchants Magazine* 3, no. 4 (October 1840): 135.

28. Rev. G. W. Burnap, "Address Delivered to the Mercantile Library Association of Baltimore," reproduced in *Hunts' Merchants Magazine* 4, no. 5 (May 1841): 417.

29. George McDuffie, "Commerce as a Liberal Pursuit," *Hunt's Merchants Magazine* 2, no. 1 (January 1840): 1.

30. Citizen of Richmond, "Commercial Cities and Towns of the United States, No. XIV," *Hunt's Merchants Magazine* 20, no. 1 (January 1849): 53.

31. Edwin Hall to Cyrus Woodman, 13 June 1837, in Larry Gara, ed., "A New Englander's View of Plantation Life: Letters of Edwin Hall to Cyrus Woodman, 1837," *Journal of Southern History* 18 (August 1952): 350–51. For similar views, see Richard Henry Dana, Jr.'s comments in his journal, 2 March 1844, in Robert F. Lucid, ed., *The Journal of Richard Henry Dana, Jr.* (Cambridge, Mass.: Belknap Press of Harvard University Press, 1968), vol. 1, p. 247.

32. Richard H. Abbott, "Yankee Farmers in Northern Virginia, 1840–1860," *Virginia Magazine of History and Biography* 76, no. 1 (January 1968): 59–60.

33. Mr. Stewart, 5 June 1832, *Register of Debates,* pp. 3274–84.

34. Amos A. Lawrence to J. S. Skinner, 18 February 1850, in A. A. Lawrence, *Letterbook,* Massachusetts Historical Society.

35. Abbott, "Yankee Farmers," p. 59.

36. Frederick Law Olmsted, "The South," *New York (Daily) Times,* 16 February 1853.

37. *New York (Daily) Times,* 20 July 1853. See also 22, 23, and 25 July 1853. On the northern desire to introduce a free-labor system to the South, see George Winston Smith, "Ante-bellum Attempts of Northern Business Interests to 'Redeem' the Upper South," *Journal of Southern History* 10 (May 1945): 177–213.

38. Frederick Law Olmsted, *A Journey in the Seaboard Slave States* (New York: n.p., 1856), pp. 145–48.

39. Ibid., p. 170.

40. S. G. Fisher, "Uncle Tom's Cabin: The Possible Amelioration of Slavery," *North American Review* 76, no. 161 (October 1853): 474–75; E. Peabody, "Slavery in the United States: Its Evils, Alleviations and Remedies," *North American Review* 73, no. 153 (October 1851): 350.

41. Stuart J. Horn, "Edward Everett and American Nationalism" (Ph.D. diss., City University of New York, 1973, University Microfilms International), pp. 125, 153.

42. Edward Everett, "Cattle Show at Denvers," 28 September 1836, in Edward Everett, *Orations and Speeches of Various Occasions,* 4 vols. (Boston: n.p., 1850–1860), vol. 2, pp. 185, 188–89.

43. Horn, *Edward Everett,* p. 173.

44. *Albany Evening Journal,* 1 December 1848.

45. Lemuel Shaw, "Slavery and the Missouri Question," *North American Review* 10, no. 26 (January 1820): 138, 143.

46. *Albany Evening Journal,* 15 January 1833; Mr. Ewing, 17 February 1832, *Register of Debates,* pp. 435–37.

47. *New York (Daily) Tribune,* 4 June 1842.

48. Horace Bushnell, *A Discourse on the Slavery Question: Delivered in the North Church, Hartford, January 10, 1839* (Hartford, Conn.: n.p., 1839), pp. 6, 15.

49. Ibid., pp. 9–10.

50. George Bourne, *Picture of Slavery in the United States of America* (Middletown,

Conn., 1834), quoted in Ronald G. Walters, *American Reformers, 1815–1860* (New York: Hill and Wang, 1978), pp. 64–65.

51. Horace Bushnell, *Politics under the Law of God: A Discourse Delivered in the North Congregational Church, Hartford, on the Annual Fast of 1844* (Hartford, Conn.: n.p., 1844), pp. 2, 12–13.

52. Emerson quoted in James Elliot Cabot, *A Memoir of Ralph Waldo Emerson*, 2 vols. (Boston: Houghton Mifflin, 1887), vol. 2, pp. 425–26.

53. Emerson, journal entry for 8 June 1838, in William H. Gilman et al., eds., *The Journals and Miscellaneous Notebooks of Ralph Waldo Emerson* (Cambridge, Mass.: Belknap Press of Harvard University Press, 1969), vol. 7, p. 6.

54. Emerson, journal entry for April [n.d.], 1840, in Gilman, *Journals and Miscellaneous Notebooks*, vol. 7, pp. 340–41.

55. Emerson, journal entry for 19 October 1842, in Gilman, *Journals and Miscellaneous Notebooks*, vol. 7, pp. 473–74.

56. Emerson, journal entry for 16 December 1826, in Edward Waldo Emerson and Waldo Emerson Forbes, eds., *Journals of Ralph Waldo Emerson, 1820–1872* (Boston: Houghton Mifflin, 1909), vol. 1, pp. 141–42. See also Ralph L. Rusk, *The Life of Ralph Waldo Emerson* (New York: Charles Scribner's Sons, 1949), p. 119.

57. Rusk, *Life of Ralph Waldo Emerson*, p. 153.

58. Emerson, journal entries for 30 October and 3 November 1838, in Gilman, *Journals and Miscellaneous Notebooks*, vol. 8, pp. 129, 139.

59. Emerson to Lillian Emerson, 8 and 9 January 1843, in Ralph L. Rusk, ed., *The Letters of Ralph Waldo Emerson* (New York: Columbia University Press, 1939), vol. 3, p. 118.

60. Emerson, "Emancipation in the British West Indies," in Edward Waldo Emerson, ed., *The Complete Works of Ralph Waldo Emerson* (Boston and New York: Houghton Mifflin, 1911), vol. 11, pp. 118–19, 125–26.

61. Emerson, journal entries for 23 May and 27 June 1846, in Emerson and Forbes, *Journals of Ralph Waldo Emerson*, vol. 7, pp. 201, 218.

62. *Albany Evening Journal*, 20 April 1849 and 29 September 1854.

63. John A. Kasson to Charles D. Kasson, 21 October 1842, in Edward Younger, ed., "A Yankee Reports on Virginia, 1842–1843: Letters of John Adam Kasson," *Virginia Historical Magazine* 56 (October 1948): 413.

64. (Philadelphia) *North American and United States Gazette*, 10 November 1849.

65. Andrew Preston Peabody, *Position and Duties of the North with Regard to Slavery* (Newburyport, Mass.: n.p., 1847), p. 5.

66. "The Political Destiny of America," *Massachusetts Quarterly Review* 3 (December 1848): 15.

67. Theodore Parker to Charles Sumner, 19 April 1850. See also Charles Sumner to Parker, 19 April 1851; William H. Seward to Parker, 11 October 1853, 4 December 1854, and 12 March 1855, all in Theodore Parker Papers, Massachusetts Historical Society.

68. Theodore Parker, Sermons, Supplement III (notes for a sermon), 2 January 1853, Theodore Parker Papers, Massachusetts Historical Society.

69. Article from the *Newark Daily Advertiser* reprinted in the *Albany Evening Journal*, 31 January 1843.

70. Caleb Cushing, "North & South," 6 June 1855, Caleb Cushing Papers, Library of Congress, Washington, D.C.

71. John Gorham Palfrey, *Papers on the Slave Power*, No. 1, *Its Foundation* (Boston: n.p., 1846), p. 1. The quotation that Palfrey used was taken from John Smith's description of the Jamestown colony.

72. Theodore Parker, *Letter to the People of the United States Touching the Matter of Slavery* (Boston: n.p., 1848), pp. 11–12.

73. Ibid., p. 12.

74. Theodore Parker quoted in Michael Fellmam, "Theodore Parker and the Abolitionist Role in the 1850s," *Journal of American History* 61 (1974): 673.

75. *Massachusetts Quarterly Review* 1 (December 1847): 2; 3 (December 1848): 15.

76. *Massachusetts Quarterly Review* 3 (December 1848): 21–30; "The Free Soil Party and the Late Election," ibid., pp. 107–18.

77. Alexander H. Everett, "Men and Manners in America," *North American Review* 38, no. 82 (January 1834): 250, 266–67.

78. Mrs. J. Ware, "The Anglo-Saxon Race," *North American Review* 73, no. 152 (July 1851): 39.

79. Such sentiments were fairly widespread. See, for example, the *Boston Atlas and Daily Bee*, 6 January 1838 and 3 March 1845; *Springfield (Daily) Republican*, 27 November 1847; *Boston Daily Advertiser*, 26 May and 22 June 1821 and 7 September 1849; *Boston Daily Evening Transcript*, 29 August 1831, 13 July 1833, and 2 February and 22 August 1835; *Pittsburgh Daily Gazette*, 25 October 1843, 6 February and 14 July 1845, 3 August 1846, 17 June, 10 July, and 4 October 1847; *Philadelphia North American and United States Gazette*, 12 December 1842 and 6 August 1846; and *Pittsburgh Daily (Evening) Mail*, 12 May 1848.

80. J. V. Matthews, " 'Whig History': The New England Whigs and a Usable Past," *New England Quarterly* 51 (June 1978): 193. See also David Brion Davis, ed., *Antebellum American Culture: An Interpretative Anthology* (Lexington, Mass.: D. C. Heath, 1979), p. 454.

81. Rev. A. D. Mayo, sermon delivered on 23 November 1856 in New York State. No location was given, but it was probably Albany, since it was reported in the *Albany Evening Journal*, 24 November 1856.

82. *Pittsburgh Daily Gazette*, 10 July 1847.

83. Eden B. Foster, *A Sermon on the Crime against Freedom* (Concord, N.H.: n.p., 1856), pp. 4–9.

84. Samuel Nott, *Slavery and the Remedy* (New York: n.p., 1856), pp. 20–21.

85. Fred Somkin, *Unquiet Eagle, Memory and Desire in the Idea of American Freedom, 1815–1860* (Ithaca, N.Y.: Cornell University Press, 1967), pp. 3–4.

86. James Freeman Clarke to Anna, 19 May 1838, in Perry-Clarke Additions, Massachusetts Historical Society.

87. *Hunt's Merchants Magazine* 21, no. 2 (August 1849): 182.

88. John A. Kasson to Maria H. Kasson, 22 November 1842, in Younger, "A Yankee Reports," pp. 419–20. Kasson helped Horace Greeley draft the Republican Party's platform at Chicago, among other things. He became assistant postmaster general in the Lincoln administration. His comments were typical as far as northern tutors were concerned. See Elizabeth Brown Pryor, "An Anomalous Person: The Northern Tutor in Plantation Society, 1773–1860," *Journal of Southern History* 48, no. 3 (August 1981): 363–92.

89. James Watson Webb, *Slavery and Its Tendencies: Letter to the* New York Courier and Enquirer (Washington, D.C.: n.p., 1856), p. 2.

90. *Albany Evening Journal*, 23 May 1854.

3. One and Inseparable?

1. Daniel Webster, Speech in the Senate, 26 and 27 January 1830, in *Webster and Hayne's Speeches* (1850; reprint, New York: Books for Libraries Press, 1971), 84.

2. Merrill D. Peterson, *The Great Triumvirate: Webster, Clay, and Calhoun* (New York and Oxford: Oxford University Press, 1987), pp. 176–78.

3. William R. Taylor, *Cavalier and Yankee: The Old South and American National Character* (1957; reprint, Cambridge, Mass., and London: Harvard University Press, 1979), p. 110.

4. Webster, *Webster and Hayne's Speeches*, p. 50.

5. Fulmer Mood, "The Origin, Evolution, and Application of the Sectional Concept, 1750–1900," in Merrill Jensen, ed., *Regionalism in America* (Madison: University of Wisconsin Press, 1952), p. 5. See also Joseph L. Davis, *Sectionalism in American Politics, 1774–1787* (Madison: University of Wisconsin Press, 1977), p. 2

6. Mood, "Origin, Evolution, and Application," pp. 25–26, 32–34.

7. Harrison Gray Otis to James Prince, 1 April 1820, and to Theodore Sedgwick, 3 January 1833; George Harrison to Otis, 4 March 1833, Harrison Gray Otis Papers, Massachusetts Historical Society (hereafter MHS).

8. J. G. Waters to Caleb Cushing, 10 February 1836; N. Cleaveland to Cushing, 10 February 1836; John Greenleaf Whittier to Cushing, 12 February 1836, Caleb Cushing Papers, Library of Congress; Amos A. to Amos Lawrene, 7 and 8 January 1836 and 10 February 1837, Amos Lawrence Papers, MHS; Samuel Downing to John P. Hale, 4 January 1844; H. W. Fuller to Hale, 31 January 1844; J. W. James to Hale, 8 January 1844; Wm. Lamprey to Hale, 25 February 1844; Charles Lanborn to Hale, 18 March 1844; John Peary to Hale, 6 February 1844; Enoch Place to Hale, 24 December 1844; Dellevon D. Marsh to Hale, 26 February 1844; John Peavey to Hale, 11 January 1844; Amos Tuck to Hale, 5 January 1844; J. B. Wiggin to Hale, 15 January 1844, John P. Hale Papers, New Hampshire Historical Society (hereafter NHHS). The Gag Rule (Pinkney gag) passed the House of Representatives on 26 May 1836. It was finally abolished in the House in 1845, but not in the Senate. See Theodore Foster to John P. Hale, 17 November 1847, John P. Hale Papers.

9. Caleb Cushing, 11 October 1822, notes for a speech on "Is Slavery Justifiable?" Caleb Cushing Papers, Library of Congress.

10. J. S. Wilder to Cushing, 8 February 1836; see also Cushing to E. Monley, 10 July 1836; Warren Ladd to Cushing, 24 January 1838; and George Cogswell to Cushing, 25 January 1838, Caleb Cushing Papers, Library of Congress.

11. James W. Ward, sermon in Abington, 28 March 1839, published as *Slavery a Sin that Concerns Non-Slaveholding States* (Boston: n.p., 1839), p. 25.

12. Mr. Stewart (Pennsylvania), House, 5 June 1832, *Register of Debates*, 22d Cong., 1st sess., vol. 3, pp. 3274–84.

13. "And Joshua made them that day hewers of wood and drawers of water for the congregation, and for the altar of the Lord, even unto this day, in the place which he should choose." Joshua 9:27.

14. Amos Lawrence to Nathan Appleton, 31 January 1832, Nathan Appleton Papers, MHS.

15. Mr. Dickerson (N.J.), Senate, 23 January 1832; John Holmes (Maine), 30 January 1832; and see Mr. Hill (N.H.), 1 February 1832, *Register of Debates*, 22d Cong., 1st sess., vol. 8, pp. 172, 217, 251.

16. *New York Evening Post*, 11 January 1839.

17. William E. Channing to Robert C. Winthrop, 30 December 1841, in *Proceedings of the Massachusetts Historical Society*, vol. 1, no. 18, p. 24.

18. Senate Document No. 4 (Commonwealth of Massachusetts), *Samuel Hoar's Expulsion from Charleston* (1844), pp. 2–3. See also Senate Document No. 31, *Report and Declaration of the Joint Special Committee Protesting against the Hostile Acts of South Carolina* (Boston, 1845), p. 13.

19. Ralph Waldo Emerson, journal entry for 15 March 1845, in Edward Waldo Emerson and Waldo Emerson Forbes, eds., *Journals of Ralph Waldo Emerson, 1820–1872* (Boston and New York: Houghton Mifflin, 1909), vol. 7, pp. 14–15, 20–22.

20. Peterson, *The Great Triumvirate*, p. 406.

21. Philip Hone, diary entries for 3 December 1840 and 13 December 1842, in Allan Nevins, ed., *The Diary of Philip Hone, 1828–1851*, rev. ed. (New York: Dodd, Mead, 1936), pp. 513,. 293. For Hone's views on northern abolitionists, see entries for 10, 12, and 14 July 1834 (pp. 134–35); on the mail and on southern violence, see 13 August 1835 (pp. 170–72); and on the Gag Rule, see 22 December 1837 (p. 293).

22. George Templeton Strong, diary entries for 9 December 1850, 26 and 28 May and 8 June 1856, in Allan Nevins and Milton Haslet Thomas, eds., *The Diary of George Templeton Strong, 1835–1875*, 4 vols. (New York: Macmillan, 1952), vol. 2, pp. 20, 274–78.

23. Everett to Winthrop, 5 December 1846, Winthrop Family Papers, MHS.

24. Robert W. Johannsen, *To the Halls of the Montezumas: The Mexican War in the American Imagination* (1985; reprint, New York and Oxford: Oxford University Press, 1987), pp. 16, 49–51.

25. "The Destiny of the Country," *American Review* 5, no. 3 (March 1847): 235–36;

"Dangers and Safeguards of the Union," *American Review* 3, no. 2 (February 1849): 112–13.

26. Mr. J. R. Ingersoll (Pennsylvania Whig), House of Representatives, 4 January 1845, *Congressional Globe*, 28th Cong., 2d sess., p. 56.

27. *Pittsburgh Daily Gazette*, 10 June 1844.

28. John Gorham Palfrey, *Papers on the Slave Power*, No. 3 (Boston: n.p., 1846), p. 7.

29. Horace Bushnell, *Barbarism the First Danger: A Discourse for Home Missions* (New York: n.p., 1847), p. 20. For additional examples of opposition to the war, see *Address of His Excellency George N. Briggs to the Two Branches of the Legislature of Massachusetts, January 1848* (Boston: n.p., 1848), pp. 11–13; Robert C. Winthrop to John Pendleton Kennedy, 21 January 1848, Winthrop Family Papers, MHS; and John Greenleaf Whittier to John P. Hale, 26 April 1848, Hale Papers, NHHS.

30. Rev. George Allen, *An Appeal to the People of Massachusetts on the Texas Question* (Boston: n.p., 1844), p. 3.

31. *New York (Daily) Tribune*, 4 June 1846. See also 9 June, 2 July, and especially 14 August 1846.

32. Robert Hughes, *American Visions: The Epic History of Art in America* (New York: Alfred A. Knopf, 1997), p. 69.

33. *New York (Daily) Tribune*, 17 July 1847.

34. Rev. Robert Morris, *Sermon to the Presbyterian Church, Newtown, Pa., 27 July 1845* (Philadelphia: n.p., 1845), p. 9.

35. *New York (Daily) Tribune*, 19 August 1846. See also *Pittsburgh Daily Gazette*, 6 February 1845, 14 July 1846, 10 July 1847, 2 October 1847.

36. *New York (Daily) Tribune*, 27 November 1846. See also *Albany Evening Journal*, 14 December 1846, 11 and 13 January, 29 July, 1 and 7 September 1847, 10 and 19 January 1848.

37. William Jay, *A Review of the Causes and Consequences of the Mexican War* (1849; reprint, New York: Books for Libraries, 1970), p. 255.

38. Johannsen, *To the Halls of the Montezumas*, pp. 271–73.

39. *Pittsburgh Daily Gazette*, 2 October 1847.

40. John P. Hale in the Senate, 10 January 1850, *Congressional Globe*, 32d Cong., 1st sess., p. 134.

41. Parker quoted in Charles Forrester Dunham, *The Attitude of the Northern Clergy toward the South, 1860–1865* (Toledo, Ohio: Gray Company, 1942), p. 82.

42. Eric Foner, *Free Soil, Free Labor, Free Men: The Ideology of the Republican Party before the Civil War* (New York: Oxford University Press, 1970), pp. 38–39.

43. Daniel Webster, "Speech in the Senate of the United Staes, March 7, 1850, on the Slavery Compromise," in *Webster and Hayne's Speeches*, p. 85; A. Merrill to Hale, 18 March 1850; see also Theodore Parker to Hale, 8 March 1850, Hale Papers, NHHS; Amelia Hickling-Nye to Thomas Hickling-Nye, 11 January 1855, Hickling-Nye Papers, MHS. For a detailed assessment of the reaction to Webster's speech, see Peterson, *The Great Triumvirate*, pp. 462–66.

44. Robert C. Winthrop to John Pendleton Kennedy, 8 October 1850 and 23 April 1851, Winthrop Family Papers, MHS.

45. Arthur W. Austin to Caleb Cushing, 3 August 1850, Caleb Cushing Papers, Library of Congress.

46. *Albany Evening Journal*, 29 August 1850; see also 9 and 18 August 1850, 24 January 1854. See also the *Springfield (Daily) Republican*, 23 October 1855, 4 March 1856.

47. *New York (Daily) Times*, 9 July 1854.

48. Rev. Daniel March, *The Crisis of Freedom, Lecture before the United Meeting in the First Church of Nashua, June 18, 1854* (Nashua, N.H.: n.p., 1854), pp. 11–12.

49. *New York (Weekly) Tribune*, 15 July 1854.

50. Henry C. Fish, *The Voice of Our Brother's Blood, Its Source and Its Summons; A Discourse Occasioned by the Sumner and Kansas Outrages* (Newark, N.J.: n.p., 1856), p. 12.

51. *New York (Daily) Times*, 23 February 1854.

52. Ibid., 18 May 1854.

53. Josiah Quincy, *Address Illustrative of the Nature and Power of the Slave States and the Duties of the Free States, 5 June 1856* (Boston: n.p., 1856), pp. 5–6.

54. David Brion Davis, *The Slave Power Conspiracy and the Paranoid Style* (Baton Rouge: Louisiana State University Press, 1969), pp. 26–31.

55. John Gorham Palfrey, *Five Year's Progress of the Slave Power* (1851; reprint, Boston: n.p., 1852), p. 84; see also pp. 3, 7, 14–19.

56. Edward Everett to Alexander Everett, 4 March 1830, Edward Everett Papers, MHS.

57. Taylor, *Cavalier and Yankee*, p. 26.

58. Peterson, *The Great Triumvirate*, p. 178.

59. Robert Cook, *Baptism of Fire: The Republican Party in Iowa, 1836–1878* (Ames: Iowa State University Press, 1994), pp. 116–22.

60. Daniel Webster, "Speech at Marshfield, September 1, 1848," in Charles M. Wiltse, ed., *The Papers of Daniel Webster: Speeches and Formal Writings*, vol. 2, *1834–1852* (Hanover, N.H., and London: University Press of New England, 1988), p. 503.

4. Firsthand Impressions

1. Frederick Law Olmsted, *A Journey in the Seaboard Slave States* (New York: n.p., 1856), pp. 516–22.

2. Olmsted, "A Tour in the Southwest," *New York (Daily) Times*, 13 May 1854.

3. Victor A. Kramer, "Olmsted as Observer," in Dana F. White and Victor Kramer, eds., *Olmsted South: Old South Critic/New South Planner* (Westport, Conn.: Greenwood Press, 1979), pp. 3–9.

4. Henry Benjamin Whipple, diary entry, 9 February 1844, in Lester B. Shippee, ed., *Bishop Whipple's Southern Diary, 1843–1844* (1844; reprint, Minneapolis: University of Minnesota Press, 1973), p. 76.

5. [Charles A. Clinton], *A Winter from Home* (New York: n.p., 1852), p. 30; Miss Mendell and Miss Hosmer, *Notes of Travel and Life* (New York: n.p., 1853), p. 195.

6. *New York (Daily) Tribune,* 24 February 1844.

7. *Bishop Whipple's Southern Diary,* p. 71. See also Paton Yoder, "Private Hospitality in the South, 1775–1850," *Mississippi Valley Historical Review* 47 (1960): 419–33; and William Cullen Bryant to William Gilmore Simms, November 1840, in William Cullen Bryant II and Thomas G. Voss, eds., *The Letters of William Cullen Bryant,* 3 vols. (New York: Fordham University Press, 1975–1981), vol. 2, p. 139.

8. *Albany Evening Journal,* 20 July 1833.

9. *Boston Daily Evening Transcript,* 1 August 1844. See also 12 and 23 July and 23 August 1844.

10. *New York (Daily) Tribune,* 24 February 1844.

11. Ibid., 1 March 1845.

12. Samuel Bowles quoted in George S. Merriam, *The Life and Times of Samuel Bowles,* 2 vols. (New York: Century Publications, 1885), vol. 1, p. 50. For similar views, see John A. Kasson to Charles Kasson, 27 December 1842, in Edward Younger, ed., "A Yankee Reports on Virginia, 1842–1843: Letters of John Adam Kasson," *Virginia Historical Magazine* 56 (October 1948): 408–30, especially 421.

13. A. H. Everett, "The Union and the States," *North American Review* 37, no. 80 (July 1833): 249; *Albany Evening Journal,* 12 February 1848; and *Bishop Whipple's Southern Diary,* 25 and 26 November 1843, pp. 30–34.

14. *Bishop Whipple's Southern Diary,* 25 November, 12 December 1843 and 6 January 1844, pp. 30, 43–44, 60–70.

15. Amos A. Lawrence to Amos Lawrence, 15 January 1836, in Amos A. Lawrence Papers, Massachusetts Historical Society (hereafter MHS). Lawrence's trip was undertaken with a view to establishing commercial links with southern traders. He was also visiting his uncle, Abbott Lawrence, who was a member of Congress at that time.

16. Amos A. Lawrence to Amos Lawrence, 12 November and 9 December 1836, in Amos A. Lawrence Papers, MHS.

17. Amos A. Lawrence to Amos Lawrence, 22 December 1836, in Amos A. Lawrence Papers, MHS.

18. Thomas H. O'Connor, *Lords of the Loom: The Cotton Whigs and the Coming of the Civil War* (New York: Charles Scribner's Sons, 1968), p. 71.

19. Bryant visited the South between February and May 1843, accompanied by his wife, Frances Bryant. He visited "Woodlands," the Roaches' plantation in Barnwell District, South Carolina (Nash Roach was the wife of William Gilmore Simms), before moving on to Georgia and Florida. His letters from this and from his 1849 trip appeared in the *New York Evening Post* between 14 March and 30 May 1843 and on 6 and 9 April 1849. These were later published in *Letters of a Traveler: Or, Notes of Things Seen in Europe and America* (London: n.p., 1850).

20. Bryant and Voss, *Letters of William Cullen Bryant,* vol. 3, p. 3.

21. Harry Houston Peckham, *Gotham Yankee: A Biography of William Cullen Bryant* (1950; reprint, New York: Russell and Russell, 1971), p. 139.

22. Howard Floan, *The South in Northern Eyes, 1831–1861* (Austin: University of Texas Press, 1958), pp. 148–54.

23. Bryant, "Richmond in Virginia," Letter IX, 2 March 1843, and "The Interior of South Carolina—A Corn Shucking," Letter XI, 29 March 1843, in Bryant, *Letters of a Traveler*, pp. 74–75, 82–89.

24. Bryant, "St. Augustine," Letter XIV, 24 April 1843, in Bryant, *Letters of a Traveler*, pp. 109–11. For additional evidence of Bryant's positive image of slavery, see Bryant to Frances Bryant, 31 March 1849, in Bryant and Voss, *Letters of William Cullen Bryant*, vol. 3, p. 18.

25. Nathaniel Parker Willis, *Health Trip to the Tropics* (New York: n.p., 1853), p. 381.

26. *Bishop Whipple's Southern Diary*, 28, 29, and 30 October 1843, pp. 12–14. See also 24 November 1843 for Whipple's description of slavery in Florida. Whipple was better known in his own day than he is in ours. See Theodore Parker to William R. Alger, 7 July 1857, Theodore Parker Papers, MHS. This letter is reproduced in part in John Weiss, *The Life and Correspondence of Theodore Parker*, 2 vols. (New York and London: n.p., 1864), vol. 2, pp. 219–20.

27. Catherine Maria Sedgwick to Miss K. M. Sedgwick, 18 June 1833, quoted in Mary E. Dewey, ed., *Life and Letters of Catherine Maria Sedgwick* (New York: Harper and Brothers, 1871), pp. 233–34.

28. Samuel Bowles quoted in Merriam, *Life and Times of Samuel Bowles*, vol. 1, p. 50.

29. Allan Nevins and Milton Halsey Thomas, eds., *The Diary of George Templeton Strong*, 4 vols. (New York: Macmillan, 1952), vol. 2, pp. 21–22.

30. John Ashworth, "The Democratic-Republicans before the Civil War: Political Ideology and Economic Change," *Journal of American Studies* 20, no. 3 (1986): 375–90; Bruce Collins, "The Ideology of the Ante-bellum Northern Democrats," *Journal of American Studies* 11 (1977): 103–21.

31. Bryant and Voss, *Letters of William Cullen Bryant*, vol. 1, p. 314 n. 2.

32. Ibid., vol. 3, pp. 191–92, 514.

33. Bryant, "Letter to the Democratic-Republican Electors of the State of New York," 15 July 1844, in ibid., p. 269.

34. *New York (Weekly) Evening Post*, 28 January and 4 November 1847.

35. Ibid., 3 February 1848. See also 27 April, 22 June, and 20 July 1848. As Ashworth has shown, this was a standard line, adopted by many Democratic-Republicans. Ashworth, "The Democratic-Republicans before the Civil War," p. 381; Floan, *The South in Northern Eyes*, pp. 148–54.

36. Bryant, letter to the *Evening Post*, 27 September 1834, quoted in Bryant and Voss, *Letters of William Cullen Bryant*, vol. 1, p. 422. For a discussion of the Democratic-Republican hostility to aristocracy, see John Mayfield, *Rehearsal for Republicanism: Free Soil and the Politics of Anti-Slavery* (New York and London: Kennikat Press, 1980), pp. 10–11.

37. Bryant to Frances Bryant, 24 May 1832, in Bryant and Voss, *Letters of William Cullen Bryant*, vol. 1, p. 330.

38. Bryant, "Southern Cotton Mills," Letter XLIV, 31 March 1849, in Bryant, *Letters of a Traveler,* pp. 345–50.

39. Bryant quoted in Floan, *The South in Northern Eyes,* p. 161.

40. Bryant to Mrs. S. Bryant, 23 August 1832, in Bryant and Voss, *Letters of William Cullen Bryant,* vol. 1, p. 357. See also Bryant to Frances Bryant, 31 March 1849, in ibid., vol. 3, p. 17.

41. Bryant, "A Journey from Richmond to Charleston," Letter X, 6 March 1843, in Bryant, *Letters of a Traveler,* pp. 80–81. See also Bryant to Richard Henry Dana, 26 May 1843, in Bryant and Voss, *Letters of William Cullen Bryant,* p. 232.

42. *New York (Daily) Tribune,* 1 March 1845.

43. Peckham, *Gotham Yankee,* p. 142.

44. Bryant, "The Ages," quoted in Fred Somkin, *Unquiet Eagle: Memory and Desire in the Idea of American Freedom, 1815–1860* (Ithaca, N.Y.: Cornell University Press, 1967), p. 54.

45. Willis, *Health Trip to the Tropics,* p. 240; [David Brown], *The Planter; or, Thirteen Years in the South, by a Northern Man* (Philadelphia: n.p., 1853), p. 18, and see pp. 20–44. See also Nehemiah Adams, *A South-Side View of Slavery: Or, Three Months at the South in 1854* (Boston: n.p., 1854).

46. Willis, *Health Trip to the Tropics,* p. 381. See also Mendell and Hosmer, *Notes of Travel and Life,* p. 125.

47. George M. Fredrickson, *The Black Image in the White Mind: The Debate on Afro-American Character and Destiny, 1817–1914* (New York: Harper and Row, 1971), p. 109. For an extended discussion of the response to northern minstrel shows, see Jean H. Baker, *Affairs of Party: The Political Culture of Northern Democrats in the Mid-Nineteenth Century* (Ithaca, N.Y., and London: Cornell University Press, 1983), pp. 213–40.

48. Dr. Thomas L. Nichols, *Forty Years of American Life,* 2 vols. (London: n.p., 1864), vol. 1, pp. 175–76. Nichols (1815–1901) enjoyed an eclectic career. He visited the South twice, first in 1845 and again in 1859. Once Civil War broke out, he left for England, where he composed *Forty Years of American Life* to help the British understand the origins of the sectional conflict.

49. Fredrickson, *The Black Image in the White Mind,* p. 5. On this point, see Nichols, *Forty Years of American Life,* vol. 1, p. 216; and [Clinton], *A Winter from Home,* pp. 25–30.

50. Nichols, *Forty Years of American Life,* vol. 1, p. 175, and see p. 252.

51. Ibid., p. 223.

52. [Brown], *The Planter,* p. 18.

53. *New York (Daily) Times,* 23 July 1853.

54. Ibid., 27 August 1853.

55. Ibid., 29 July 1853.

56. Nichols, *Forty Years of American Life,* vol. 1, pp. 176–77, 233–37.

57. Olmsted, *Journey in the Seaboard Slave States,* p. 18.

58. *New York (Daily) Times,* 15 August 1853.

59. Nichols, *Forty Years of American Life*, vol. 1, pp. 191–94, 189, 226, 249.

60. Willis, *Health Trip to the Tropics*, p. 329. See also Mendell and Hosmer, *Notes of Travel and Life*, p. 162.

61. Nichols, *Forty Years of American Life*, vol. 1, pp. 148–49.

62. Willis, *Health Trip to the Tropics*, p. 349.

63. David Bertelson, *The Lazy South* (New York: Oxford University Press, 1967), pp. 179–80; William R. Taylor, *Cavalier and Yankee: The Old South and American National Character* (1961; reprint, Cambridge, Mass., and London: Harvard University Press, 1979).

64. Walter Sommerville, "Impressions of the South upon a Native Northerner," *New York (Daily) Times*, 25 July 1853.

65. *New York (Daily) Times*, 29 July 1853.

66. Adams, *A South-Side View of Slavery*, p. 44.

67. Willis, *Health Trip to the Tropics*, pp. 236–37, 349; Nichols, *Forty Years of American Life*, vol. 1, pp. 175–76.

68. [Clinton], *A Winter from Home*, pp. 28–32.

69. Mendell and Hosmer, *Notes of Travel and Life*, pp. 125–26. See also Eliza Potter, *A Hairdresser's Experience in High Life* (Cincinnati: n.p., 1859), p. 182.

70. The most extreme examples were Rev. Philo Tower, *Slavery Unmasked: Being a Truthful Narrative of Three Years' Residence and Journeying in Eleven Southern States; to Which Is Added, The Invasion of Kansas, Including the Last Chapter of Her Wrongs* (Rochester, N.Y.: n.p., 1856), and C. G. Parsons, MD, *Inside View of Slavery: Or, a Tour among the Planters* (Boston and Ohio: n.p., 1855). To complicate matters further, Tower incorporated large sections of Parsons's work, which itself was a mix of material culled from Olmsted and others.

71. Parsons, *Inside View of Slavery*, p. 237.

72. Anon. [A Former Resident of the Slaves States], *Influence of Slavery upon the White Population* (New York and Boston: Anti-Slavery Tracts, n.d.), p. 3. This pamphlet is undated, but the frequent references to Topsy and Little Eva (characters in Harriet Beecher Stowe's *Uncle Tom's Cabin*) place it post-1851, probably post-1852.

73. Parsons, *Inside View of Slavery*, p. 28.

74. Ibid., p. 52, and see pp. 129–35.

75. John Stevens Cabot Abbot, *South and North; or, Impressions Received during a Trip to Cuba and the South* (New York: n.p., 1860), pp. 90–92. See also Tower, *Slavery Unmasked*, p. 399.

76. Parsons, *Inside View of Slavery*, p. 62.

77. Nichols, *Forty Years of American Life*, p. 211.

78. Abbot, *South and North*, pp. 154, 181, 274–76.

79. Ibid., p. 145.

80. Somkin, *Unquiet Eagle*, p. 29.

81. John Hope Franklin, *A Southern Odyssey: Travelers in the Antebellum North* (Baton Rouge: Louisiana State University Press, 1975), p. xii.

82. Details of Olmsted's book sales can be found in Laura Wood Roper, *FLO: A*

Biography of Frederick Law Olmsted (Baltimore: Johns Hopkins University Press, 1973), p. 112; and in Laura Wood Roper, "Frederick Law Olmsted in the 'Literary Republic,'" *Mississippi Valley Historical Review* 39 (December 1952): 459–82.

83. Olmsted, *Journey in the Seaboard Slave States*, p. 178.

84. There is a wealth of material on Olmsted and the South. See Arthur M. Schlesinger, "Was Olmsted an Unbiased Critic of the South?" *Journal of Negro History* 37, no. 2 (April 1952): 173–87; John C. Inscoe, "Olmsted in Appalachia: A Connecticut Yankee Encounters Slavery and Racism in the Southern Highlands," *Slavery and Abolition* 9, no. 2 (September 1988): 171–82; Gary A. Donaldson, "Antebellum Criticism: Frederick Law Olmsted in Mississippi, 1853–1854," *Journal of Mississippi History* 50, no. 4 (November 1988): 317–33. All concur with Olmsted that the information available to northerners about the South was either inaccurate or written from an abolitionist perspective and that Olmsted's reports were, by contrast, more objective.

85. Clement Eaton is one who sees Olmsted as both objective and influenced by his New England background against the South. See his introduction to Frederick Law Olmsted, *A Journey in the Back Country*, Clement Eaton, ed. (New York: Schocken Books, 1970), pp. xi–xiii. Others see Olmsted as entirely flawed in his assessment of the Old South, most notably Robert William Fogel and Stanley Engerman in *Time on the Cross: The Economics of American Negro Slavery* (London: Wildwood House, 1974), pp. 179–218. For a more balanced view, see Dana F. White, "A Connecticut Yankee in Cotton's Kingdom," in White and Kramer, *Olmsted South*, pp. 11–49.

86. Melvin Kalfus, *Frederick Law Olmsted: The Passion of a Public Artist* (New York and London: New York University Press, 1990), p. 160.

87. This was the introduction to Olmsted's series, *New York (Daily) Times*, 16 February 1853.

88. *Savannah (Georgia) Republican*, 9 March 1853.

89. *New York (Daily) Times*, 27 July 1853.

90. Timothy J. Crimmins argues that Olmsted approached the South like a nineteenth-century social worker, believing his position as an outsider to be a positive benefit, in "Frederick Law Olmsted and Jonathan Baxter Harrison: Two Generations of Social Critics of the American South," in White and Kramer, *Olmsted South*, pp. 137–51, especially pp. 146–47.

91. Olmsted to Charles Loring Brace, 22 December 1852, in Charles Capen McLaughlin et al., eds., *The Papers of Frederick Law Olmsted*, 6 vols. (Baltimore: Johns Hopkins University Press, 1977–1992), vol. 2, p. 92.

92. Olmsted, "The South," No. 7, *New York (Daily) Times*, 17 March 1853.

93. Roper, *FLO*, pp. 112–13.

94. Olmsted, "The South," No. 2, *New York (Daily) Times*, 19 February 1853.

95. Ibid., No. 9, 5 April 1953. For more in the same vein, see letters 7, 8, 10, and 14, which appeared in the *Times* on 17 and 30 March, 8 and 28 April 1853.

96. Charles E. Beveridge, introduction to McLaughlin et al., *Olmsted Papers*, vol. 2, pp. 2–8.

97. Olmsted, "The South," No. 14, *New York (Daily) Times*, 28 April 1853.

98. Olmsted, *Journey in the Seaboard Slave States*, p. 502.

99. Beveridge, introduction to McLaughlin et al., *Olmsted Papers*, vol. 2, pp. 14–15. For examples, see "The South" Nos. 7, 8, 12, and 19, which appeared in the *New York (Daily) Times* on 17 and 30 March, 20 April, and 24 May 1853. Letters 12 and 19 later appeared in *Journey in the Seaboard Slave States*, pp. 149–52, 357–67. One additional letter (No. 14, 28 April 1853), which Beveridge and McLaughlin list as not appearing in *Journey in the Seaboard Slave States*, actually does so (p. 140).

100. Olmsted, "The South," No. 8, *New York (Daily) Times*, 30 March 1853.

101. Ibid., No. 44, 22 November 1853, and Olmsted, *Journey in the Back Country*, p. 223.

102. Broadus Mitchell, *Frederick Law Olmsted: A Critic of the Old South* (Baltimore: Johns Hopkins University Press, 1924), pp. 68–69. This continues to be the accepted view of Olmsted's attitude at the outset of his southern tour. See White and Kramer, *Olmsted South*, pp. xviii–xix; Roper, *FLO*, p. 85; and Thomas D. Clark, ed., *Travels in the Old South: A Bibliography*, vol. 3, *The Antebellum South, 1825–1860* (Norman: University of Oklahoma Press, 1959), p. 370.

103. Beveridge regards the Kansas-Nebraska Act as crucial but argues that the Mexican War saw the beginning of a change in Olmsted's views; see his introduction in McLaughlin et al., *Olmsted Papers*, vol. 2, pp. 2–3. See also Clark, *Travels in the Old South*, p. 370, and Kalfus, *Frederick Law Olmsted*, p. 167.

104. Olmsted, "The South," No. 10, *New York (Daily) Times*, 8 April 1853.

105. Olmsted, *Journey in the Seaboard Slave States*, p. 136.

106. Olmsted, "The South," No. 46, *New York (Daily) Times*, 12 January 1854.

107. Ibid.

108. Beveridge, introduction in McLaughlin et al., *Olmsted Papers*, vol. 2, pp. 16–17. On the subject of Olmsted's meeting with Allison, see also Donaldson, "Antebellum Criticism," p. 323, and Roper, *FLO*, pp. 92–95.

109. Olmsted to Charles Loring Brace, 1 December 1853, in McLaughlin et al., *Olmsted Papers*, vol. 2, pp. 234–35.

110. Olmsted, *Journey in the Seaboard Slave States*, pp. 489, 491.

111. Ibid., pp. 402, 404.

112. Ibid., p. 515.

113. Olmsted, "How Ruffianism in Washington and Kansas is Regarded in Europe," *New York (Daily) Times*, 10 July 1856.

114. Frederick Law Olmsted, "Letter to a Southern Friend," introduction to *A Journey through Texas* (1857; reprint, Austin: University of Texas Press, 1978), p. vii.

115. Frederick Law Olmsted, introduction to T. H. Gladstone's *The Englishman in Kansas; or, Squatter Life and Border Warfare* (1857; reprint, Lincoln: University of Nebraska Press, 1971), in McLaughlin et al., *Olmsted Papers*, vol. 2, pp. 416–18.

116. Kalfus, *Frederick Law Olmsted*, pp. 16–17.

117. Olmsted, introduction to *Englishman in Kansas*, in McLaughlin et al., *Olmsted Papers*, vol. 2, pp. 410–16.

118. Review of *A Journey in the Seaboard Slave States* by S. W. S. Dutton, *New Englander* 14, no. 2 (May 1856): 273–81.

119. Anonymous review of *A Journey in the Back Country, North American Review* 91, no. 189 (October 1860): 571.

5. Representative Mann

1. Fred Somkin, *Unquiet Eagle: Memory and Desire in the Idea of American Freedom, 1815–1860* (Ithaca, N.Y.: Cornell University Press, 1967), p. 9.

2. Eric Foner, *Free Soil, Free Labor, Free Men: The Ideology of the Republican Party before the Civil War* (New York: Oxford University Press, 1970), chap. 2.

3. Merrill D. Peterson, *The Great Triumvirate: Webster, Clay, and Calhoun* (New York and Oxford: Oxford University Press, 1987), p. 178.

4. Horace Mann, in a speech outlining his reasons for accepting the Whig nomination, in *Horace Mann: Speeches,* "Liberty, and Miscellaneous Notes on Slavery, Drayton and Sayres Case" [1848], in Horace Mann Papers, Massachusetts Historical Society (hereafter MHS).

5. Mann to Samuel Gridley Howe, 22 April 1848, in Mann Papers, MHS.

6. Mann to Mary P. Mann, 21, 23, 25, and 26 May and 2 June 1848, in Mann Papers, MHS.

7. *Speech of Mr. Horace Mann, on the Right of Congress to Legislate for the Territories of the United States and Its Duty to Exclude Slavery Therefrom, Delivered in the House of Representatives, in Committee of the Whole, 30 June 1848* (Boston: n.p., 1848), p. 16; William Gregg, *Essays on Domestic Industry, or an Enquiry into the Expediency of Establishing Cotton Manufactures in South Carolina* (Charleston, S.C.: n.p., 1845), p. 19; Broadus Mitchell, *William Gregg: Factory Master of the Old South* (Chapel Hill: University of North Carolina Press, 1928), p. 20.

8. Speech by Hon. W. C. Preston, *Columbia Telescope,* January 1837; J. G. Palfrey, "The New England Character," *North American Review* 44, no. 94 (January 1837). Preston's speech was reprinted eighteen years later in C. G. Parsons, *Inside View of Slavery; or a Tour among the Planters* (Boston: n.p., 1855).

9. *Pittsburgh Daily Gazette,* 25 October 1843. The article was reprinted from the *Cincinnati Gazette.*

10. A Slaveholder of West Virginia [Rev. Henry Ruffner, D.D.], *Address to the People of West Virginia; Showing that Slavery Is Injurious to the Public Welfare, and that It May Be Gradually Abolished, without Detriment to the Rights and Interests of Slaveholders* (Lexington, 1847), quoted in Horace Mann, *Slavery: Letters and Speeches* (Boston: n.p., 1851), pp. 73–83.

11. Jonathan Messerli, *Horace Mann: A Biography* (New York: Alfred A. Knopf, 1972), p.108.

12. For further examples of Mann's economic critique of the South, see *New Dan-*

gers to Freedom, and New Duties for Its Defenders: A Letter by the Hon. Horace Mann, to His Constituents, May 3rd, 1850 (Boston: n.p., 1850).

13. Horace Mann, "An Oration Delivered before the Authorities of the City of Boston, July 4th, 1842," in Mary Mann and George C. Mann, eds., *Life and Works of Horace Mann*, 5 vols. (1865; reprint, Washington, D.C.: National Education Association, 1937), vol. 4, pp. 350–51, 372.

14. Mann to George Combe, 28 February 1842, Combe Papers, National Library of Scotland (hereafter NLS).

15. Horace Mann, "Twelfth Annual Report of the Secretary of the Board of Education of Massachusetts," in Mann and Mann, *Life and Works*, vol. 3, pp. 682–83, 688–89.

16. David Nasaw, *Schooled to Order: A Social History of Public Schooling in the United States* (New York: Oxford University Press, 1979), pp. 38–42. See also Ruth Miller Elson, *Guardians of Tradition* (Lincoln: University of Nebraska Press, 1964), pp. 289–93.

17. On this point, see John McCardell, *The Idea of a Southern Nation: Southern Nationalists and Southern Nationalism, 1830–1860* (New York: W. W. Norton, 1979), pp. 19–20, and especially pp. 132–33.

18. *The North and the South* (New York: *New York Tribune* Office, 1854), pp. 16–17.

19. R. Freeman Butts and Lawrence A. Cremin, *A History of Education in American Culture* (New York and London: Holt, Rinehart and Winston, 1953), p. 217.

20. "Twelfth Annual Report," in Mann and Mann, *Life and Works*, vol. 3, p. 689.

21. Nasaw, *Schooled to Order*, p. 47; Horace Mann, *Fifth Annual Report of the Secretary of the Board of Education of Massachusetts* (Boston: Dutton and Wentworth, 1842); John Hardin Best and Robert T. Sidwell, *The American Legacy of Learning: Readings in the History of Education* (Philadelphia and New York: J. B. Lippincott, 1967), pp. 184–88.

22. *New York Daily Times*, 5 April 1852.

23. Miscellaneous Notes, 12 [184–] Education, Mann Papers, MHS.

24. Richard H. Abbott, *Cotton and Capital: Boston Businessmen and Antislavery Reform, 1854–1868* (Amherst: University of Massachusetts Press, 1991), p. 6.

25. See Mann to Mary Peabody, 25 June 1837; Mann to Samuel J. May, 22 September 1848, in Mann Papers, MHS.

26. William R. Taylor, *Cavalier and Yankee: The Old South and American National Character* (1957; reprint, Cambridge, Mass., and London: Harvard University Press, 1979).

27. Edward Everett, "The Importance of the Mechanic Arts," 20 September 1837, in Edward Everett, *Orations and Speeches on Various Occasions*, 4 vols. (Boston: n.p., 1850–1860), vol. 2, pp. 252–55.

28. Mr. Ewing (Ohio), Senate, 17 February 1832, *Register of Debates*, 22d Cong., 1st sess., vol. 8, p. 437.

29. George M. Dallas (Pennsylvania), Senate, 27 February 1832, *Register of Debates*, 22d Cong., 1st sess, vol. 8, p. 468.

30. Theodore Parker, *Letter to the People of the United States Touching the Matter of Slavery* (Boston: n.p., 1848), pp. 42, 47.

31. *Boston Daily Courier*, 29 March 1850; *Albany Evening Journal*, 22 June and 12 September 1854; *New York Daily Times*, 22 October 1852, 25 July and 23 August 1855, and 7 March 1857.

32. *New York (Weekly) Tribune*, 7 January 1854. See also *Albany Evening Journal*, 12 September and 21 December 1854; *New York (Daily) Tribune*, 8 January 1848 and 30 November 1850.

33. Mann, Speech of 30 June 1848, in Horace Mann, *Slavery: Letters and Speeches* (Miami: Mnemosyne Publishing, 1969), p. 25.

34. See "Universal Liberty Necessitates Labor," in *Notes on Slavery* [n.d.]; "Education," in *Lectures, Sermons, Speeches, Legal Notes*, 12 [184–]; and "Education" [1854], in Mann Papers, MHS.

35. Horace Mann, "The Necessity of Education in a Republican Government" (1838), in Mann and Mann, *Life and Works*, vol. 2; *Annual Reports of the Secretary of the Board of Education of Massachusetts for the Years 1837–1838, to which Are Prefixed Lectures on Education* (Boston: n.p., 1891), pp. 143, 149, 150–51, 180.

36. See, for example, Mann's "An Historical View of Education; Showing Its Dignity and Its Degradation" and "An Oration Delivered before the Authorities of the City of Boston, July 4th, 1842", in Mann and Mann, *Life and Works*, vol. 2, pp. 241–93, and vol. 4, pp. 341–403.

37. Mann to Mary Peabody Mann, 12 March 1850, in Mann Papers, MHS. In this letter, Mann added that he believed that slavery, if restricted geographically, would die a natural death, and he expanded on his theme of the "intellectual deficiencies" of the South and the lack of education there.

38. *Speech of Horace Mann, of Massachusetts, on the Subject of Slavery in the Territories, and the Consequence of a Dissolution of the Union, House of Representatives, 15 February 1850* (Boston: n.p., 1850), pp. 4–5, 19.

39. Horace Bushnell, *Barbarism the First Danger* (New York: American Home Missionary Society, 1847), pp. 27–28. Bushnell's sermon was delivered throughout the northern states during the summer of 1847 and, as one biographer noted, represents "one of the best known and most striking of [Bushnell's] public utterances." See Mary B. Cheney, ed., *Life and Letters of Horace Bushnell* (London: n.p., 1880), p. 184.

40. Mann, Speech of June 1848, in Mann, *Slavery: Letters and Speeches*, p. 29.

41. Somkin, *Unquiet Eagle*, pp. 33, 44.

42. Rush Welter, *Popular Education and Democratic Thought in America* (New York and London: Columbia University Press, 1962), pp. 83, 98. Welter describes Mann as "one of the country's leading social theorists" (p. 98).

43. Henry Ward Beecher, *A Discourse Delivered at the Plymouth Church, Brooklyn, New York, upon Thanksgiving Day, November 25, 1847* (New York: n.p., 1848), p. 15.

44. Frederick Law Olmsted, conclusion to "The South," No. 47, *New York (Daily) Times*, 26 January 1854.

45. *Boston Daily Courier*, 3 July 1848.

46. Ralph Waldo Emerson, "Emancipation in the British West Indies" (1844), in

Edward Waldo Emerson, ed., *The Complete Works of Ralph Waldo Emerson* (Boston: Houghton Mifflin, 1911), vol. 11, pp. 125–26.

47. Howard R. Floan, *The South in Northern Eyes, 1831–1861* (Austin: University of Texas Press, 1958), pp. 52–61; Philip Butcher, "Emerson and the South," *Phylon* 17 (1956): 279–85; Len Gougeon, "Abolition, the Emersons, and 1837," *New England Quarterly* 54 (March–December 1981): 345–64, and "Emerson and Abolition: The Silent Years, 1837–1844," *American Literature* 54, no. 4 (December 1982): 560–75; and Marjory M. Moody, "The Evolution of Emerson as an Abolitionist," *American Literature* 17 (March 1945–January 1946): 1–21.

48. Emerson to John Boynton Hill, 12 March 1822, in Ralph L. Rusk, ed., *The Letters of Ralph Waldo Emerson* (New York: Columbia University Press, 1939), vol. 1, p. 107.

49. Emerson to John Boynton Hill, 28 February 1823, in Rusk, *Letters of Ralph Waldo Emerson*, vol. 1, p. 130.

50. Journal entry for October 1837, in Edward Waldo Emerson and Waldo Emerson Forbes, eds., *Journals of Ralph Waldo Emerson, 1820–1872* (Boston and New York: Houghton Mifflin, 1909), vol. 4, pp. 312–13.

51. Nasaw, *Schooled to Order*, p. 31.

52. Mann to Mary Mann, 4 March 1849, in Mann Papers, MHS.

53. *New York (Daily) Times*, 24 July 1854.

54. Mann, *New Dangers to Freedom*, pp. 14, 30.

55. Mann, *The Institution of Slavery: Speech of the Hon. Horace Mann, of Massachusetts, on the Institution of Slavery. Delivered in the U.S. House of Representatives, August 17, 1852* (Boston: n.p., 1852), p. 22. See also Mann, *New Dangers to Freedom*, p. 30, and Mann to Mr. and Mrs. Combe, 5 December 1851, Combe Papers, NLS.

56. Larry Gara, "Slavery and the Slave Power: A Crucial Distinction," *Civil War History* 15 (1969): 6. See also Russell B. Nye, "The Slave Power Conspiracy: 1830–1860," *Science and Society* 10 (1946): 262–74.

57. Mann to Mary Peabody Mann, 23 April 1848, Mann Papers, MHS.

58. Mann, *The Institution of Slavery*, p. 24.

59. See Mann to Mr. and Mrs. Combe, 15 November 1850, in Combe Papers, NLS. For a more comprehensive analysis of the Speakership debate at the start of the 31st Congress, see Messerli, *Horace Mann*, p. 507.

60. Mann to Mary Mann, 15 March 1850, Mann Papers, MHS.

61. See Mann to Mary Mann, 9 and 13 June 1848, Mann Papers, MHS. He writes: "it is said we have yielded to the demands of the South again and again; that they always ask for once more; and that we may yield and yield forever, and still they will require us to do it *once more.*"

62. Ralph Waldo Emerson, "The Fugitive Slave Law" (1851), in Edward Waldo Emerson, ed., *The Complete Works of Ralph Waldo Emerson*, vol. 11, *Miscellanies* (Boston and New York: Houghton Mifflin, 1911), p. 211. For an analysis of Emerson's hostility toward Daniel Webster over the Fugitive Slave Act issue, see Carl Straunch,

"The Background and Meaning of the 'Ode Inscribed to W. H. Channing,'" *Emerson Society Quarterly* 42 (1966 supplement): 3–14.

63. Emerson "The Fugitive Slave Law," p. 180.

64. Ibid., p. 206.

65. Horace Mann, *Speech on the Fugitive Slave Law, Delivered at Lancaster, May 19, 1851* (Boston: n.p., 1851), pp. 2–3.

66. Mann to Mary Mann, 8 and 14 March, 8, 14, 15, and 17 September 1850; Mann to Samuel Downer, 1 March 1850; Mann to Mr. and Mrs. Combe, 15 November 1850; Mann to Samuel Gridley Howe, 3 January [1851]; and *Speeches: Liberty and Miscellaneous Notes . . .* [1848], in an extract in which Mann outlines his reasons for accepting the Whig nomination. The date is doubtless post-1850, possibly even post-1854. All in Mann Papers, MHS.

67. Mann to Mary Mann, 14 March 1850, in Mann Papers, MHS.

68. Mann to Mary Mann, 18 and 28 August and 6, 15, 17, 20, and 21 September 1850; Mann to Samuel Downer, 22 December 1850; Mann to Mr. and Mrs. Combe, 5 December 1851 and 8 May 1852, in Mann Papers, MHS.

69. Mann to Mr. George Combe, 8 May 1852, in Mann, *Life and Works*, vol. 1, p. 364.

70. Miscellaneous—Education, 1854, Mann Papers, MHS.

71. Wendell Phillips quoted in Richard Hofstadter, *The American Political Tradition and the Men Who Made It* (1948; reprint, New York: Vintage Books, 1989), p. 150.

72. Parker, *Letter to the People of the United States*, pp. 63–64.

73. Journal entry for 18 February 1850, in Emerson and Forbes, *Journals of Ralph Waldo Emerson*, vol. 8, pp. 100–101.

74. Lewis P. Simpson, *Mind and the American Civil War: A Meditation on Lost Causes* (Baton Rouge: Louisiana State University Press, 1989), pp. 50, 35.

75. Mann to George Combe, 12 April 1849 and 15 November 1850; Mann to Samuel Gridley Howe, 22 February 1850; and Mann to Mary Mann, 28 December 1848 and 18 May 1850, Mann Papers, MHS.

76. Mann to Mary Mann, 6 February 1850, in Mann Papers, MHS.

77. Mann, *Speech of Horace Mann in the House of Representatives, 15 February 1850*, p.19.

78. Mann, *Fifth Annual Report*.

79. William R. Brock, *Parties and Political Conscience: American Dilemmas, 1840–1850* (New York: Kto Press, 1979), p. 140.

80. Somkin, *Unquiet Eagle*, p. 27.

6. When Is a Nation Not a Nation?

1. W. H. Furness to Charles Sumner, 9 November 1856, quoted in Larry Gara, "Slavery and the Slave Power: A Crucial Distinction," *Civil War History* 15 (1969): 17.

2. H. Bennet (New York), House of Representatives, 10 May 1854, *Congressional Globe,* 33d Cong., 1st sess., appendix, pp. 694–95; emphasis in original.

3. *Springfield (Daily) Republican,* 21 February 1854; emphasis in original. See also 3 and 6 March 1854.

4. Charles Francis Adams to Theodore Parker, 4 June 1854, in Theodore Parker Papers, Massachusetts Historical Society (hereafter MHS); C. W. Upham (Massachusetts), House of Representatives, 10 May 1854, *Congressional Globe,* 33d Cong., 1st sess., appendix, pp. 710–13, and "Kansas and Nebraska," *North American Review* 80, no. 166 (January 1855): 110.

5. Israel Washburn (Maine), House of Representatives, 10 May 1854, *Congressional Globe,* 33d Cong., 1st sess., appendix, pp. 714–15. This view was shared by some Democrats; see the speech of Thomas Davis (Rhode Island), House of Representatives, 9 May 1854, in ibid., pp. 636–42, and the *Springfield (Daily) Republican,* 8 February 1854.

6. *Albany Evening Journal,* 19 May 1854.

7. Ibid., 1 December 1854.

8. *Springfield (Daily) Republican,* 6 June 1854.

9. Amos A. Lawrence to Giles Richards, 1 June 1854, A. A. Lawrence, *Letterbook,* MHS.

10. Thomas Wentworth Higginson, sermon preached in Worcester, 4 June 1854. It appeared in the *Worcester Daily Spy* the following week and was later published in pamphlet form as *Massachusetts in Mourning* (Boston, 1854), p. 5. For similar sentiments, see Rev. Daniel March, *The Crisis of Freedom* (Nashua, N.H., 1854), pp. 5–9.

11. *Boston Courier,* 22 December 1854.

12. *Springfield (Daily) Republican,* 1 July 1854.

13. Ralph Waldo Emerson's second address on "The Fugitive Slave Law" (1854), in Edward Waldo Emerson, ed., *The Complete Works of Ralph Waldo Emerson,* vol. 11, *Miscellanies* (Boston and New York: Houghton Mifflin, 1911), p. 219.

14. Theodore Parker, *Some Thoughts on the New Assault upon Freedom in America, and the General State of the Country* (Boston, 1854), quoted in David Brion Davis, *The Slave Power Conspiracy and the Paranoid Style* (Baton Rouge: Louisiana State University Press, 1969), p. 60.

15. Josiah Quincy, *Address Illustrative of the Nature and Power of the Slave States and the Duties of the Free States,* 5 June 1856 (Boston: n.p., 1856); Higginson, *Massachusetts in Mourning,* p. 11.

16. *The North and the South* (New York: *New York Tribune* Office, 1854), pp. 6–8. This was a pamphlet reprinted from the *New York (Daily and Weekly) Tribune.*

17. *Albany Evening Journal,* 24 January 1854. See also *Springfield (Daily) Republican,* 23 October 1855 and 4 March 1856.

18. *The North and the South,* p. 21.

19. *New Hampshire Statesman,* 31 May 1856. See also Quincy, *Address Illustrative of the Nature and Power,* p. 4.

20. Edward Everett to Sir Henry Holland, 3 June 1856, Edward Everett Papers, MHS.

21. Samuel P. Chase to Theodore Parker, 23 June 1856, and John P. Hale to Theodore Parker, 25 May 1856, Parker Papers, MHS.

22. Robert Winthrop to J. H. Cifford, 6 July 1856, Winthrop Family Papers, MHS.

23. F. H. Morse to William Pitt Fessenden, 25 May 1856, William Pitt Fessenden Papers, Library of Congress.

24. George Templeton Strong, diary entries for 26 and 29 May and 8 June 1856, in Allan Nevins and Milton Halsey Thomas, eds., *The Diary of George Templeton Strong, 1835–1875*, 4 vols. (New York: Macmillan, 1952), vol. 2, pp. 274–78.

25. William E. Gienapp argues that Strong had defended the South prior to Brooks's attack on Sumner and only afterward came to regard southerners as barbarians. William E. Gienapp, "The Crime against Sumner: The Caning of Charles Sumner and the Rise of the Republican Party," *Civil War History* 25 (September 1979): 218–45. Strong certainly defended the South's ownership of slaves against the northern abolitionists, but even then he drew a clear distinction between slaveholding and "the expediency of slave-holding." In general, Strong's comments on the South were far from favorable. Strong, 9 September and 25 November 1850, in Nevins and Thomas, *Diary*, pp. 20, 29–30.

26. *Springfield (Daily) Republican*, 17 May 1856.

27. Henry Wilson (Massachusetts), Senate, 13 June 1856, *Congressional Globe*, 34th Cong., 1st sess., pp. 1400–1403. See also Edward Stabler to William Pitt Fessenden, 16 June 1856, Fessenden Papers, Library of Congress; and E. Peake to Lyman Trumbull, 26 May 1856, Lyman Trumbull Papers, Library of Congress.

28. Horace Greeley to Mrs. R. M. Whipple, 8 June 1856, Horace Greeley Papers, Library of Congress. For responses to the attacks on Greeley and Sumner and to the Willard hotel incident, see *Albany Evening Journal*, 31 January 1856; *New York (Daily) Times*, 24, 26–28 May, 3, 4, 6 June, and 14, 16, 22, 25 July 1856.

29. Jeter Allen Isely, *Horace Greeley and the Republican Party, 1853–1861* (Princeton, N.J.: Princeton University Press, 1947), p. 186.

30. Theodore Parker, *A Sermon Preached at the Music Hall, Boston, 25 May 1856* (Boston: n.p., 1856), p. 8.

31. The exception was Herbert, who was arrested for killing the waiter. Brooks probably would have been censured by Congress—procedures to do so were under way—but he died before any action could be taken against him.

32. Apart from newspaper coverage, which was extensive, see Henry C. Fish, *The Voice of Our Brother's Blood, Its Source and Its Summons: A Discourse Occasioned by the Sumner and Kansas Outrages* (Newark, N.J.: n.p., 1856), pp. 6–7; and James Watson Webb, *Slavery and Its Tendencies: A Letter from General J[ames] Watson Webb to the New York Courier and Enquirer, May 24, 1856* (Washington, D.C.: n.p., 1856), p. 3.

33. Quincy, *Address Illustrative of the Nature and Power*, pp. 7–8.

34. *New York (Daily) Times*, 22 July 1856. See also the *Boston Daily Evening Transcript*, 23, 26 May and 3 June 1856.

35. *New York (Weekly) Evening Post*, 23 May 1856.

36. Strong, 29 May 1856, in Nevins and Thomas, *Diary*, vol. 2, pp. 275–76.

37. *New York (Daily) Times,* 6 March 1854.

38. Henry Wilson (Massachusetts), Senate, 13 June 1856, and Israel Washburn (Maine), House of Representatives, 21 June 1856, in *Congressional Globe,* 34th Cong., 1st sess., pp. 1401–3 and appendix, pp. 635–41.

39. George Melville Weston, *The Poor Whites of the South; The Federal Union: It Must Be Preserved, No. 1; Southern Slavery Reduces Northern Wages; Will the South Dissolve the Union?* and *Who Are Sectional?* (Washington, D.C.: n.p., 1856); *The Progress of Slavery in the United States* (Washington, D.C.: n.p., 1857); and *Disunion—Its Remedy* (Washington, D.C.: n.p., 1860).

40. Weston, *The Progress of Slavery,* p. 51.

41. Quincy, *Address Illustrative of the Nature and Power,* pp. 27–28.

42. Ralph Waldo Emerson, "The Assault upon Mr. Sumner," in Emerson, *Complete Works,* vol. 11, p. 248; and journal entry for February 1857, in Edward Waldo Emerson and Waldo Emerson Forbes, eds., *Journals of Ralph Waldo Emerson* (Boston and New York: Houghton Mifflin, 1909), vol. 9, p. 121.

43. Nathaniel Prentiss Banks, *Address Delivered at the Merchant's Exchange, New York, on Thursday, September 25, 1856* (Republican Documents, 1856), pp. 6–12, in Nathaniel Prentiss Banks Papers, Library of Congress.

44. The phrase was Richard Henry Dana's, quoted in William E. Gienapp, *The Origins of the Republican Party, 1852–1856* (1987; paperback reprint, New York and Oxford: Oxford University Press, 1988), p. 192. Gienapp argues that Seward's speeches "The Dominant Class in the Republic" and "The Political Parties of the Day," taken together with his 1855 speeches at Albany and Buffalo, constituted "the most carefully reasoned statement of Republican principles until after 1856" (p. 361 n. 54).

45. William H. Seward, "Speech at Albany," 12 October 1855; see also his speech at Buffalo a few days later (19 October 1855), both in George E. Baker, ed., *The Works of William H. Seward,* 5 vols. (Boston: n.p., 1853–1884), vol. 4, pp. 226–27, 243 ff.

46. William H. Seward, "Speech at a Whig Mass Meeting," 29 October 1844, in Baker, *Works,* vol. 3, pp. 269–70.

47. Webb, *Slavery and Its Tendencies,* p. 2.

48. John Murray Forbes quoted in Bruce Levine, *Half Slave and Half Free: The Roots of Civil War* (New York: Hill and Wang, 1992), p. 123.

49. David M. Potter, *The Impending Crisis, 1848–1861* (New York and London: Harper and Row, 1976), p. 256. See also William E. Gienapp, "Nativism and the Creation of a Republican Majority in the North before the Civil War," *Journal of American History* 72, no. 3 (December 1985): 186–205; Fred Harvey Harrington, "The First Northern Victory," *Journal of Southern History* 5 (1939): 186–205; and Joel Silbey, "After 'The First Northern Victory': The Republican Party Comes to Congress, 1855–1856," *Journal of Interdisciplinary History* 20, no. 2 (autumn 1989): 1–24.

50. John P. Hale to Theodore Parker, 16 December 1855, Parker Papers, MHS.

51. Edwin Barber Morgan to his brother, 3 February 1856, in Temple R. Hollcroft, ed., "A Congressman's Letters on the Speaker Election in the Thirty-fourth Congress," *Mississippi Valley Historical Review* 43 (1954): 445.

52. William Herndon to Theodore Parker, 16 February 1856, Parker Papers, MHS. For additional examples of this kind of sentiment, see O. H. White to Banks, 6 February 1856; Charles Congdon to Banks, 5 February 1856; A. J. Banks to Banks, 6 February 1856; J. V. Peck to Banks, 4 February 1856; Isaac Parker to Banks, 6 February 1856; and William E. Waller to Banks, 7 February 1856, Banks Papers, Library of Congress.

53. *Albany Evening Journal,* 4 February 1856. For similar responses in the press, see *New York (Daily) Tribune,* 8 December 1855; *New York (Daily) Times,* 28 December 1855 and 4, 9 February 1856; *Springfield (Daily) Republican,* 25 February 1856; *Philadelphia North American and United States Gazette,* 24 December 1855.

54. Weston, *Who Are Sectional?* p. 7.

55. Charles Sumner to the Massachusetts Committee, 25 February 1856, in *The Complete Works of Charles Sumner,* 15 vols. (1856; reprint, Boston: Houghton Mifflin, 1900), vol. 5, p. 97.

56. Potter, *The Impending Crisis,* p. 259.

57. Eric Foner, *Free Soil, Free Labor, Free Men: The Ideology of the Republican Party before the Civil War* (New York: Oxford University Press, 1970), p. 227.

58. *New York (Daily) Times,* 23 June 1854.

59. Reinhold Niebuhr and Alan Heimert, *A Nation so Conceived: Reflections on the History of America from Its Early Visions to Its Present Power* (London: Faber and Faber, 1963), pp. 31–32.

60. *New York (Daily) Tribune,* 25 April and 4 July 1856.

61. *New York (Daily) Times,* 22 September 1851.

62. *Albany Evening Journal,* 24 December 1842.

63. Perry Miller, *The Life of the Mind in America: From the Revolution to the Civil War* (New York: Harcourt, Brace and World, 1965), p. 12.

64. Richard Carwardine, *Evangelicals and Politics in Antebellum America* (New Haven, Conn., and London: Yale University Press, 1993), pp. 241, 321.

65. Charles A. Dana quoted in Tyler Anbinder, *Nativism and Slavery: The Northern Know-Nothings and the Politics of the 1850s* (New York and Oxford: Oxford University Press, 1992), p. 278.

66. *Springfield (Daily) Republican,* 21 February 1854.

67. Samuel J. May, *Liberty or Slavery: The Only Question* (Syracuse, N.Y.: n.p., 1856). This was a Fourth of July oration that May delivered at Jamestown.

68. Weston, *The Federal Union: It Must Be Preserved,* pp. 4–5; *Will the South Dissolve the Union?* p. 6.

69. Gideon Welles to Preston King, 25 November 1854; Welles to General Houston, 26 February and 23 April 1855; and Welles to James F. Babcock, 14 March 1855, Gideon Welles Papers, Library of Congress.

70. *New York (Daily) Tribune,* 25 November 1856.

71. *Springfield (Daily) Republican,* 8 November 1856.

72. For an extended analysis of Republican support in the 1856 election, see Gienapp, *Origins of the Republican Party,* pp. 413–48.

73. *Springfield (Daily) Republican*, 5 May 1857.

74. William H. Seward to Theodore Parker, 11 October 1853, Parker Papers, MHS.

75. Stephen A. Douglas, House of Representatives, 3 June 1844, *Congressional Globe*, 28th Cong., 1st sess., appendix, p. 601.

76. B. D. Murray et al. to John P. Hale, 20 May 1854, John P. Hale Papers, New Hampshire Historical Society.

77. Robert Everest to Theodore Parker, 7 November 1856, Parker Papers, MHS.

78. *Albany Evening Journal*, 2 October 1855.

79. Ibid., 8 December 1855.

80. William J. Cooper, *Liberty and Slavery: Southern Politics to 1860* (New York: Alfred A. Knopf, 1983), p. 38.

81. Rev. Henry Dana Ward, 25 May 1856, *Diary*, Manuscript Division, New York Public Library. The line "to escape the Southern masters" was scored through in the diary.

82. Horace Greeley quoted in Bertram Wyatt-Brown, *Yankee Saints and Southern Sinners* (Baton Rouge: Louisiana State University Press, 1985), pp. 6–7.

83. Michael Holt, *The Political Crisis of the 1850s* (New York: John Wiley and Sons, 1978), p. 190.

84. Peter Dobkin Hall, *The Organization of American Culture, 1700–1900: Private Institutions, Elites, and the Origins of American Nationality* (New York: New York University Press, 1984), pp. 214–15.

85. Abraham Lincoln, "Speech at Peoria, Illinois," 16 October 1854, in Roy P. Basler, ed., *The Collected Works of Abraham Lincoln*, 11 vols. (1953; reprint, New Brunswick, N.J.: Rutgers University Press, 1988), vol. 2, p. 255.

86. Earl J. Hess, *Liberty, Virtue, and Progress: Northerners and Their War for the Union* (New York: New York University Press, 1988), p. 1.

87. Strong, 2 July 1856, in Nevins and Thomas, *Diary*, p. 283.

88. This point is made in Major L. Wilson, *Space, Time and Freedom: The Quest for Nationality and the Irrepressible Conflict, 1815–1861* (Westport, Conn.: Greenwood Press, 1974), pp. 188–89.

89. Rush Welter, *The Mind of America, 1820–1860* (New York and London: Columbia University Press, 1975), p. 39.

90. Edward Everett to Henry Holland, 6 April 1857; see also Everett Diary, 24 January, 10 May, 17 June, 25 July 1856, Everett Papers, MHS.

91. Amos Lawrence quoted in Richard H. Abbott, *Cotton and Capital: Boston Businessmen and Antislavery Reform, 1854–1868* (Amherst: University of Massachusetts Press, 1991), p. 53; Amos A. Lawrence to Charles Hale, 8 October 1858, A. A. Lawrence, *Letterbook*, MHS.

92. Peter Alter, *Nationalism*, 2d ed. (London: Edward Arnold, 1994), p. 1.

93. *New York (Daily) Times*, 26 May 1854.

94. Emerson quoted in James Elliot Cabot, *A Memoir of Ralph Waldo Emerson*, 2 vols. (Boston: n.p., 1887), vol. 2, pp. 600–601.

95. Hall, *Organization of American Culture*, p. 221. On this point, see also Lewis P.

Simpson, *Mind and the American Civil War: A Meditation on Lost Causes* (Baton Rouge: Louisiana State University Press, 1989), pp. 61–64.

96. Theodore Parker to William Herndon, 17 November 1856, Parker Papers, MHS.

97. Hall, *Organization of American Culture*, p. 216.

Epilogue: From Hell to Holy

1. *Springfield (Daily) Republican*, 8 January 1857.

2. Amos A. Lawrence to Hon. A. B. Ely, 7 August 1856, A. A. Lawrence, *Letterbook*, Massachusetts Historical Society (hereafter MHS).

3. Amos A. Lawrence to Moses G. Cobb, 7 and 8 July 1857, A. A. Lawrence Papers, MHS.

4. James A. Dorr, *Justice to the South!* (New York: n.p., 1856), p. 4.

5. Amos A. Lawrence to Charles Hale, 8 October 1858, A. A. Lawrence, *Letterbook*, MHS.

6. Amos A. Lawrence to Moses G. Cobb, 6 October 1858, A. A. Lawrence Papers, MHS.

7. Nathaniel Hawthorne to Horatio Bridge, 26 May 1861, in Louis P. Masur, ed., *The Real War Will Never Get in the Books: Selections from Writers during the Civil War* (1993; reprint, New York and Oxford: Oxford University Press, 1995), p. 164.

8. Frederick Douglass, "Emancipation, Racism, and the Work before Us," address delivered in Philadelphia, 4 December 1863, in Masur, *The Real War*, pp. 118–19.

9. Harriet Beecher Stowe, "The Chimney Corner," *Atlantic Monthly*, 15 January 1865, in Masur, *The Real War*, p. 251.

10. Merrill D. Peterson, *The Jefferson Image in the American Mind* (New York: Oxford University Press, 1960), p. 218; Randall C. Jimerson, *The Private Civil War: Popular Thought during the Sectional Conflict* (Baton Rouge: Louisiana State University Press, 1988), p. 36.

11. Henry Adams to Charles Francis Adams, Jr., 22 May 1862, in Masur, *The Real War*, p. 8.

12. *Boston Post*, 16 May 1861.

13. Henry James, *Hawthorne* (London: English Men of Letters Series, 1879), p. 144, quoted in George M. Fredrickson, *The Inner Civil War: Northern Intellectuals and the Crisis of the Union* (1965; paperback reprint, New York: Harper and Row, 1968), p. 1.

14. Abraham Lincoln, "First Inaugural Address," 4 March 1861, in Roy F. Basler, ed., *The Collected Works of Abraham Lincoln*, 11 vols. (1953; reprint, New Brunswick, N.J.: Rutgers University Press, 1988), vol. 4, p. 269.

15. Ibid., p. 266.

16. Abraham Lincoln, "Address at Gettysburg," 19 November 1863, in ibid., vol. 7, p. 23.

17. Gladstone quoted in Peter J. Parish, *The American Civil War* (New York: Alfred A. Knopf, 1975), p. 448.

18. Richard E. Beringer et al., *Why the South Lost the Civil War* (Athens, Ga., and London: Georgia University Press, 1986), p. 77.

19. See Drew Gilpin Faust, *Confederate Nationalism: Ideology and Identity in the Civil War South* (Baton Rouge: Louisiana State University Press, 1988); Gary Gallagher, *The Confederate War* (Cambridge, Mass., and London: Harvard University Press, 1997).

20. Gallagher, *The Confederate War*, p. 73.

21. Parish, *The American Civil War*, p. 637.

22. Reid Mitchell, *Civil War Soldiers: Their Expectations and Their Experiences* (1988; reprint, New York: Simon and Schuster, 1989), p. 1.

23. James M. McPherson, *What They Fought For, 1861–1865* (Baton Rouge: Louisiana State University Press, 1994), pp. 9, 28.

24. Peter J. Parish, "The Road Not Quite Taken: The Constitution of the Confederate States of America," in Thomas J. Barron, Owen Dudley Edwards, and Patricia J. Storey, eds., *Constitutions and National Identity* (Edinburgh: Quadriga, 1993), p. 113.

25. Quotation from Washington's "Farewell Address," 1796, in Robert Birley, ed., *Speeches and Documents in American History* (New York: Oxford University Press, 1951), vol. 1, p. 223.

26. Jefferson Davis, "Message to the Confederate Congress," 29 April 1861, in Birley, *Speeches and Documents*, vol. 2, p. 261. Davis was referring to Article X of the Bill of Rights.

27. John Lothrop Motley, "The Causes of the American Civil War: A Paper Contributed to the *London Times*" (New York, 1861), in Frank Freidel, ed., *Union Pamphlets of the Civil War, 1861–1865*, 2 vols. (Cambridge, Mass.: Harvard University Press, 1967), vol. 1, pp. 31, 42, 48, 51. Motley's article first appeared in the paper on 23 and 24 May 1861.

28. Abraham Lincoln, "Speech at Indianapolis," 11 February 1861; "Message to Congress in Special Session," 4 July 1861; and "Annual Message to Congress," 3 December 1861, in Basler, *Collected Works of Abraham Lincoln*, vol. 4, pp. 196, 426; and vol. 5, p. 51.

29. Clement Laird Vallandigham, "The Great Civil War in America" (speech in the House of Representatives, 14 January 1863), in Freidel, *Union Pamphlets*, vol. 2, p. 700.

30. Lincoln to Erastus Corning et al., 12 June 1863, in Basler, *Collected Works of Abraham Lincoln*, vol. 6, p. 264.

31. John O'Sullivan quoted in Fredrickson, *The Inner Civil War*, pp. 132, 144.

32. Fredrickson, *The Inner Civil War*, p. 132.

33. Charles Janeway Stillé, "How a Free People Conduct a Long War: A Chapter from English History" (Philadelphia, 1862), reproduced in Freidel, *Union Pamphlets*, vol. 1, p. 397.

34. Fredrickson, *The Inner Civil War*, pp. 133, 135.

35. Ibid., p. 150. For an extended and detailed discussion of the intellectual response to the war, see especially pp. 130–50.

36. Ibid., p. 185. The poem under discussion is James Russell Lowell's "Com-

memoration Ode" (1865), which can be found, together with comments on it, in Richard Marius, ed., *The Columbia Book of Civil War Poetry: From Whitman to Walcott* (New York and Chichester: Columbia University Press, 1994), p. 372.

37. McPherson, *What They Fought For*, p. 23.

38. Liah Greenfeld, *Nationalism: Five Roads to Modernity* (Cambridge, Mass., and London: Harvard University Press, 1992), p. 473.

39. Abraham Lincoln, letter to Horace Greeley, 22 August 1862, in Basler, *Collected Works of Abraham Lincoln*, vol. 5, p. 388.

40. Lincoln, "Gettysburg Address" and "First Inaugural," in Basler, *Collected Works of Abraham Lincoln*, vols. 7, p. 23; vol. 4, p. 271.

41. Frances E. W. Harper, "We Are All Bound up Together," from *Proceedings of the Eleventh Women's Rights Convention* (1866), in Karen L. Kilcup, ed., *Nineteenth-Century American Women Writers: An Anthology* (Cambridge, Mass., and Oxford: Blackwell, 1997), p. 157.

42. Charles Sumner, "Are We a Nation?" (1867), quoted in Greenfeld, *Nationalism*, p. 480.

43. Anthony D. Smith, *The Ethnic Origins of Nations* (1983; reprint, London: Blackwell, 1993), pp. 206–7.

44. Gerald F. Linderman, *Embattled Courage: The Experience of Combat in the American Civil War* (New York: Free Press, 1987), pp. 271–80.

45. Paul Buck, *The Road to Reunion* (Boston: Little, Brown, 1937); Stuart McConnell, *Glorious Contentment: The Grand Army of the Republic, 1865–1900* (Chapel Hill: University of North Carolina Press, 1992), p. xv; Celia O'Leary, "'American All': Reforging a National Brotherhood, 1876–1917," *History Today* 44 (October 1994): 19–27.

46. McConnell, *Glorious Contentment*, pp. 220–23.

47. Gaines M. Foster, *Ghosts of the Confederacy: Defeat, the Lost Cause, and the Emergence of the New South* (1987; reprint, New York and Oxford: Oxford University Press, 1988), p. 69.

48. O'Leary, "'American All,'" p. 26.

49. Merrill D. Peterson, *Lincoln in American Memory* (1994; reprint, New York: Oxford University Press, 1995), p. 29; Scott A. Sandage, "A Marble House Divided: The Lincoln Memorial, the Civil Rights Movement, and the Politics of Memory, 1939–1963," *Journal of American History* 80, no. 1 (June 1993): 135–67.

50. Sherman quoted in Linderman, *Embattled Courage*, pp. 283–84.

51. William Pencak, *For God and Country: The American Legion, 1919–1941* (Boston: Northeastern University Press, 1989), pp. 29–30.

52. Lincoln, "Message to Congress in Special Session," 4 July 1861, in Basler, *Collected Works of Abraham Lincoln*, vol. 4, p. 439.

Selected Bibliography

Manuscripts

John A. Andrew Papers, Massachusetts Historical Society
William Henry Anthon, *Letterbook,* New York Public Library
Appleton Family Papers, Massachusetts Historical Society
Nathaniel Prentiss Banks Papers, Library of Congress
Henry Whitney Bellows Papers, Massachusetts Historical Society
Simon Cameron Papers, Library of Congress
Zachariah Chandler Papers, Library of Congress
Schuyler Colfax Papers, Library of Congress
George Combe Papers, National Library of Scotland
Caleb Cushing Papers, Library of Congress
Richard Henry Dana, Jr., Papers, Massachusetts Historical Society
Dana Family Papers, Massachusetts Historical Society
Denison Papers, Library of Congress
James Rood Doolittle, *Letters* (1848–1892), New York Public Library
Edward Everett Papers, Massachusetts Historical Society
William Pitt Fessenden Papers (microfilm), Library of Congress
Azariah Flagg Papers, New York Public Library
Horace Greeley Papers, Library of Congress
Horace Greeley Papers, New Hampshire Historical Society
Horace Greeley Papers, New York Public Library
Greeley-Colfax Papers (microfilm) New York Public Library
John P. Hale Papers, Dartmouth College
John P. Hale Papers, New Hampshire Historical Society
John P. Hale Scrapbook, New Hampshire Historical Society
Hale-Chandler Papers, Dartmouth College
Hannibal Hamlin Papers (microfilm), Library of Congress
Hickling-Nye Papers, Massachusetts Historical Society
Thomas W. Higginson Papers, Houghton Library, Harvard University
Thomas W. Higginson Papers, Library of Congress
Amos Lawrence Papers, Massachusetts Historical Society
Amos A. Lawrence Papers, Massachusetts Historical Society
Amos A. Lawrence, *Letterbook,* Massachusetts Historical Society
Horace Mann Papers, Houghton Library, Harvard University

Horace Mann Papers, Massachusetts Historical Society
Edward McPherson Papers, Library of Congress
Frederick Law Olmsted Papers, Library of Congress
Harrison Gray Otis Papers, Massachusetts Historical Society
John Gorham Palfrey Papers, Houghton Library, Harvard University
Theodore Parker Papers (microfilm), Massachusetts Historical Society
Perry-Clarke Additions, Massachusetts Historical Society
Franklin Pierce Papers, New Hampshire Historical Society
Sears Family Papers, Massachusetts Historical Society
Sedwick II Papers, Massachusetts Historical Society
William H. Seward Papers, New York Public Library
Thaddeus Stevens Papers (microfilm), Library of Congress
Charles Sumner Papers (microfilm), Houghton Library, Harvard University
Charles Turner Torrey Papers, Congregational Library, Boston
Lyman Trumbull Papers, Library of Congress
John C. Underwood Papers, Library of Congress
Rev. Henry Dana Ward, *Diary*, New York Public Library
Israel Washburn, Jr., Papers, Library of Congress
Elihu B. Washburne Papers, Library of Congress
Daniel Webster Papers, New Hampshire Historical Society
Thurlow Weed Papers (microfilm), Library of Congress
Gideon Welles Papers, Library of Congress
Gideon Welles Papers, New York Public Library
Henry Wilson Papers, Library of Congress
Winthrop Family Papers, Massachusetts Historical Society
Horatio Woodman Papers, Massachusetts Historical Society

Published Primary Sources

Abbot, John Stevens Cabot. *South and North; or, Impressions Received during a Trip to Cuba and the South.* New York: n.p., 1860.
Adams, Henry. *The Education of Henry Adams.* Boston: Houghton Mifflin, 1973.
Adams, Nehemiah, D.D. *A South-Side View of Slavery; or, Three Months at the South, in 1854.* Boston: n.p., 1854.
Atwater, H. Cowles. *Incidents of a Southern Tour: Or, the South as Seen through Northern Eyes.* Boston: n.p., [1851].
Bailey, Gamaliel. *The Record of Sectionalism.* Washington, D.C.: n.p., 1856.
Baker, George E., ed. *The Works of William H. Seward.* 5 vols. Boston: n.p., 1853–1884.
Bartlett, John Russell. *Personal Narrative of Explorations and Incidents in Texas.* 2 vols. New York and London: n.p., 1854.
Basler, Roy, ed. *The Collected Works of Abraham Lincoln.* 11 vols. 1953. Reprint, New Brunswick, N.J.: Rutgers University Press, 1988.

Best, John Hardin, and Robert T. Sidwell. *The American Legacy of Learning: Readings in the History of Education.* Philadelphia and New York: J. B. Lippincott, 1967.

[Brown, David]. *The Planter: Or, Thirteen Years in the South, by a Northern Man.* Philadelphia: n.p., 1853.

Bryant, William Cullen. *Letters of a Traveller: Or, Notes of Things Seen in Europe and America.* 3d ed. New York: n.p., 1851.

Bryant, William Cullen II, and Thomas G. Voss, eds. *The Letters of William Cullen Bryant.* 3 vols. New York: Fordham University Press, 1975–1981.

Butts, R. Freeman, and Lawrence A. Cremin. *A History of Education in American Culture.* New York and London: Holt, Rinehart and Winston, 1953.

Cabot, James Elliot. *A Memoir of Ralph Waldo Emerson.* 2 vols. Boston: n.p., 1887.

Chamberlain, Joshua Lawrence. *The Passing of the Armies: The Last Campaign of the Armies.* 1915. Reprint, Gettysburg, Pa.: Stan Clark Military Books, 1994.

Chase, Salmon P. *The Diary and Correspondence of Salmon P. Chase.* Vol. 2 of *Annual Report of the American Historical Association.* Washington, D.C.: U.S. Government Printing Office, 1903.

Cheney, Mary B., ed. *Life and Letters of Horace Bushnell.* London: n.p., 1880.

[Clinton, Charles A.] *A Winter from Home.* New York: n.p., 1852.

Cobbe, Francis Power. *The Collected Works of Theodore Parker.* 15 vols. 1863–1871. Reprint, Boston: American Unitarian Association, 1907–1912.

Cutler, Wayne, ed. *North for Union: John Appleton's Journal of a Tour to New England Made by President Polk in June and July, 1847.* Nashville, Tenn.: Vanderbilt University Press, 1986.

Dana, Richard Henry III, ed. *Richard Henry Dana, Jr.: Speeches in Stirring Times.* Boston and New York: n.p., 1910.

Dewey, Mary E., ed. *Life and Letters of Catherine Maria Sedgwick.* New York: n.p., 1871.

Emerson, Edward Waldo, ed. *The Complete Works of Ralph Waldo Emerson.* Vol. 11, *Miscellanies.* Boston and New York: Houghton Mifflin, 1911.

Emerson, Edward Waldo, and Waldo Emerson Forbes, eds. *Journals of Ralph Waldo Emerson, 1820–1872.* Boston and New York: Houghton Mifflin, 1909.

Everett, Edward. *Orations and Speeches on Various Occasions.* 4 vols. Boston: n.p., 1850–1860.

Gara, Larry, ed. "A New Englander's View of Plantation Life: Letters of Edwin Hall to Cyrus Woodman, 1837." *Journal of Southern History* 18 (August 1952): 343–54.

Gilman, William H. et al., eds. *The Journals and Miscellaneous Notebooks of Ralph Waldo Emerson.* Cambridge, Mass.: Belknap Press of Harvard University Press, 1969.

Gladstone, T. H. *The Englishman in Kansas; or, Squatter Life and Border Warfare.* 1857. Reprint, Lincoln: University of Nebraska Press, 1971.

Godwin, Parke. *A Biography of William Cullen Bryant, with Extracts from His Private Correspondence.* 2 vols. New York: n.p., 1883.

———, ed. *The Prose Writings of Willian Cullen Bryant.* Vol. 1, *Essays, Tales, and Orations.* Vol. 2, *Travels, Addresses, and Comments.* New York: n.p., 1864.

Greeley, Horace. *Recollections of a Busy Life.* New York: n.p., 1868.

Gregg, William. *Essays on Domestic Industry: Or, an Enquiry into the Expediency of Establishing Cotton Manufactures in South Carolina.* Charleston, S.C.: n.p., 1845.

Hale, Sarah Josepha. *Northwood: Or, Life North and South, Showing the True Character of Both.* Rev. ed. New York: n.p., 1852.

———. *Sidney Romelee: A Tale of New England.* 3 vols. Boston: n.p., 1827.

———. *Sketches of American Character.* Boston: n.p., 1829.

Hall, D. H., ed. "A Yankee Tutor [Charles W. Holbrook] in the Old South." *New England Quarterly* 32 (1960): 82–91.

Hall, John D., ed. *Forty Years' Familiar Letters of James W. Alexander, D.D.* 2 vols. New York: n.p., 1860.

Hildreth, Richard. *Despotism in America; or, an Inquiry into the Nature and Results of the Slave-Holding System in the United States.* Boston: n.p., 1840.

Hollcroft, Temple R., ed. "A Congressman's [Edwin Barber Morgan (N.Y.), 1806–1881] Letters on the Speaker Election in the Thirty-fourth Congress." *Mississippi Valley Historical Review* 43 (1954): 444–58.

Hughes, Sarah Forbes, ed. *Letters and Recollections of John Murray Forbes.* 2 vols. Boston and New York: n.p., 1899.

Jay, William. *A Review of the Causes and Consequences of the Mexican War.* 1849. Reprint, New York: Books for Libraries Press, 1970.

Lawrence, William R. *Extracts from the Diary and Correspondence of the Late Amos Lawrence: With a Brief Account of Some Incidents in His Life.* Boston: n.p., 1855.

———. *Life of Amos A. Lawrence, with Extracts from His Diary and Correspondence, by His Son, William Lawrence.* Boston: n.p., 1888.

Lucid, Robert F., ed. *Journal of Richard Henry Dana, Jr.* 3 vols. Cambridge, Mass.: Belknap Press of Harvard University Press, 1968.

Manly, H. *The South Vindicated from the Treason and Fanaticism of the Northern Abolitionists.* Philadelphia: n.p., 1836. Reprint, New York: Greenwood Press, 1969.

Mann, Horace. *Slavery: Letters and Speeches.* Miami, Fla.: Mnemosyne Publishing, 1969.

Mann, Horace, and Charles Sumner. *American Slavery Discussed in Congress: Speeches of the Hon. Horace Mann and the Hon. Charles Sumner.* Introduction by Sir George Stephen. London: n.p., 1853.

Mann, Mary, and George C. Mann, eds. *Life and Works of Horace Mann.* 5 vols. 1865. Reprint, Washington, D.C.: National Education Association, 1937.

May, Samuel J. *The Fugitive Slave Law and Its Victims.* 1861. Reprint, New York: Books for Libraries Press, 1970.

McLaughlin, Charles Capen et al., eds. *The Papers of Frederick Law Olmsted.* 6 vols. (Baltimore: Johns Hopkins University Press, 1977–1992.

Mendall, Miss, and Miss Hosmer. *Notes of Travel and Life.* New York: n.p., 1853.

Merriam, George S. *The Life and Times of Samuel Bowles.* 2 vols. New York: n.p., 1885.

Moody, Loring. *Facts for the People: Showing the Relations of the United States Government to Slavery.* 1847. Reprint, New York: Books for Libraries Press, 1971.

Moody, Robert E., ed. *The Papers of Leverett Saltonstall, 1816–1845*. Vol. 1, *1816–1830*. Vol. 2, *1831–June 1940*. Boston: Massachusetts Historical Society, 1978, 1981.

Moore, John H. "The Abiel Abbot Journals: A Yankee Preacher in Charleston Society, 1818–1827." *South Carolina History Magazine* 68 (1967): 51–73.

Morris, Rev. Thomas Asbury. *Miscellany: Consisting of Essays, Biographical Sketches, and Notes of Travel*. Cincinnati: n.p., 1852.

Morrison, Samuel Eliot. *The Life and Letters of Harrison Gray Otis, Federalist, 1765–1848*. 2 vols. Boston: n.p., 1913.

Nevins, Allan, ed. *The Diary of Philip Hone, 1828–1851*. Rev. ed. New York: Dodd, Mead, 1936.

Nevins, Allan, and Milton Halsey Thomas, eds. *The Diary of George Templeton Strong*. 4 vols. New York: Macmillan, 1952.

Nichols, Dr. Thomas L. *Forty Years of American Life*. 2 vols. London: n.p., 1864.

Niven, John, ed. *The Salmon P. Chase Papers*. 3 vols. Kent, Ohio: Kent State University Press, 1993–1994.

O'Connor, John. *Wanderings of a Vagabond: An Autobiography*. Ed. John Morris [pseud.]. New York: n.p., 1873.

Olmsted, Frederick Law. *A Journey in the Back Country, 1853–1854*. 1860. Reprint, New York: Shocken Books, 1970.

———. *A Journey in the Seaboard Slave States; with Remarks on Their Economy*. New York: n.p., 1856.

———. *A Journey through Texas*. 1857. Reprint, Austin: University of Texas Press, 1978.

———. *Walks and Talks of an American Farmer in England*. 1852. Rev. ed., Columbus, Ohio: n.p., 1859.

Parker, Theodore. *Additional Speeches, Addresses, and Occasional Sermons*. Vol. 1. Boston: n.p., 1855.

Parsons, C. G., M.D. *Inside View of Slavery: Or, a Tour among the Planters*. Boston and Ohio: n.p., 1855.

Paxton, Philip [Samuel A. Hammett]. *A Stray Yankee in Texas*. New York: n.p., 1853.

Potter, Eliza. *A Hairdresser's Experience in High Life*. Cincinnati: n.p., 1859.

Redpath, James [pseud.]. *The Roving Editor: Or, Talks with Slaves in the Southern States*. New York: n.p., 1859.

Rusk, Ralph L., ed. *The Letters of Ralph Waldo Emerson*. New York: Columbia University Press, 1939.

Sargent, Nathan. *Public Men and Events, from the Commencement of Mr. Monroe's Administration, in 1817, to the Close of Mr. Fillmore's Administration, in 1853*. 2 vols. Philadelphia: n.p., 1875.

Sumner, Charles. *The Complete Works of Charles Sumner*. 15 vols. 1856. Reprint, Boston: Houghton Mifflin, 1900.

Tower, Rev. Philo. *Slavery Unmasked: Being a Truthful Narrative of a Three Years' Residence and Journeying in Eleven Southern States; to Which Is Added the Invasion of Kansas, Including the Last Chapter of Her Wrongs*. Rochester, N.Y.: n.p., 1856.

Tryon, Warren S., ed. *A Mirror for Americans: Life and Manners in the United States 1790–1870 as Recorded by American Travelers.* Vol. 2, "The Cotton Kingdom." Chicago: University of Chicago Press, 1952.

Weed, Harriet A., and Thurlow Weed Barnes, eds. *Life of Thurlow Weed, Including His Autobiography and a Memoir.* 2 vols. Boston: n.p., 1883–1884.

Weiss, John. *The Life and Correspondence of Theodore Parker.* 2 vols. New York and London: n.p., 1864.

Weston, George Melville. *The Progress of Slavery in the United States.* Washington, D.C.: n.p., 1857.

Whipple, Bishop Henry Benjamin. *Bishop Whipple's Southern Diary, 1843–1844.* Ed. Lester B. Shippee. Minneapolis: University of Minnesota Press, 1937.

William, Father [pseud.]. *Recollections of Rambles in the South.* New York: n.p., 1856.

Willis, Nathaniel Parker. *Health Trip to the Tropics.* New York: n.p., 1853.

Wiltse, Charles M. et al., eds. *The Papers of Daniel Webster: Speeches and Formal Writings.* 14 vols. Hanover, N.H., and London: University Press of New England, 1974–1989.

Younger, Edward, ed. "A Yankee Reports on Virginia, 1842–1843: Letters of John Adam Kasson." *Virginia Historical Magazine* 56 (October 1948): 408–30.

Newspapers and Periodicals

Albany Evening Journal
American Quarterly Review (Philadelphia)
American Review: A Whig Journal of Politics, Literature, Art and Science (Philadelphia)
Atlas and Daily Bee (Boston)
Boston Daily Advertiser
Boston (Daily) Courier
Boston (Daily) Evening Transcript
Boston Post
Boston Semi-Weekly Advertiser
Godey's Lady's Book and Ladies' American Magazine (Philadelphia)
Harper's (New) Monthly Magazine (New York)
Hunt's Merchants Magazine and Commercial Review (New York)
Massachusetts Quarterly Review (Boston)
New Englander (New Haven)
New Hampshire (Daily) Patriot (Concord)
New Hampshire Statesman
New York Evening Post
New York (Weekly) Evening Post
New York Herald
New York Times
New York (Daily) Tribune

New York (Weekly) Tribune
North American and United States Gazette (Philadelphia)
North American Review (Boston)
Pittsburgh Allegheny Gazette
Pittsburgh American
Pittsburgh (Daily) Gazette and Advertiser
Pittsburgh Weekly Dispatch and Temperance Banner
Springfield (Daily) Republican

Pamphlets

Adams, Charles Francis. *What Makes Slavery a Question of National Concern?* Boston, 1855.

Address of the Committee Appointed by a Public Meeting, held at Faneuil Hall, September 24, 1846, for the Purpose of Considering the Recent Case of Kidnapping from Our Soil, and of Taking Measures to Prevent the Recurrence of Similar Outrages. Boston, 1846.

Allen, Rev. Geo. *An Appeal to the People of Massachusetts on the Texas Question.* Boston, 1844.

Andrew, John A. *Address of His Excellency, John A. Andrew, to the Two Branches of the Legislature of Massachusetts.* Senate Document No. 2. Boston, 1861.

Anon. *The North and the South.* New York: *New York Tribune* Office, 1854.

Appleton, General James. *The Missouri Compromise: Or, the Extension of the Slave Power.* Boston, n.d.

Appleton, Nathan. *Letter to the Hon. Wm. C. Rives, of Virginia, on Slavery and the Union.* Boston, 1860.

——. *Speech in Reply to Mr. McDuffie, of South Carolina, on the Tariff. House of Representatives, May 30, 1832.* Washington, D.C., 1832.

Banks, Nathaniel Prentiss. *Address of His Excellency Nathaniel Prentiss Banks to the Two Branches of the Legislature of Massachusetts.* Senate Document No. 1. Boston, 1858.

——. *Address of Hon. N. P. Banks . . . Delivered from the Steps of the Merchants' Exchange . . . September 25th, 1856.* New York: Republican Documents, 1856.

——. *A Letter to Samuel B. Ruggles, Esq., of New York.* New York, 1856.

Batchelder, S. *The Responsibility of the North in Relation to Slavery.* Cambridge, Mass., 1856.

Beecher, Henry Ward. *A Discourse Delivered at the Plymouth Church, Brooklyn, New York, upon Thanksgiving Day, Nov. 25, 1847.* New York, 1848.

Boutwell, George S. *Address of His Excellency—to the Two Branches of the Legislature of Massachusetts.* Senate Document No. 3. Boston, 1851.

Briggs, George N. *Address of His Excellency—to the Two Branches of the Legislature of Massachusetts.* Boston, 1844, 1846, 1847, 1848, 1849, 1850.

Bushnell, Horace. *Barbarism the First Danger.* New York: American Home Missionary Society, 1847.

————. *A Discourse on the Slavery Question: Delivered in the North Church, Hartford, January 10, 1839.* Hartford, Conn., 1839.

————. *Politics under the Law of God: A Discourse Delivered in the North Congregational Church, Hartford, on the Annual Fast of 1844.* Hartford, Conn., 1844.

Child, David Lee. *The Despotism of Freedom: A Speech at the First Anniversary of the New England Anti-Slavery Society.* Boston: Abolitionists' Library No. 1, 1834.

Clifford, John H. *Address of His Excellency—to the Two Branches of the Legislature of Massachusetts.* Boston, 1853.

A Conservative Whig. *The Duty of Conservative Whigs in the Present Crisis: A Letter to the Hon. Rufus Choate.* Boston, 1856.

Davis, John. *Address of His Excellency—to the Two Branches of the Legislature of Massachusetts.* Boston, 1841.

Dorr, James A. *Justice to the South!* New York, 1856.

Everett, Edward. *Address of His Excellency to the Two Branches of the Legislature on the Organization of the Government for the Political Year Commencing January 6, 1836.* House Document No. 6. Boston, 1836.

————. *Address of His Excellency. . . . January 3, 1838.* House Document No. 3. Boston, 1838.

————. *Address of His Excellency . . . January 2, 1839.* Senate Document No. 1. Boston, 1839.

Everett, Edward et al. *The Nebraska Question, Comprising Speeches in the United States Senate by. . . .* Boston, 1854.

Fish, Henry C. *Freedom or Despotism. The Voice of Our Brother's Blood: Its Source and Its Summons.* Newark, N.J., 1856.

A Former Resident of Slave States. *Influence of Slavery upon the White Population.* New York and Boston: Anti-Slavery Tracts No. 9, n.d.

Foster, Eden B. *A North-Side View of Slavery: A Sermon on the Crime against Freedom in Kansas and Washington, Preached at Henniker, N.H., August 31, 1856.* Concord, N.H., 1856.

Gannett, Rev. Ezra S. *Relation of the North to Slavery: A Discourse Preached in the Federal Street Meetinghouse in Boston on Sunday, June 11, 1854.* Boston, 1854.

Gardner, H. J. *Address of His Excellency—to the Two Branches of the Legislature of Massachusetts.* Boston, 1855, 1856, 1857.

Hedrick, Benjamin S. *Are North Carolinians Freemen?* Boston, [1856].

Higginson, Thomas Wentworth. *Massachusetts in Mourning: A Sermon Preached in Worcester, on Sunday, June 4, 1854.* Boston, 1854.

Lafon, Thomas. *The Great Obstruction to the Conversion of Souls at Home and Abroad.* Boston, 1843.

Mann, Horace. *Letters on the Extension of Slavery into California and New Mexico; and on the Duty of Congress to Provide the Trial by Jury for Alleged Fugitive Slaves.* West Newton, Mass., 1850.

————. *New Dangers to Freedom, and New Duties for Its Defenders: A Letter by the Hon. Horace Mann, to His Constituents, May 3, 1850.* Boston, 1850.

————. *Speech in the House, February 23, 1849, on Slavery in the U.S. and the Slave Trade in the District of Columbia.* Boston, 1849.

————. *Speech of Horace Mann, of Massachusetts, on the Subject of Slavery in the Territories, and the Consequences of a Dissolution of the Union, House of Representatives, February 15, 1850.* Boston, 1850.

————. *Speech on the Fugitive Slave Law, Delivered at Lancaster, May 19, 1851.* Boston, 1851.

————. *Speech on the Institution of Slavery, in the House of Representatives, August 17, 1852.* Washington, D.C., 1852.

————. *Speech on the Right of Congress to Legislate for the Territories and Its Duty to Exclude Slavery Therefrom; to Which Is Added a Letter from Martin Van Buren and Joshua Leavitt.* Boston, 1848.

March, Rev. Daniel. *The Crisis of Freedom: Remarks on the Duty which All Christian Men and Good Citizens Owe to Their Country in the Present State of Public Affairs.* Nashua, N.H., 1854.

May, Samuel J. *"Liberty or Slavery, the Only Question." Oration: Delivered on the Fourth of July, 1856, at Jamestown, Chatauque Co., New York.* Syracuse, N.Y., 1856.

Morris, Rev. Robert D. *Slavery: Its Nature, Evils, and Remedy: A Sermon Preached to the Congregation of the Presbyterian Church, Newtown, Pennsylvania, July 27, 1845.* Philadelphia, 1845.

A Northern Presbyter. *A Letter of Inquiry to Ministers of the Gospel of All Denominations, on Slavery.* Boston, 1854.

Nott, Samuel. *The Necessities and Wisdom of 1861. A Supplement to the Sixth Edition of* Slavery and the Remedy. Boston, 1861.

————. *The Present Crisis: With a Reply and Appeal to European Advisers.* Boston, 1860.

————. *Slavery, and the Remedy; or, Principles and Suggestions for a Remedial Code.* 1st and 5th eds., with *A Review of the Supreme Court in the Case of Dred Scott.* New York, 1856, 1857.

Palfrey, John Gorham. *An Address to the Society of Middlesex Husbandmen and Manufacturers, Delivered at Concord, October 7, 1846.* Cambridge, Mass., 1846.

————. *Five Year's Progress of the Slave Power: A Series of Papers.* Boston, 1852.

————. *Papers on the Slave Power.* Boston, 1846.

Parker, Theodore. *Letter to the People of the United States Touching the Matter of Slavery.* Boston, 1848.

Peabody, Andrew Preston. *Position and Duties of the North with Regard to Slavery.* Newburyport, Mass., 1847.

Quincy, Josiah. *Address Illustrative of the Nature and Power of the Slave States and the Duties of the Free States.* Boston, 1856.

————. *Whig Policy Analyzed and Illustrated.* Boston, 1856.

Report and Declaration of the Joint Special Committee Protesting against the Hostile Acts of South Carolina. Massachusetts Senate Document No. 31, 1845. Response by a Member of Congress from South Carolina. *Massachusetts and South Carolina: An Examination of the Controversy between Them.* Washington, D.C., 1845.

Rockwood, Rev. S. L. *Rev. S. L. Rockwood's Sermon upon the "Signs of the Times."* Massachusetts, 1854.

Samuel Hoar's Expulsion from Charleston. Old South Leaflets No. 140. Reprint of Senate Document No. 4, Commonwealth of Massachusetts. Boston, 1845.

Sumner, Charles. *The Slave Oligarchy and Its Usurpation.* Washington, D.C., 1855.

Ward, James W. *Slavery a Sin that Concerns Non-Slaveholding States: A Sermon Delivered on the Day of the Annual Fast in Massachusetts, March 28, 1839.* Boston, 1839.

Webb, James Watson. *Slavery and Its Tendencies: A Letter from General J. Watson Webb to the* New York Courier and Enquirer. Washington, D.C., 1856.

Weston, George Melville. *Disunion—Its Remedy.* Washington, D.C., 1860.

——. *The Federal Union—It Must be Preserved, No. 1.* Washington, D.C., 1856.

——. *The Poor Whites of the South.* Washington, D.C., 1856.

——. *Southern Slavery Reduces Northern Wages. An Address by George M. Weston, Delivered in Washington, D.C., March 25, 1856.* Washington, D.C., 1856.

——. *Who Are Sectional?* Washington, D.C., 1856.

——. *Will the South Dissolve the Union?* Washington, D.C., 1856.

Whipple, Charles K. *The Family Relation, as Affected by Slavery.* Cincinnati, n.d.

Books and Articles

Abbott, Richard H. *Cotton and Capital: Boston Businessmen and Antislavery Reform, 1854–1868.* Amherst: University of Massachusetts Press, 1991.

——. "Yankee Farmers in Northern Virginia, 1840–1860." *Virginia Magazine of History and Biography* 76, no. 1 (January 1968): 56–63.

Adams, Charles Francis. *Richard Henry Dana: A Biography.* 2 vols. 1890. Reprint, Boston and New York: Houghton Mifflin, 1895.

Adams, Michael C. C. *Our Masters the Rebels: A Speculation on Union Military Failure in the East, 1861–1865.* Cambridge, Mass., and London: Harvard University Press, 1978.

Albrecht, Robert C. *Theodore Parker.* New York: Twayne, 1971.

Alter, Peter. *Nationalism.* 2d ed. London: Edward Arnold, 1994.

Anbinder, Tyler. *Nativism and Slavery: The Northern Know-Nothings and the Politics of the 1850s.* New York and Oxford: Oxford University Press, 1992.

Anderson, Benedict. *Imagined Communities: Reflections on the Origin and Spread of Nationalism.* Rev. ed. London and New York: Verso, 1991.

Anderson, Virginia de John. *New England's Generation: The Great Migration and the Formation of Society and Culture in the Seventeenth Century.* New York and Cambridge: Cambridge University Press, 1991.

Appleby, Joyce. *Liberalism and Republicanism in the Historical Imagination.* Cambridge, Mass.: Harvard University Press, 1992.

Archard, David. "Myths, Lies and Historical Truth: A Defence of Nationalism." *Political Studies* 43, no. 3 (1995): 472–81.

Armstrong, John. *Nations before Nationalism*. Chapel Hill: University of North Carolina Press, 1982.

Ashley, Perry J., ed. *American Newspaper Journalists, 1690–1872*. Detroit: Bruccoli Clark, 1985.

Ashworth, John. *"Agrarians" and "Aristocrats": Party Political Ideology in the United States, 1837–1846*. New York and Cambridge: Cambridge University Press, 1987.

———. "The Democratic-Republicans before the Civil War: Political Ideology and Economic Change." *Journal of American Studies* 20, no. 3 (1986): 375–90.

Azbug, Robert H., and Stephen E. Maizlish, eds. *New Perspectives on Race and Slavery in America*. Lexington: University of Kentucky Press, 1986.

Baker, Jean H. *Affairs of Party: The Political Culture of Northern Democrats in the Mid-Nineteenth Century*. Ithaca, N.Y.: Cornell University Press, 1983.

———. "The Ceremonies of Politics: Nineteenth-Century Rituals of National Affirmation." In William J. Cooper et al., eds. *A Master's Due: Essays in Honor of David Herbert Donald*. Baton Rouge and London: Louisiana State University Press, 1985.

Banner, James M., Jr. *To the Hartford Convention: The Federalists and the Origins of Party Politics in Massachusetts, 1789–1815*. New York: Alfred A. Knopf, 1970.

Barnes, Gilbert Hobbs. *The Antislavery Impulse, 1830–1844*. 1933. Reprint, New York: Harcourt, Brace and World, 1964.

Baxter, Maurice G. *One and Inseparable: Daniel Webster and the Union*. Cambridge, Mass.: Belknap Press of Harvard University Press, 1984.

Bell, Alan. *Sydney Smith: A Biography*. New York: Oxford University Press, 1982.

Belohlavek, John M., and Lewis N. Wynne. *Divided We Fall: Essays on Confederate Nation Building*. Saint Leo, Fla.: Saint Leo College Press, 1991.

Bender, Thomas. *The Antislavery Debate: Capitalism and Abolitionism as a Problem in Historical Interpretation*. Berkeley: University of California Press, 1992.

Bensel, Richard Franklin. *Yankee Leviathan: The Origins of Central State Authority in America, 1859–1877*. Cambridge: Cambridge University Press, 1990.

Berger, Meyer. *The Story of the* New York Times, *1851–1951*. New York: Simon and Schuster, 1951.

Bertelson, David. *The Lazy South*. New York: Oxford University Press, 1967.

Blight, David. "'For Something beyond the Battlefield': Frederick Douglass and the Struggle for the Memory of the Civil War." *Journal of American History* 75, no. 4 (March 1989): 1156–78.

Bolt, Christine, and Seymour Drescher, eds. *Anti-Slavery, Religion, and Reform: Essays in Memory of Roger Anstey*. Kent, England: Dawson-Anchor, 1980.

Bonner, James C. "Profile of a Late Ante-bellum Community." *American Historical Review* 49 (July 1944): 663–80.

Boorstin, Daniel. *The Americans: The National Experience*. 1965. Reprint, New York and London: Sphere Books, 1988.

Borrit, Gabor S., ed. *The Historian's Lincoln: Pseudohistory, Psychohistory, and History*. 1988. Reprint, Urbana and Chicago: University of Illinois Press, 1996.

Boyer, Paul. *Urban Masses and Moral Order in America, 1820–1920.* Cambridge, Mass.: Harvard University Press, 1978.

Bradshaw, Michael. *Regions and Regionalism in the United States.* London: Macmillan, 1988.

Brauer, Kinley J. *Cotton versus Conscience: Massachusetts Whig Politics and Southwestern Expansion, 1843–1848.* Lexington: University of Kentucky Press, 1967.

Braverman, William. "James Benjamin Clark and the Southern Experience at Harvard College in the Civil War Era." *Harvard Library Bulletin* 34 (fall 1986): 396–414.

Brock, William R. *Conflict and Transformation: The United States, 1844–1877.* 1973. Reprint, London: Penguin Books, 1978.

———. *Parties and Political Conscience: American Dilemmas, 1840–1850.* New York: Kto Press, 1979.

Brown, Charles H. *William Cullen Bryant.* New York: Scribners, 1971.

Buchan, John. *Two Ordeals of Democracy.* Boston and New York: Houghton Mifflin, 1925.

Buck, Paul. *The Road to Reunion.* Boston: Little, Brown, 1937.

Burbick, Joan. *Healing the Republic: The Language of Health and the Culture of Nationalism in Nineteenth-Century America.* Cambridge: Cambridge University Press, 1994.

Butcher, Philip. "Emerson and the South [1822–1875]." *Phylon* 17 (1975): 279–85.

Campbell, Stanley. *The Slave Catchers: Enforcement of the Fugitive Slave Bill, 1850–1860.* 1968. Paperback reprint, New York and London: W. W. Norton, 1972.

Carwardine, Richard. *Evangelicals and Politics in Antebellum America.* New Haven, Conn., and London: Yale University Press, 1993.

Caudill, Edward, and Susan L. Caudill. "Nation and Section: An Analysis of Key Symbols in the Antebellum Press." *Journalism History* 15, no. 1 (spring 1988): 16–24.

Chadwick, John. *Theodore Parker: Preacher and Reformer.* Boston: Little, Brown, 1900.

Chamberlain, Joseph Edgar. *The* Boston Transcript: *A History of Its First Hundred Years.* 1930. Reprint, New York: Books for Libraries, 1969.

Chevigny, Bell Dale. *The Woman and the Myth: Margaret Fuller's Life and Writings.* New York: Feminist Press, 1976.

Clinton, Catherine. *The Plantation Mistress: Woman's World in the Old South.* New York: Pantheon Books, 1982.

Clive, John, and Bernard Bailyn. "England's Cultural Provinces: Scotland and America." *William and Mary Quarterly* 9 (October 1954): 207–29.

Cole, Arthur C. *The Irrepressible Conflict: 1850–1865.* New York: Macmillan, 1934. Reprint, Reprint Service Corporation, 1971, 1993.

Collins, Bruce. "The Ideology of the Ante-bellum Northern Democrats." *Journal of American Studies* 11 (1977): 103–21.

Commager, Henry Steele. *Theodore Parker: Yankee Crusader.* 1936. Reprint, Boston: Beacon Press, 1947.

Compayre, Gabriel. *Horace Mann and the Public Schools in the United States.* New York: Thomas Y. Crowell, 1907.

Connor, Walker. "A Nation Is a Nation, Is a State, Is an Ethnic Group." *Ethnic and Racial Studies* 1, no. 4 (1978): 377–400.

Converse, Philip E. "The Nature of Belief Systems in Mass Publics." In David E. Apter, ed. *Ideology and Discontent.* Vol. 5 of *International Yearbook of Political Behaviour.* New York: Free Press of Glencoe, 1964.

Cook, Robert. *Baptism of Fire: The Republican Party in Iowa, 1836–1878.* Ames: Iowa State University Press, 1994.

Cooper, William J., Jr. *The South and the Politics of Slavery, 1828–1856.* Baton Rouge and London: Louisiana State University Press, 1978.

Craven, Avery O. *The Growth of Southern Nationalism, 1848–1861.* Vol. 6 of Wendell H. Stephenson and E. Merton Coulter, eds., *A History of the South.* Baton Rouge: Louisiana State University Press, 1953.

Cremin, Lawrence. *The Republic and the School: Horace Mann on the Education of Free Men.* New York: Teachers College, 1957.

Cross, Barbara M. *Horace Bushnell: Minister to a Changing America.* Chicago: University of Chicago Press, 1958.

Crouch, Barry A. "Amos A. Lawrence and the Formation of the Constitutional Union Party: The Conservative Failure in 1860." *Historical Journal of Massachusetts* 8, no. 2 (June 1980): 46–58.

Culver, Raymond B. *Horace Mann and Religion in the Massachusetts Public Schools.* New Haven, Conn.: Yale University Press, 1929.

Current, Richard N. *Daniel Webster and the Rise of National Conservatism.* Boston: Little, Brown, 1955.

———. *Old Thad. Stevens: A Study of Ambition.* 1942. Reprint, Westport, Conn.: Greenwood Press, 1980.

Curry, Richard O., and Thomas M. Brown, eds. *Conspiracy: The Fear of Subversion in American History.* New York: Holt, Rinehart and Winston, 1972.

Curti, Merle. *The Roots of American Loyalty.* New York: Columbia University Press, 1946.

———. *The Social Ideas of American Educators.* 1935. Reprint, Totowa, N.J.: Littlefield, Adams, 1966.

Curtiss, George Ticknor. *Life of Daniel Webster.* New York: n.p., 1870.

Dalzell, Robert F., Jr. *Daniel Webster and the Trial of American Nationalism, 1843–1852.* Boston: Houghton Mifflin, 1973.

———. *Enterprising Elite: The Boston Associates and the World They Made.* 1987. Reprint, New York and London: W. W. Norton, 1993.

Dangerfield, George. *The Awakening of American Nationalism, 1815–1828.* New York and London: Harper Torchbooks, 1965.

Davis, David Brion. *The Problem of Slavery in the Age of Revolution, 1770–1823.* Ithaca, N.Y., and London: Cornell University Press, 1975.

———. *The Slave Power Conspiracy and the Paranoid Style.* Baton Rouge: Louisiana State University Press, 1969)

———. *Slavery and Human Progress.* 1984. Reprint, New York and Oxford: Oxford University Press, 1986.

———. "Some Recent Directions in American Cultural History." *American Historical Review* 73, no. 3 (February 1968): 696–707.

———. "Some Themes of Counter-Subversion: An Analysis of Anti-Masonic, Anti-Catholic, and Anti-Mormon Literature." *Mississippi Valley Historical Review* 47, no. 2 (September 1960): 205–24.

———, ed. *Ante-bellum Reform.* New York: Harper and Row, 1967.

———. *The Fear of Conspiracy: Images of Un-American Activities from the Revolution to the Present.* Ithaca, N.Y., and London: Cornell University Press, 1971.

Davis, Joseph L. *Sectionalism in American Politics, 1774–1787.* Madison: University of Wisconsin Press, 1977.

Degler, Carl. "Thesis, Antithesis, Synthesis: The South, the North, and the Nation." *Journal of Southern History* 53, no. 1 (February 1987): 5–18.

Dill, William A. "Growth of Newspapers in the United States." *University of Kansas Bulletin* (1928).

Donald, David Herbert. "A Generation of Defeat." In Walter J. Fraser, Jr., and Winfred B. Moore, eds. *From the Old South to the New: Essays on the Transitional South.* Westport, Conn.: Greenwood Press, 1981.

Donaldson, Gary A. "Antebellum Criticism: Frederick Law Olmsted in Mississippi, 1853–1854." *Journal of Mississippi History* 50, no. 4 (November 1988): 317–33.

Downs, Robert B. *Horace Mann: Champion of Public Schools.* New York: Twayne Publishers, 1974.

Dunham, Charles Forrester. *The Attitude of the Northern Clergy toward the South, 1860–1865.* Toledo, Ohio: Gray Company, 1942.

Eaton, Clement. "Censorship of the Southern Mails." *American Historical Review* 48 (January 1943): 266–80.

Edelstein, Tilden G. *Strange Enthusiasm: A Life of Thomas Wentworth Higginson.* New Haven, Conn., and London: Yale University Press, 1968.

Ellis, Richard E. *The Union at Risk: Jacksonian Democracy, States' Rights and the Nullification Crisis.* New York: Oxford University Press, 1987.

Emerson, Edward Waldo. *The Early Years of the Saturday Club, 1855–1870.* Boston and New York: Houghton Mifflin, 1918.

Ericson, David F. *The Shaping of American Liberalism: The Debates over Ratification, Nullification and Slavery.* Chicago and London: University of Chicago Press, 1993.

Falk, Byron A., and Valerie R. Falk. *Personal Names Index to "The* New York Times *Index," 1851–1974.* 22 vols. Succasunna, N.J.: Roxbury Data Interface, 1976–1983.

Faust, Drew Gilpin. *The Creation of Confederate Nationalism: Ideology and Identity in the Civil War South.* Baton Rouge and London: Louisiana State University Press, 1988.

Fellman, Michael. "Theodore Parker and the Abolitionist Role in the 1850s." *Journal of American History* 61 (1974): 667–84.

Fischer, David Hackett. *Albion's Seed: Four British Folkways in America.* New York: Oxford University Press, 1989.

Floan, Howard R. "The *New York Evening Post* and the Ante-bellum South." *American Quarterly* 8, no. 3 (fall 1956): 243–53.

———. *The South in Northern Eyes, 1831–1861.* Austin: University of Texas Press, 1958.

Foner, Eric. *Free Soil, Free Labor, Free Men: The Ideology of the Republican Party before the Civil War.* New York: Oxford University Press, 1970.

———. *Politics and Ideology in the Age of the Civil War.* New York and Oxford: Oxford University Press, 1980.

———. "The Wilmot Proviso Revisited." *Journal of American History* 56 (1969): 262–79.

Foote, Kenneth E. *Shadowed Ground: America's Landscapes of Violence and Tragedy.* Austin: University of Texas Press, 1997.

Foster, Gaines M. *Ghosts of the Confederacy: Defeat, the Lost Cause, and the Emergence of the New South.* 1987. Reprint, New York and Oxford: Oxford University Press, 1988.

Franklin, John Hope. "The North, the South, and the American Revolution." *Journal of American History* 62 (1975): 5–23.

———. *A Southern Odyssey: Travelers in the Antebellum North.* Baton Rouge: Louisiana State University Press, 1975.

Fredrickson, George M. *The Black Image in the White Mind: The Debate on Afro-American Character and Destiny, 1817–1914.* New York: Harper and Row, 1971.

———. *The Inner Civil War: Northern Intellectuals and the Crisis of the Union.* 1965. Reprint, New York: Harper and Row, 1968.

———, ed. *A Nation Divided: Problems and Issues of the Civil War and Reconstruction.* Minneapolis: Burgess Publishing Company, 1975.

Freehling, William W. *The Road to Disunion.* Vol. 1, *Secessionists at Bay, 1776–1854.* New York and Oxford: Oxford University Press, 1990.

Frothingham, Octavious Brooks. *Theodore Parker.* Boston: James R. Osgood, 1874.

Frothingham, P. R. *Edward Everett, Orator and Statesman.* Boston: Houghton Mifflin, 1925.

Gaines, Francis Pendleton. *The Southern Plantation: A Study in the Development and the Accuracy of a Tradition.* New York: Columbia University Press, 1925.

Gara, Larry. *The Liberty Line: The Legend of the Underground Railroad.* Lexington: University of Kentucky Press, 1961.

———. "Slavery and the Slave Power: A Crucial Distinction." *Civil War History* 15 (1969): 5–18.

Gatell, Frank Otto. "'Conscience and Judgment': The Bolt of the Massachusetts Conscience Whigs." *Historian* 21 (November 1958): 18–45.

———. *John Gorham Palfrey and the New England Conscience.* Cambridge, Mass.: Harvard University Press, 1963.

———. "Palfrey's Vote, the Conscience Whigs and the Election of Speaker Winthrop." *New England Quarterly* 31, no. 2 (June 1958): 218–31.

———. "The Slaveholder and the Abolitionist." *Journal of Southern History* 27, no. 3 (August 1961): 368–91.

Geertz, Clifford. *The Interpretation of Cultures.* London: Hutchinson, 1975.

Gellner, Ernest. *Nations and Nationalism.* 1983. Reprint, London: Blackwell, 1990.

———. *Thought and Change.* London: Weidenfeld and Nicolson, 1964.

Gerster, Patrick, and Nicholas Cords, eds. *Myth and Southern History.* 2d ed. 2 vols. Urbana and Chicago: University of Illinois Press, 1989.

Gienapp, William E. "The Crime against Sumner: The Caning of Charles Sumner and the Rise of the Republican Party." *Civil War History* 25 (1979): 218–45.

———. "Nativism and the Creation of a Republican Majority before the Civil War." *Journal of American History* 72 (December 1985): 529–59.

———. *The Origins of the Republican Party, 1852–1856*. 1987. Paperback reprint, New York and Oxford: Oxford University Press, 1988.

Gienapp, William E. et al. *Essays on American Antebellum Politics, 1840–1860*. Arlington: University of Texas/Texas A&M University Presses, 1982.

Ginger, Ray, ed. *The Nationalizing of American Life, 1877–1900*. New York: Free Press, 1965.

Glickstein, Jonathan A. *Concepts of Free Labor in Antebellum America*. New Haven, Conn., and London: Yale University Press, 1991.

Goodman, Paul. "Ethics and Enterprise: The Values of a Boston Elite, 1800–1860." *American Quarterly* 18 (1966): 437–51.

Gougeon, Len. "Abolition, the Emersons, and 1837." *New England Quarterly* 54 (June 1981): 345–64.

———. "Emerson and Abolition: The Silent Years, 1837–1844." *American Literature* 54, no. 4 (December 1982): 560–75.

Grant, Susan-Mary. "'The Charter of its Birthright': The Civil War and American Nationalism." *Nations and Nationalism* 4, no. 2 (1998): 163–85.

———. "Making History: Myth and the Construction of American Nationhood." In Geoffrey Hosking and George Schöpflin, eds. *Myths and Nationhood*. London: Hurst and Company, 1997.

———. "Representative Mann: Horace Mann, the Republican Experiment and the South." *Journal of American Studies* 32, no. 1 (1998): 105–23.

———. "When Is a Nation Not a Nation? The Crisis of American Nationalism in the Mid-Nineteenth Century." *Nations and Nationalism* 2, no. 1 (1996): 105–29.

Grantham, Dewey W., Jr. *The Regional Imagination: The South and Recent American History*. Nashville: Vanderbilt University Press, 1979.

———, ed. *The South and the Sectional Image: The Sectional Theme since Reconstruction*. New York and London: Harper and Row, 1967.

Gray, Richard. *Writing the South: Ideas of an American Region*. 1986. Reprint, Cambridge: Cambridge University Press, 1989.

Green, Fletcher M. "Northern Missionary Activities in the South, 1846–1861." *Journal of Southern History* 21, no. 2 (May 1955): 147–72.

———. *The Role of the Yankee in the Old South*. Athens: University of Georgia Press, 1972.

Greenfeld, Liah. *Nationalism: Five Roads to Modernity*. Cambridge, Mass., and London: Harvard University Press, 1992.

Gregory, Frances W. *Nathan Appleton, Merchant and Entrepreneur, 1779–1861*. Charlottesville: University Press of Virginia, 1975.

———. "A Tale of Three Cities: The Struggle for Banking Stability in Boston, New York, and Philadelphia, 1839–1841." *New England Quarterly* 56, no. 1 (March 1983): 3–38.

Hall, Peter Dobkin. *The Organization of American Culture, 1700–1900: Private Institu-

tions, Elites, and the Origins of American Nationality. New York: New York University Press, 1984.

Hamilton, Holman. *Prologue to Conflict: The Crisis and Compromise of 1850*. 1964. Reprint, New York: W. W. Norton, 1966.

Hamlin, Charles Eugene. *The Life and Times of Hannibal Hamlin*. 2 vols. 1899. Reprint, New York: Kennikat Press, 1970.

Harrington, Fred Harvey. *Fighting Politician: Major General N. P. Banks*. Philadelphia and London: University of Pennsylvania/Oxford University Presses, 1948.

———. "The First Northern Victory." *Journal of Southern History* 5 (1939): 186–205.

———. "Nathaniel Prentiss Banks: A Study in Anti-Slavery Politics." *New England Quarterly* 9 (1936): 626–54.

Hayne, Barnie. "Yankee in the Patriarchy: T. B. Thorpe's Reply to *Uncle Tom's Cabin*." *American Quarterly* 20 (1968): 180–95.

Hess, Earl J. *Liberty, Virtue, and Progress: Northerners and Their War for the Union*. New York: New York University Press, 1988.

Hijiya, James A. *J. W. De Forest and the Rise of American Gentility*. Hanover, N.H.: University Press of New England for Brown University Press, 1988.

Hinsdale, Burke. *Horace Mann and the Common School Revival in the United States*. New York: Charles Scribner's Sons, 1898.

Hobsbawn, Eric J. *Nations and Nationalism since 1780: Programme, Myth, Reality*. London: Canto, 1990.

Hoffman, Charles, and Tess Hoffman. *North by South: The Two Lives of Richard James Arnold*. Athens, Ga., and London: University of Georgia Press, 1988.

Hofstadter, Richard. *The Paranoid Style in American Politics and Other Essays*. 1965. Reprint, New York: Alfred A. Knopf, 1966.

Holt, Michael F. *The Political Crisis of the 1850s*. New York: John Wiley and Sons, 1978.

Hooker, Richard. *The Story of an Independent Newspaper: One Hundred Years of the* Springfield Republican. 1924. Reprint, New York: Johnson Reprint Corporation, 1969.

Howard, Michael. *The Lessons of History*. Oxford: Oxford University Press, 1991.

Howe, Daniel Walker. *The Political Culture of the American Whigs*. Chicago and London: University of Chicago Press, 1979.

Hubbell, George Allen. *Horace Mann, Educator, Patriot and Reformer: A Study in Leadership*. Philadelphia: Wm. F. Fell Company, 1910.

Hubbell, Jay B. *Southern Life in Fiction*. Athens: University of Georgia Press, 1960.

Hudson, Frederic. *Journalism in the United States from 1690–1872*. 1873. Reprint, New York: Haskell House Publishers, 1968.

Hunt, H. Draper. *Hannibal Hamlin of Maine: Lincoln's First Vice-President*. New York: Syracuse University Press, 1969.

Ignatieff, Michael. *Blood and Belonging: Journeys into the New Nationalism*. London: Vintage Books, 1994.

Ingersoll, Lurton D. *The Life of Horace Greeley*. 1873. Reprint, New York: Beekman Publishers, 1974.

Inscoe, John C. "Olmsted in Appalachia: A Connecticut Yankee Encounters Slavery and Racism in the Southern Highlands." *Slavery and Abolition* 9, no. 2 (September 1988): 171–82.

Isely, Jeter Allen. *Horace Greeley and the Republican Party, 1853–1861.* Princeton, N.J.: Princeton University Press, 1947.

Jensen, Merrill, ed. *Regionalism in America.* Madison: University of Wisconsin Press, 1952.

Jimerson, Randall C. *The Private Civil War: Popular Thought during the Sectional Conflict.* Baton Rouge: Louisiana State University Press, 1988.

Johannsen, Robert W. *Lincoln, the South and Slavery: The Political Dimension.* Baton Rouge: Louisiana State University Press, 1991.

———, ed. *The Union in Crisis, 1850–1877.* New York: Free Press, 1962.

Johnson, Curtiss S. *Politics and a Belly-full: The Journalistic Career of William Cullen Bryant, Civil War Editor of the* New York Evening Post. New York: Vantage Books, 1962.

Kalfus, Melvin. *Frederick Law Olmsted: The Passion of a Public Artist.* New York and London: New York University Press, 1990.

Kamenka, Eugene, ed. *Nationalism: The Nature and Evolution of an Idea.* London: Edward Arnold, 1976.

Kammen, Michael. *Mystic Chords of Memory: The Transformation of Tradition in American Culture.* New York: Alfred A. Knopf, 1991.

———. *A Season of Youth: The American Revolution and the Historical Imagination.* New York: Alfred A. Knopf, 1978.

Kerber, Linda. *Federalists in Dissent: Imagery and Ideology in Jeffersonian America.* 1970. Reprint, Ithaca, N.Y., and London: Cornell University Press, 1983.

King, Clyde S. *Horace Mann, 1796–1859: A Bibliography.* New York: Oceana Publications, 1966.

Kirby, Jack Temple. *Media-Made Dixie: The South in the American Imagination.* Rev. ed. Athens: University of Georgia Press, 1986.

Kohn, Hans. *American Nationalism: An Interpretative Essay.* New York: Macmillan, 1957.

———. *The Idea of Nationalism: A Study in Its Origins and Background.* New York: Macmillan, 1945.

Korngold, Ralph. *Thaddeus Stevens: A Being Darkly Wise and Rudely Great.* New York: Harcourt, Brace, 1955.

Lader, Lawrence. *The Bold Brahmins: New England's War against Slavery, 1831–1863.* New York: E. P. Dutton, 1961.

Lawrence, Rt. Rev. William. "Memoirs of Amos A. Lawrence." *Proceedings of the Massachusetts Historical Society* 12 (January 1898): 130–37.

Lee, Alfred M. *The Daily Newspaper in America: The Evolution of a Social Instrument.* New York: Macmillan, 1937.

Levin, Harry. "Some Meanings of Myth." *Daedalus: Journal of the American Academy of Arts and Sciences* 88, no. 2 (spring 1959): 223–31.

Levine, Bruce. *Half Slave and Half Free: The Roots of Civil War.* New York: Hill and Wang, 1992.

Linderman, Gerald F. *Embattled Courage: The Experience of Combat in the American Civil War.* 1987. Reprint, New York: Free Press, 1989.

Linn, William Alexander. *Horace Greeley: Founder of the* New York Tribune. 1903. Reprint, New York: Beekham Publishers, 1974.

Lipset, Seymour Martin. *The First New Nation: The United States in Historical and Comparative Perspective.* 1963. Reprint, London: W. W. Norton, 1979.

Llobera, Josep R. *The God of Modernity: The Development of Nationalism in Western Europe.* Oxford: Berg, 1994.

Lowry, Thomas P. *The Story the Soldiers Wouldn't Tell: Sex and the American Civil War.* Mechanicsburg, Pa.: Stackpole Books, 1994.

Lunde, Erik S. *Horace Greeley.* Boston: Twayne, 1981.

Maizlish, Stephen E., and John J. Kushman, eds. *Essays on American Antebellum Politics, 1840–1860.* Arlington: Texas A&M University Press, 1982.

Malik, Kenan. *The Meaning of Race: Race, History and Culture in Western Society.* London: Macmillan, 1996.

Marx, Leo. *The Machine in the Garden: Technology and the Pastoral Ideal in America.* New York: Oxford University Press, 1964.

Matthews, Donald G. "The Abolitionists on Slavery: The Critique behind the Social Movement." *Journal of Southern History* 33, no. 2 (May 1967): 163–82.

——. "The Methodist Schism of 1844 and the Popularization of Antislavery Sentiment." *Mid-America* 51 (1969): 21–27.

Matthews, J. V. "'Whig History': The New England Whigs and a Usable Past." *New England Quarterly* 51 (June 1978): 193–208.

Maverick, Augustus. *Henry J. Raymond and the New York Press, for Thirty Years: Progress of American Journalism from 1840 to 1870.* Hartford, Conn.: A. S. Hale, 1870.

Mayfield, John. *The New Nation, 1800–1845.* Rev. ed. New York: Hill and Wang, 1982.

——. *Rehearsal for Republicanism: Free Soil and the Politics of Anti-Slavery.* New York and London: Kennikat Press, 1980.

McCardell, John. *The Idea of a Southern Nation: Southern Nationalists and Southern Nationalism, 1830–1860.* New York and London: W. W. Norton, 1979.

McConnell, Stuart. *Glorious Contentment: The Grand Army of the Republic, 1865–1900.* Chapel Hill: University of North Carolina Press, 1992.

McKivigan, John R. "John Ball, Jr., Alias the Roving Editor Alias James Redpath." Part I, *Manuscripts* 40, no. 4 (fall 1988): 307–17. Part 2, *Manuscripts* 41, no. 1 (winter 1989): 19–29.

——. *The War against Proslavery Religion: Abolitionism and the Northern Churches, 1830–1865.* Ithaca, N.Y.: Cornell University Press, 1984.

McPherson, James M. *What They Fought For, 1861–1865.* Baton Rouge: Louisiana State University Press, 1994.

Merritt, Richard L. "The Emergence of American Nationalism: A Quantitative Approach." *American Quarterly* 17 (summer 1965): 319–34.

Messerli, Jonathan. *Horace Mann: A Biography.* New York: Alfred A. Knopf, 1972.

Miller, David. *On Nationality.* Oxford: Clarendon Press, 1995.

Miller, Perry. *The Life of the Mind in America: From the Revolution to the Civil War*. New York: Harcourt, Brace and World, 1965.

Mitchell, Broadus. *Frederick Law Olmsted: A Critic of the Old South*. Baltimore: Johns Hopkins University Press, 1924; New York: Russell and Russell, 1968.

———. *William Gregg: Factory Master of the Old South*. Chapel Hill: University of North Carolina Press, 1928.

Mitchell, Reid. *Civil War Soldiers: Their Expectations and Their Experiences*. 1988. Reprint, New York: Simon and Schuster, 1989.

———. *The Vacant Chair: The Northern Soldier Leaves Home*. 1993. Reprint, New York and Oxford: Oxford University Press, 1995.

Mommsen, Wolfgang. "Power, Politics, Imperialism, and National Emancipation, 1870–1914." In G. W. Moody, ed., *Nationality and the Pursuit of National Independence*. Belfast: Appletree Press for the Irish Committee of Historical Sciences, 1978.

Monroe, Paul. *Founding of the American Public School System: A History of Education in the United States*. New York: Macmillan, 1940.

Moody, Marjory M. "The Evolution of Emerson as an Abolitionist." *American Literature* 17 (March 1945–January 1946): 1–21.

Morgan, Joy Elmer. *Horace Mann: His Ideas and Ideals*. Washington, D.C.: National Home Library, 1936.

Morris, Thomas. *Free Men All: The Personal Liberty Laws of the North, 1780–1861*. Baltimore and London: Johns Hopkins University Press, 1974.

Morrison, Chaplain W. *Democratic Politics and Sectionalism: The Wilmot Proviso Controversy*. Chapel Hill: University of North Carolina Press, 1967.

Morse, Grant W. *Guide to the Incomparable* New York Times *Index*. New York: Fleet Academic Edition, 1980.

Mott, Frank Luther. *American Journalism. A History: 1690–1960*. 3d ed. New York: Macmillan, 1962.

———. *A History of American Magazines, 1741–1850*. 5 vols. Cambridge, Mass.: Belknap Press of Harvard University Press, 1938–1968.

Mulkern, John R. *The Know-Nothing Party in Massachusetts: The Rise and Fall of a People's Movement*. Boston: Northeastern University Press, 1990.

Murrin, John M. "A Roof without Walls: The Dilemma of American National Identity." In Richard Beeman et al., eds., *Beyond Confederation: Origins of the Constitution and American National Identity*. Chapel Hill and London: University of North Carolina Press, 1987.

Nagel, Paul C. *One Nation Indivisible: The Union in American Thought, 1776–1861*. New York and Oxford: Oxford University Press, 1964.

———. *This Sacred Trust: American Nationality, 1798–1898*. New York and Oxford: Oxford University Press, 1971.

Nasaw, David. *Schooled to Order: A Social History of Public Schooling in the United States*. New York: Oxford University Press, 1979.

Nevins, Allan. "American Journalism and Its Historical Treatment." *Journalism Quarterly* 36 (1959): 411–519.

———. *The Evening Post, A Century of Journalism*. New York: Boni and Liveright, 1922.

————. *Ordeal of the Union.* Vol. 1, pt. 1, *Fruits of Manifest Destiny, 1847–1852.* Vol. 1, pt. 2, *A House Dividing, 1852–1857.* Vol. 2, pt. 1, *The Emergence of Lincoln: Douglas, Buchanan and Party Chaos, 1857–1859.* 1947–1971. Paperback reprint, New York: Macmillan, 1992.

Newman, Simon P. *Parades and the Politics of the Street: Festive Culture in the Early American Republic.* Philadelphia: University of Pennsylvania Press, 1997.

Nichols, H. G. "Uncle Tom's Cabin, 1852–1952." *History Today* 11, no. 6 (June 1952): 413–20.

Niebuhr, Reinhold, and Alan Heimert. *A Nation so Conceived: Reflections on the History of America from Its Early Visions to Its Present Power.* London: Faber and Faber, 1963.

Niven, John. *Gideon Welles: Lincoln's First Secretary of the Navy.* New York: Oxford University Press, 1973.

North, S. N. D. *History and Present Condition of the Newspaper and Periodical Press of the United States with a Catalogue of the Publications of the Census Year.* Washington, D.C.: U.S. Government Printing Office, 1884.

Nye, Russell B. *Fettered Freedom: Civil Liberties and the Slavery Controversy, 1830–1860.* Rev. ed. East Lansing: Michigan State University Press, 1963.

————. "The Slave Power Conspiracy, 1830–1860." *Science and Society* 10 (summer 1946): 262–74.

————. *Society and Culture in America, 1830–1860.* New York and London: Harper and Row, 1974.

O'Brien, Conor Cruise. *God Land: Reflections on Religion and Nationalism.* Cambridge, Mass.: Harvard University Press, 1988.

O'Brien, Michael. *The Idea of the American South, 1920–1941.* Baltimore and London: Johns Hopkins University Press, 1979.

O'Connor, Thomas H. *Bibles, Brahmins and Bosses: A Short History of Boston.* 2d rev. ed. Boston: Trustees of the Public Library of the City of Boston, 1984.

————. *Lords of the Loom: The Cotton Whigs and the Coming of the Civil War.* New York: Charles Scribner's Sons, 1968.

O'Leary, Celia. "'American All': Reforging a National Brotherhood, 1876–1917." *History Today* 44 (October 1994): 19–27.

Osofsky, Gilbert. "Abolitionists, Irish Immigrants and the Dilemmas of Romantic Nationalism." *American Historical Review* 80, no. 4 (October 1975): 889–912.

Owsley, Frank L., and Harriet C. Owsley. "The Economic Basis of Society in the Late Ante-bellum South." *Journal of Southern History* 6 (1940): 24–45.

Parish, Peter J. "American Nationalism and the Nineteenth Century Constitution." In Joseph Smith, ed., *The American Constitution: The First Two Hundred Years, 1787–1987.* Exeter Studies in History No. 16. Exeter: Exeter University, 1987.

————. "Confidence and Anxiety in Victorian America." *Uppsala North American Studies Reports,* No. 6 (1991).

————. "Daniel Webster, New England, and the West." *Journal of American History* 54, no. 3 (December 1967): 524–49.

————. "An Exception to Most of the Rules: What Made American Nationalism Different in the Mid-Nineteenth Century?" *Prologue: Quarterly of the National Archives* 27, no. 3 (fall 1995): 219–29.

———. "The Road Not Quite Taken: The Constitution of the Confederate States of America." In Thomas J. Barron, Owen Dudley Edwards, and Patricia Storey, eds., *Constitutions and National Identity*. Edinburgh: Quadriga, 1993.

Pease, William H., and Jane H. Pease. *The Web of Progress: Private Values and Public Styles in Boston and Charleston, 1828–1843*. New York: Oxford University Press, 1985.

Peckham, Harry Houston. *Gotham Yankee: A Biography of William Cullen Bryant*. 1950. Reprint, New York: Russell and Russell, 1971.

Pencak, William. *For God and Country: The American Legion, 1919–1941*. Boston: Northeastern University Press, 1989.

Perkins, Howard C. "The Defence of Slavery in the Northern Press on the Eve of Civil War." *Journal of Southern History* 9 (1943): 501–31.

Pessen, Edward. "How Different from Each Other Were the Antebellum North and South?" *American Historical Review* 65 (1980): 1119–49.

Peterson, Merrill D. *The Great Triumvirate: Webster, Clay, and Calhoun*. New York and Oxford: Oxford University Press, 1987.

———. *The Jefferson Image in the American Mind*. New York: Oxford University Press, 1960.

———. *Lincoln in American Memory*. 1994. Reprint, New York: Oxford University Press, 1995.

Piercy, J. W. "The Newspaper as a Source of Historical Information." *Indiana Historical Bulletin* 10 (1933): 387–96.

Potter, David M. "Horace Greeley and Peaceable Secession." *Journal of Southern History* 7, no. 2 (May 1941): 145–59.

———. *The Impending Crisis, 1848–1861*. Completed and edited by Don. E. Fehrenbacher. New York and London: Harper and Row, 1976.

———. *People of Plenty: Economic Abundance and the American Character*. 1954. Reprint, Chicago and London: University of Chicago Press, 1973.

———. *The South and the Sectional Conflict*. Baton Rouge: Louisiana State University Press, 1968.

Potter, David M., and Thomas G. Manning. *Nationalism and Sectionalism in America, 1775–1877: Select Problems in Historical Interpretation*. New York: Holt, Rinehart and Winston, 1966.

Pressly, Thomas J., and Stephen Maizlish, eds. *Essays on Antebellum American Politics, 1840–1860*. Arlington: Texas A&M University Press, 1982.

Pryor, Elizabeth Brown. "An Anomalous Person: The Northern Tutor in Plantation Society, 1773–1860." *Journal of Southern History* 47, no.3 (August 1981): 363–92.

Ratner, Lorman. "Northern Concern for Social Order as Cause for Rejecting Anti-Slavery, 1831–1840." *Historian* 28, no. 1 (November 1965): 1–18.

Rawley, James P. *Race and Politics: "Bleeding Kansas" and the Coming of the Civil War*. New York and Philadelphia: J. B. Lippincott, 1969.

Rayback, Joseph G. *Free Soil: The Election of 1848*. Lexington: University Press of Kentucky, 1970.

Reed, John Shelton. *Southern Folk, Plain and Fancy: Native White Social Types*. Athens: University of Georgia Press, 1986.

Reid, Brian Holden. *The Origins of the American Civil War*. London and New York: Longman, 1996.

Reid, Ronald F. *Edward Everett: Unionist Orator*. Hartford, Conn: Greenwood Press, 1990.

Rhodes, James Ford. "Newspapers as Historical Sources." *Atlantic Monthly* 102 (1909): 650–57.

Richards, Leonard L. *"Gentlemen of Property and Standing": Anti-Abolition Mobs in Jacksonian America*. New York: Oxford University Press, 1970.

Roberts, Diane. *The Myth of Aunt Jemima: Representations of Race and Region*. London: Routledge, 1994.

Roland, Charles P. *An American Iliad: The Story of the Civil War*. Lexington: University Press of Kentucky, 1991.

Roper, Laura Wood. *FLO: A Biography of Frederick Law Olmsted*. Baltimore: Johns Hopkins University Press, 1973.

———. "Frederick Law Olmsted and the Western Texas Free-Soil Movement." *American Historical Review* 56 (October 1950): 58–64.

———. "Frederick Law Olmsted in the 'Literary Republic.'" *Mississippi Valley Historical Review* 39 (December 1952): 459–82.

Rose, Alan Henry. "The Image of the Negro in the Pre–Civil War Novels of John Pendleton Kennedy and William Gilmore Simms." *Journal of American Studies* 4 (February 1971): 217–26.

Sandage, Scott A. "A Marble House Divided: The Lincoln Memorial, the Civil Rights Movement, and the Politics of Memory, 1939–1963." *Journal of American History* 80, no. 1 (June 1993): 135–67.

Satterwhite, Joseph N. "The Tremulous Formulae: Form and Technique in *Godey's* Fiction." *American Quarterly* 8, no. 2 (summer 1956): 99–113.

Saum, Lewis O. *The Popular Mood of Pre–Civil War America*. Westport, Conn.: Greenwood Press, 1980.

Schlesinger, Arthur M. "Was Olmsted an Unbiased Critic of the South?" *Journal of Negro History* 37, no. 2 (April 1952): 173–87.

Schwartz, Harold. "Fugitive Slave Days in Boston." *New England Quarterly* 27 (1954): 191–212.

Schwarzlose, Richard A. *Newspapers: A Reference Guide*. New York: Greenwood Press, 1987.

Scott, Donald M. "The Popular Lecture and the Creation of a Public in Mid-Nineteenth Century America." *Journal of American History* 66, no. 4 (March 1980): 791–809.

Sehr, Timothy J. "Leonard Bacon and the Myth of the Good Slaveholder." *New England Quarterly* 49 (June 1976): 194–213.

Seitz, Don C. *Horace Greeley: Founder of the* New York Tribune. Indianapolis: Bobbs-Merrill, 1926.

Seton-Watson, Hugh. *Nations and States: An Inquiry into the Origins of Nations and the Politics of Nationalism.* London: Methuen, 1977.

Sewell, Richard H. *Ballots for Freedom: Antislavery Politics in the United States, 1837–1860.* New York: Oxford University Press, 1976.

——. "John P. Hale and the Liberty Party, 1847–1848." *New England Quarterly* 37, no. 2 (June 1964): 200–23.

——. *John P. Hale and the Politics of Abolition.* Cambridge, Mass.: Harvard University Press, 1965.

——. "The John P. Hale Papers." *Dartmouth College Library Bulletin* 10, no. 2 (April 1970): 70–78.

Shapiro, Samuel. *Richard Henry Dana, Jr., 1815–1882.* East Lansing: Michigan State University Press, 1961.

Shy, John. *A People Numerous and Armed: Reflections on the Military Struggle for American Independence.* Rev. ed. Ann Arbor: University of Michigan Press, 1990.

Silber, Nina. "Intemperate Men, Spiteful Women, and Jefferson Davis: Northern Views of the Defeated South." *American Quarterly* 41, no. 4 (December 1989): 615–35.

——. *The Romance of Reunion: Northerners and the South, 1865–1900.* Chapel Hill and London: University of North Carolina Press, 1993.

Silber, Nina, and Mary Beth Sievens, eds. *Yankee Correspondence: Civil War Letters between New England Soldiers and the Home Front.* Charlottesville and London: University Press of Virginia, 1996.

Silbey, Joel. "After 'The First Northern Victory': The Republican Party Comes to Congress, 1855–1856." *Journal of Interdisciplinary History* 20 (1989): 1–24.

——. *The American Political Nation, 1838–1893.* Stanford, Calif.: Stanford University Press, 1991.

——. *The Transformation of American Politics, 1840–1860.* Princeton, N.J.: Prentice-Hall, 1967.

Simpson, Lewis P. *The Man of Letters in New England and the South: Essays on the History of the Literary Vocation in America.* Baton Rouge: Louisiana State University Press, 1973.

——. *Mind and the American Civil War: A Meditation on Lost Causes.* Baton Rouge: Louisiana State University Press, 1989.

——. "Slavery and the Cultural Imperialism of New England." *Southern Review* 25 (January 1989): 1–29.

Sloan, Wm. David, ed. *American Journalism History: An Annotated Bibliography.* New York: Greenwood Press, 1989.

Smith, Anthony D. *The Ethnic Origins of Nations.* 1983. Reprint, London: Blackwell, 1993.

——. *National Identity.* London: Penguin Books, 1991.

——. *Nationalism in the Twentieth Century.* Oxford: Martin Roberston, 1979.

——. "Origin of Nation." *Times Higher Education Supplement* 8 (January 1993): 15–16.

——. "The Origins of Nations." *Ethnic and Racial Studies* 12, no. 3 (1989): 340–67.

Smith, George Winston. "Ante-bellum Attempts of Northern Business Interests to 'Redeem' the Upper South." *Journal of Southern History* 10 (May 1945): 177–213.

Smith, Henry Nash. *Virgin Land: The American West as Symbol and Myth.* Cambridge, Mass.: Harvard University Press, 1950.

Sokolow, Jayme A. "The Jerry McHenry Rescue and the Growth of Northern Antislavery Sentiment during the 1850s." *Journal of American Studies* 16, no. 3 (December 1982): 427–43.

Somkin, Fred. *Unquiet Eagle: Memory and Desire in the Idea of American Freedom, 1815–1860.* Ithaca, N.Y.: Cornell University Press, 1967.

Stampp, Kenneth M. *America in 1857: A Nation on the Brink.* 1990. Paperback reprint, New York and Oxford: Oxford University Press, 1992.

Stevenson, Elizabeth. *Park Maker: A Life of Frederick Law Olmsted.* New York: Macmillan, 1977.

Stoddard, Henry Luther. *Horace Greeley: Printer, Editor, Crusader.* New York: Putnam's, 1946.

Storey, Moorfield. "Dana as an Antislavery Leader." *Proceedings,* Cambridge Historical Society, Publications X, 26 January–26 October 1915 (1917).

Strauch, Carl. "The Background and Meaning of the 'Ode Inscribed to W. H. Channing.'" *Emerson Society Quarterly* (1966 supplement): 3–14.

Sydnor, Charles S. *The Development of Southern Sectionalism, 1819–1848.* 1948. Paperback reprint, Baton Rouge: Louisiana State University Press, 1968.

Taylor, William R. *Cavalier and Yankee: The Old South and American National Character.* 1957. Reprint, Cambridge, Mass., and London: Harvard University Press, 1979.

Tharp, Louise Hall. *Until Victory: Horace Mann and Mary Peabody.* Boston: Little, Brown, 1953.

Thelen, David. "The Movie Maker as Historian: Conversations with Ken Burns." *Journal of American History* 81, no. 3 (December 1994): 1031–50.

Thomas, John L. "Romantic Reform in America, 1815–1865." *American Quarterly* 17 (winter 1965): 656–81.

Thomas, M. Wynn. "Whitman and the American Democratic Identity before and during the Civil War." *Journal of American Studies* 15, no. 1 (April 1981): 73–93.

Thornton, Tamara Plakins. *Cultivating Gentlemen: The Meaning of Country Life among the Boston Elite, 1785–1860.* New Haven, Conn., and London: Yale University Press, 1989.

Toplin, Robert Brent, ed. *Ken Burns's* The Civil War: *Historians Respond.* New York and Oxford: Oxford University Press, 1996.

Turner, Frederick Jackson. *The Significance of Sections in American History.* Introduction by Max Farrand. Gloucester, Mass.: Peter Smith, 1959.

Tuveson, Ernest Lee. *Redeemer Nation: The Idea of America's Millennial Role.* (Chicago and London: University of Chicago Press, 1968.

Van Deusen, Glyndon G. *Horace Greeley, Nineteenth Century Crusader.* Philadelphia: University of Pennsylvania Press, 1953.

————. *Thurlow Weed, Wizard of the Lobby.* Boston: Little, Brown, 1947.

Vandiver, Frank E., ed. *The Idea of the South: Pursuit of a Central Theme.* Chicago and London: University of Chicago Press, 1964.

Vinovskis, Maris. "Horace Mann on the Economic Productivity of Education." *New England Quarterly* 43 (1970): 550–71.

Waldstreicher, David. *In the Midst of Perpetual Fetes: The Making of American Nationalism, 1776–1820.* Chapel Hill and London: University of North Carolina Press, 1997.

Walters, Ronald G. *American Reformers, 1815–1860.* New York: Hill and Wang, 1978.

————. *The Antislavery Appeal: American Abolitionism after 1830.* 1978. Reprint, New York: W. W. Norton, 1984.

————. "Signs of the Times: Clifford Geertz and the Historians." *Social Research* 47 (1980): 537–56.

Warren, Robert Penn. *The Legacy of the Civil War: Meditations on the Centennial.* New York: Random House, 1961.

Watkins, Floyd C. "James Kirke Paulding and the South." *American Quarterly* 5, no. 3 (fall 1953): 219–30.

Weinberg, Albert K. *Manifest Destiny: A Study of Nationalist Expansion in American History.* 1935. Reprint, Gloucester, Mass.: Peter Smith, 1958.

Wells, Anna Mary. *Dear Preceptor: The Life and Times of Thomas Wentworth Higginson.* Boston: Houghton Mifflin, 1963.

Welter, Rush. *The Mind of America, 1820–1860.* New York and London: Columbia University Press, 1975.

————. *Popular Education and Democratic Thought in America.* New York and London: Columbia University Press, 1962.

Wesson, Kenneth R. "Travelers' Accounts of the Southern Character: Antebellum and Early Postbellum Period." *Southern Studies* 17 (1978): 305–18.

White, Dana F., and Victor A. Kramer, eds. *Olmsted South: Old South Critic/New South Planner.* Westport, Conn., and London: Greenwood Press, 1979.

Williams, Edward I. F. *Horace Mann: Educational Statesman.* New York: Macmillan, 1937.

Williams, Frank J. et al., eds. *Abraham Lincoln: Sources and Style of Leadership.* Westport, Conn: Greenwood Press, 1994.

Wills, Garry. *Lincoln at Gettysburg: The Words that Remade America.* New York: Simon and Schuster, 1992.

Wilson, Major L. *Space, Time and Freedom: The Quest for Nationality and the Irrepressible Conflict, 1815–1861.* Westport, Conn.: Greenwood Press, 1974.

Winthrop, Robert C. "Memoir of Nathan Appleton." *Proceedings of the Massachusetts Historical Society* 5 (October 1861): 249–308.

Wolff, Gerald W. *The Kansas-Nebraska Bill: Party, Section, and the Coming of the Civil War.* 1977. Reprint, New York: Revisionist Press, 1980.

Woodward, C. Vann. *American Counterpoint: Slavery and Racism in the North/South Dialogue.* 1964. Reprint, Boston: Little, Brown, 1971.

———. "The Antislavery Myth." *American Scholar* 31, no. 2 (spring 1962): 312–28.

Yoder, Paton. "Private Hospitality in the South, 1775–1850." *Mississippi Valley Historical Review* 47 (1960): 419–33.

Zelinsky, Wilbur. *Nation into State: The Shifting Symbolic Foundations of American Nationalism.* Chapel Hill and London: University of North Carolina Press, 1988.

Dissertations

Angert, Carol. "The Role of Education in a Changing America, 1820–1850: Horace Mann and the Public Schools." Master's diss., University of London, 1971.

Beveridge, Charles E. "Frederick Law Olmsted: The Formative Years, 1822–1865." Ph.D. diss., University of Wisconsin, 1966.

Butler, Randall R. II. "New England Journalism and the Questions of Slavery, the South, and Abolitionism: 1820–1861." Ph.D. diss., Brigham Young University, 1980. University Microfilms International.

Christian, William Kenneth. "The Mind of Edward Everett." Ph.D. diss., Michigan State College of Agriculture and Applied Science, 1952. Microfilms International.

Day, Laura A. "'A History of Every One of Us': A Gender Study of America's Antebellum Travel Writers." Ph.D. diss., Purdue University, 1988.

Fasburg, Michael. "The Formation of the Republican Party in Maine: A Study of Hannibal Hamlin's Change in Party Affiliation." Masters' thesis, Columbia University, 1967.

Green, Alan. "The Legacy of Illusion: The Image of the Negro in the Pre–Civil War North, 1787–1857." Ph.D. diss., Claremont Graduate School, 1968.

Horn, Stuart Joel. "Edward Everett and American Nationalism." Ph.D. diss., City University of New York, 1973. University Microfilms International.

Vogt, Allen Roy. "'An Honest Fanatic': The Images of the Abolitionist in the Antebellum and Historical Minds." Ph.D. diss., University of Houston, 1984.

Index